MW00642009

THE SOCIAL GOSPEL IN AMERICAN RELIGION

The Social Gospel in American Religion

A History

Christopher H. Evans

NEW YORK UNIVERSITY PRESS

New York

NEW YORK UNIVERSITY PRESS
New York
www.nyupress.org

© 2017 by New York University
All rights reserved

References to Internet websites (URLs) were accurate at the time of writing. Neither the author nor New York University Press is responsible for URLs that may have expired or changed since the manuscript was prepared.

ISBN: 978-1-4798-6953-4 (hardback)
ISBN: 978-1-4798-8857-3 (paperback)

For Library of Congress Cataloging-in-Publication data, please contact the Library of Congress.

Manufactured in the United States of America

10 9 8 7 6 5 4 3 2 1

Also available as an ebook

CONTENTS

ACKNOWLEDGMENTS

I am indebted to many individuals who enabled this book to be written. Above all, I am grateful to Jennifer Hammer, my editor at New York University Press, for her support and encouragement of this project. Jennifer's critique of earlier versions of this manuscript and keen editorial eye challenged me to improve the book while inspiring me onward in the task of writing. I couldn't ask for a better colleague in this endeavor.

A number of people read and commented on various parts of the manuscript. Above all, I am thankful to the amazing scholars in the Boston Historians of American Religion Group, with particular gratitude to Jon Roberts, Peggy Bendroth, Cliff Putney, Chris Beneke, M. J. Farrelly, Patricia Appelbaum, Jess Parr, and Roberta Wollons for their helpful comments on various chapter drafts. I was fortunate to receive invaluable research assistance from two outstanding graduate students at Boston University, Laura Chevalier and Matthew Preston. This book also reflects my gratitude for my current and former students at Boston University and Colgate Rochester Crozer Divinity School. Their questions and engagement with me over the years have inspired a great deal of my scholarship and make me grateful for the opportunities that I've had in my career as a teacher. As always, I am thankful to Robin, Peter, and Andrew for the ways that they have indulged my passion for history.

Introduction

In 1958 Martin Luther King Jr. acknowledged his intellectual debt to a movement in American religious history commonly called the "social gospel." Citing the impact of the early twentieth-century church leader Walter Rauschenbusch, King noted that Rauschenbusch's social gospel had pushed Christian theology beyond a concern for individual salvation to engage questions of social justice. At its core, religious faith needed to address questions of systemic political change. "It has been my conviction ever since reading Rauschenbusch that any religion which professes to be concerned about the souls of men and is not concerned about the social and economic conditions that scar the soul, is a spiritually moribund religion only waiting for the day to be buried."[1]

In 1996 another religious activist concurred with King, contending that religion had an implicit mission to change the social fabric of modern life. This author affirmed that Rauschenbusch and King were part of a wider history of American religious political engagement, "the story of slumbering faith awakening from the pews and flowing into school board meetings, courtrooms, slums, and state capitols."[2] What is perhaps surprising is that this second activist was not a theological liberal but the longtime head of the conservative-based Christian Coalition, Ralph Reed.

Reed's gloss of American religious history ignored important nuances in historians' definitions of the social gospel. At the same time, the fact that Reed sought to recast a religious heritage with deep-seated connections to theological and political liberalism is significant. Reed's identification of the Christian Coalition with the social gospel is indicative of how broadly defined—and historically contested—the movement has been in American history.

Largely associated with late nineteenth- and early twentieth-century American Protestantism, the social gospel was a religious movement that applied a liberal theology to a range of social reform measures that would become associated with the political left. However, as Ralph Reed's uncritical use of this term suggests, the social gospel is a somewhat elastic concept, often used broadly to denote any sort of religious engagement with social issues. To trace the rise of the social gospel in American religious history and its legacy in the twentieth century is the purpose of this book.

Defining and Interpreting the Social Gospel

While many scholars date the social gospel's origin and apex roughly to the Progressive Era of the late nineteenth and early twentieth centuries, they have long debated precise definitions of the social gospel, what persons/groups fall under the rubric of this term, and when this tradition ended.[3] In 1921 Shailer Mathews, professor of New Testament interpretation at the University of Chicago Divinity School, presented one of the most cited (and innocuous) definitions of the social gospel as "the application of the teaching of Jesus and the total message of the Christian salvation to society, the economic life, and social institutions such as the state, the family, as well as to individuals."[4] Mathews's phrase "the application of the teaching of Jesus" illustrates how certain religious leaders have interpreted the social gospel as a unique model of "applied" religion. Specifically, Mathews noted that the social gospel modeled a modern tradition of religious ethics. There was nothing particularly novel about understanding a religious tradition, like Christianity, through ethical engagement. Yet the social gospel embodied a new understanding of social engagement that challenged earlier suppositions coming out of previous religious movements in America, especially in the nation's Protestant churches.

As a way to orient the reader, I offer a definition of the social gospel that will anchor the discussion in this book: *The social gospel was an offshoot of theological liberalism that strove to apply a progressive theological vision to engage American social, political, and economic structures.[5] Rooted in wider historical-theological developments in American Protestantism in the late nineteenth and early twentieth centuries, the social gospel integrated evangelical and liberal theological strands in ways that advocated for systemic, structural changes in American institutions. The movement had a wide-ranging impact on religion and society through-*

out the twentieth century, cresting during the civil rights movement of the 1950s and 1960s.[6] This definition stresses three characteristics of the social gospel as a broadly based religious movement in American history: first, its social idealism, emanating from its distinctive liberal synthesis; second, a belief that a primary objective of religion was to advocate for systemic social changes along politically progressive and, at times, radical lines; and finally, a motivation to promote a vision of America as a religiously and culturally pluralistic society.[7]

The social gospel's religious idealism developed out of the movement's unique origins in nineteenth-century American Protestantism. Although this book's narrative seeks to broaden the religious base for understanding the social gospel as a theological tradition, it pays close attention to how this movement emerged out of distinctive currents of evangelical and liberal Protestantism. This intersection helped to fuse earlier visions of Protestantism's mission to an emerging late nineteenth-century belief that equated Christian teachings with specific social-economic reform efforts. Part of this book's goal is to analyze what many scholars have identified as the classic social gospel era, corresponding roughly from the final quarter of the nineteenth century through the first quarter of the twentieth century. In the context of post–Civil War America, many religious leaders were coming to terms with a nation that was coping with immigration, industrialization, urbanization, and new manifestations of institutional racism. Those who embraced what became known as the social gospel were alarmed by the social inequalities that existed in American society and increasingly challenged taken-for-granted assumptions about the inherent goodness of laissez-faire capitalism For some scholars, the social gospel has been interpreted as the religious wing of the Progressive Era, in that its major leaders embraced a long-standing belief that the nation's moral-ethical fabric depended upon the strength of its religious—chiefly Protestant—institutions.[8]

However, this book argues that far from disappearing, the social gospel continued to exert a strong influence in North America long after the end of the Progressive Era, both within and outside religious organizations.[9] While many Protestant churches and institutions went through a period after World War I of reassessing their missional identities, the core theological ideals of the social gospel continued to have a wide impact on American religious and secular institutions.[10] One might argue that the period between the early 1920s and the early 1960s could be called the long social gospel era, when many aspects of the original movement's theology were being rethought and reapplied in American society.

In examining the history of the social gospel, we need to explore how the theological heritage of the movement extended throughout the twentieth century. Indeed, in order to trace the history of what some have called the religious left in America, we need to examine and interpret the history of the social gospel. Although this book follows a historical chronology, it pays particular attention to four significant aspects of the social gospel as a distinctive movement in American religious history: its evangelical heritage, its relationship to theological liberalism, its connections with the political left, and its institutional legacy.

1. Evangelical Heritage

When early historians of the social gospel searched for theological roots of the tradition, they tended to concentrate on developments coming out of New England Unitarianism.[11] There is no doubt that early nineteenth-century Unitarianism, with its emphasis on human goodness and its proclivity to look at religion through an ethical rather than doctrinal lens played an important role in the foundation of American theological liberalism. Yet when one looks at the emergence of the social gospel in the late nineteenth century, and especially examines the movement as it matured in the early twentieth century, the echoes of a larger historical tradition of nineteenth-century evangelical Protestantism are unmistakable.

For much of the nineteenth century, American Protestantism was dominated by churches and denominations steeped in numerous currents of evangelicalism. Largely associated with a tradition of revivalism coming out of the First and Second Great Awakenings of the mid-eighteenth and early nineteenth centuries, Protestant evangelicalism stressed the importance of an individual's conversion experience, often referred to by evangelicals as the "new birth." While conversion was primarily personal, this piety had a societal component as well. Extending back to the founding of the first English-speaking American colonies in the 1600s, Protestant evangelicalism was strongly millennial. This belief in Christ's imminent second coming often expressed itself in efforts to make society more righteous in advance of this event. Evangelical optimism was especially evident in America during the early nineteenth century leading up to the Civil War. This millennial spirit, which scholars have called postmillennialism, manifested itself in a variety of Protestant efforts at social reform, including long-standing Protestant crusades for temperance, economic reform, women's rights, and most especially, the abolition of slavery. While it is true that nineteenth-century revivalists like Charles Finney were primarily concerned with individual salvation, they stressed that personal conversion could lead to lives of personal holiness that would be marked by changed societal behavior.[12]

By the early 1870s, discernible changes were beginning to occur in many Protestant churches. For several evangelicals, themes surrounding Christ's imminent return became more apocalyptic. Instead of seeing millennialism in a socially progressive light, emerging movements of what became known as premillennialism insisted that societal conditions would grow worse in advance of the second coming.[13] In a sense, the social gospel, especially in its classic phase, embraced aspects of the evangelical tradition of postmillennialism rather than premillennialism. Although social gospelers were not obsessed by the idea of a literal second coming, they believed that a central goal of Christianity was to create a righteous society that could approximate a heavenly kingdom on earth. At a time in the late nineteenth century when increasing numbers of evangelicals were turning toward premillennialism, those who became associated with the social gospel often expressed earlier themes of evangelical postmillennialism through a liberal theological lens.[14]

In the late nineteenth century, numerous Protestants continued to manifest earlier interests in social reform, reflected in an array of evangelical movements from the Salvation Army to the ministries associated with the urban revivalist Dwight Moody. Many social gospel leaders supported these forms of outreach. Yet what differentiated the social gospelers was their growing insistence that social reform required more than individual conversions or charitable giving to the poor. Modern evangelicalism needed to inject its spirit into the social structures of the nation. "To become fully Christian the Church must come out of its spiritual isolation," Walter Rauschenbusch asserted in 1912. "Like all the rest of us, the Church will get salvation by finding the purpose of its existence outside of itself, in the Kingdom of God, the perfect life of the race."[15]

The exact shape of this "kingdom of God" meant different things to different groups of Protestants, and the term becomes even more suspect when one looks at examples of social reform in Judaism and Catholicism. However, for many social gospelers, the kingdom of God was a powerful and dynamic theological concept. It served as a prism to judge religion's role in seeking to change American social institutions, including government, businesses, families, and even cultural structures. Put another way, social gospel leaders believed that salvation was not about escaping the sins of the world, it was about saving the world.

Importantly, many of the social gospel's primary leaders, especially during its inception and maturity at the turn of the twentieth century, did not define themselves primarily as social reformers. Their commitments to social reform emerged out of a desire to stave off the growing influence in American religion of various apocalyptic theologies that saw the world as an evil place that would come to an end in the near future. Social gospel leaders like Walter Rauschenbusch were vigorously denounced by religious leaders who later were branded "fundamentalists." At the same time, social gospelers strongly identified themselves as part of a wider Protestant heritage that was being contested by a range of other theological and missional viewpoints during the late nineteenth and early twentieth centuries.[16]

Despite the critical role that the social gospel played in American religion, the theological legacy of the movement has largely been interpreted through the lens of neo-orthodox and crisis theologians who emerged in the 1920s and 1930s, particularly Reinhold Niebuhr. The common perception created by these theologians—that the social gospel offered a myopic vision of social progress and lacked an adequate understanding of human sin and depravity—was a gross caricature. Most social gospelers took for granted that their message, like that of Jesus and the prophets of the Hebrew Scriptures, would be rejected by the majority of society and by their own religious traditions. Reflecting back on his ministry in 1912, Rauschenbusch described his early commitment to the social gospel as a time of great uncertainty and, to a degree, of being forced to work as a pariah in the churches. "We were few, and we shouted in the wilderness. . . . Our older friends remonstrated with us for wrecking our career. We ourselves saw the lions' den plainly before us, and only wondered how the beasts would act this time."[17] Such sentiment was not unique. Part of what historians have sometimes overlooked is that even though the social gospel did have a discernible impact on the shape of institutional Protestantism in the early years of the twentieth century, many social gospelers took upon themselves the role of what R. Laurence Moore has called "religious outsiders."[18] Even as someone like Rauschenbusch could speak confidently in 1912 of "Christianizing the social order," he and other social gospelers worried that churches needed to be vigilant in the face of societal forces that were working against the achievement of justice.

One historian used the metaphor of a "God of battles" to characterize the social gospel's theological vision.[19] Social gospelers believed that God worked in history to transform the conditions of individuals and societies to create a just world. However, those who did the work of God had to confront a society made up of forces that opposed these changes. Whether it was combating the misguided teachings of religious conservatives or opposing the forces of big-money capitalism, the social gospelers were engaged in a battle for the soul of the nation, a struggle that often required them to suffer the consequences of their faith in the face of an unbelieving world. At times, this zeal led proponents of the social gospel into many examples of prophetic action. Yet, like earlier examples in the history of American Protestantism, it also led social gospelers to a false sense of their own cherished place in American society.

2. Theological Liberalism

The major difference between the social gospel and other forms of religiously based social reform that developed during the Progressive Era is that the social gospel movement represented a unique outcropping of theological liberalism. The roots of American liberalism go back into the eighteenth century, but it wasn't until the early nineteenth century that liberalism emerged as a distinctive theological heritage in North America.[20] Historically, liberals tended to affirm a positive view of human capacities, rejecting orthodox theologies of original sin and human depravity. As the nineteenth century progressed, those who became associated with theological liberalism also embraced emerging trends in biblical higher criticism, intellectual developments in the natural sciences, such as Darwinian views of evolution, and quite often new currents of Western philosophy, particularly schools of liberalism rooted in nineteenth-century German theology. These trends contributed to what scholars frequently call a "modernist" view of religion, which was committed to the goal of harmonizing religious beliefs with the developing intellectual currents of a reason-dominated Enlightenment world.

Yet many of these modernist liberals showed little or no interest in engaging questions of social reform. What tended to differentiate the liberalism of the social gospel from other theological liberals was the desire to use theology as the basis for creating a mandate to structurally change society. As the social ethicist Gary Dorrien points out, "the notion that Christianity has a mission to transform the structures of society is distinctly modern."[21]

This modern view of religion's role—what many in the social gospel movement called "social salvation"—extends beyond Protestantism. In the late nineteenth century, modernist arguments in philosophy, theology, and the social sciences were also impacting a range of figures in Judaism and Catholicism. Although there were of course significant differences among these various religious voices, they shared a common belief that religion was central to the redemption of society, along decidedly ethical lines. As expressed by Walter Rauschenbusch, the goal of religion was not simply to change individual behavior; religion's goal was to change people such that the chief goal of a person was to serve the common good. "When we submit to God, we submit to the supremacy of the common good. Salvation is the voluntary socializing of the soul."[22]

Although social gospel adherents reflected varying degrees of commitment toward liberal theology, they shared a conviction that the central purpose of religious faith was the creation of a just society, defined initially along politically progressive lines.[23] Like other figures associated with the Progressive Era of the early twentieth century, social gospelers advocated for the creation of government initiatives to protect the rights of the poor, such as the regulation of working hours and the creation of a minimum wage. By the end of World War I, however, many proponents of the social gospel increasingly pushed the parameters of this progressivism by arguing for more radical social-political changes in American society. This broader passion to address political processes emerged from social gospel leaders' interpretation of scripture. By the early twentieth century, representatives of the social gospel were galvanized by a theological fixation on the prophets of the Hebrew Scriptures and the model of the "historical Jesus" presented in the synoptic gospels of the New Testament—the shared tradition of the historical Jesus in the books of Matthew, Mark, and Luke.[24] However, what drove their interpretation of scripture was an idealistic belief that men and women, in partnership with God, could change the course of history.[25] Not only did religion need to address questions of social-political import, but it needed to engage these questions in ways that led to positive social change—change that often focused on a wide range of left-leaning political ideologies.[26]

This book argues that the social gospel's staying power had much to do with its impact as a movement of liberal idealism that traversed a wide range of religious and secular institutions. By the mid-twentieth century, the social gospel was often caricatured by its critics as theologically naïve and overoptimistic. However, the tradition showed its ability to evolve theologically and institutionally. By the end of World War II, the social gospel ideology was not only anchored in churches and religious institutions, but was increasingly expressed in a range of religious and secular movements that impacted emerging social movements of the 1950s, 1960s, and beyond.

3. The Political Left

A central contention of this book is that we cannot understand the social gospel without examining its contributions to the politics of the political left. Earlier scholarship on the social gospel has tended to emphasize the tradition's identity as a middle-class movement and its fidelity to preserving long-standing social and religious institutions.[27] While this assertion is partially accurate, it does not fully capture how the social gospel impulse interpenetrated a wide cross section of religious movements. This is especially evident when one looks at the tendency of scholars to separate the conservative aspects of the social gospel from more radical movements of social Christianity, commonly called Christian socialism. James Dombrowski, who in 1936 wrote one of the first critical studies on the social gospel, lauded the movement for its claim that religion had a fundamental mission to change social structures. Yet he tended to define the social gospel as a politically conservative movement, in juxtaposition to more radical forms of social Christianity that embraced concrete models of political socialism.[28]

While it is important to examine how the concept of Christian socialism was interpreted, it is also necessary to explore how the broader social gospel movement wrestled with the implications of this ideal as it was translated into various theological and political commitments. If anything, socialism in its various forms represents a foil for the social gospel tradition. There may not have been broad support for the political platform of the Socialist Party in America in the early twentieth century, but the idealism that led socialists to advocate for workers' rights, critique capitalist wealth, and aspire to a harmonious social order appealed to a cross section of social gospel liberals.

What ties together the persons and groups discussed in this book under the label "social gospel" is that they embody what the historian Doug Rossinow describes as the "left-liberal" political tradition. This tradition was rooted in a vision of societal progress that wanted to reform preexisting American institutions, such as churches, while also introducing more radical models of social change. Advocates of the social gospel "believed that the country was in the midst of a fundamental transformation into a new society that held the potential to become more democratic, egalitarian, and united," offering an alternative to the unregulated wealth and materialism of American capitalism.[29] Although Rossinow's understanding of the left-liberal tradition encompasses a wide range of secular and religious movements, it is very helpful for understanding the reform mindset of many social gospelers, including reformers coming out of Protestantism, Catholicism, and Judaism who possessed varying degrees of sympathy with political socialism.[30] John Ryan's 1906 book *A Living Wage* stresses themes similar to those of Protestant reformers like Walter Rauschenbusch, affirming a belief that government had a moral obligation to protect the rights of the poor. However, an extensive history of American anti-Catholicism often made it difficult for Catholics and Protestants to work in partnership.[31] Similar barriers were also evident for American Jewish leaders who critiqued social injustice while staving off the anti-Semitism of many of their Protestant colleagues. These intersections between Protestants, Catholics, and Jews were not without tension. However, they underscore the fact that often what held the social gospel movement together was a shared desire to fuse religion and progressive political action.

This wider tradition of religiously inspired political engagement was especially evident in the nation's African American churches, as many prominent clergy and laity in these traditions embraced various aspects of the social gospel.[32] The greatest failure of the early social gospel movement, coming out of predominantly white Protestant churches, was an inability to systemically engage issues of racism that created, in W. E. B. Du Bois's, words "two souls" in America. At the same time, the writings of social gospel leaders like Washington Gladden, Richard Ely, Shailer Mathews, and Walter Rauschenbusch permeated the intellectual underpinnings of many movements of African American social reform. In many ways, Walter Rauschenbusch's legacy was cemented not just by what he did during his lifetime, but by the ways African American leaders during the civil rights era of the 1950s appropriated and reinterpreted his thought.[33]

The social gospel was birthed in a particular array of predominantly white Protestant churches that took for granted their central location in American society. By the same token, many of the political values espoused by the tradition—the redistribution of economic resources, racial justice, and a growing commitment to a vision of America as a religiously pluralistic society—pushed the social gospel beyond its initial base within a Protestant vision of a Christian America. Throughout the twentieth century, the social gospel heritage broadened to embody a social-religious message that embraced the importance of religious and cultural pluralism.[34] This particular contribution of the social gospel remains an underappreciated part of its legacy.

4. Institutional Legacy

Finally, to understand the development of the social gospel in American religion requires that we take seriously the various institutional manifestations of this movement. In the early nineteenth century, religious bodies in the United States were dominated by the concept of volunteerism. Many Americans believed that religious faith was determined by what the sixteenth-century Protestant reformer Martin Luther called the "priesthood of all believers," mainly, that religious meaning needed to be interpreted by the masses, rather than by elite individuals and groups. In the early national period, Protestants, Jews, and Catholics often relied on the efforts of dedicated laity in their churches or synagogues to fulfill a range of leadership roles in areas related to worship, administration, and fund raising. The social gospel emerged at a period in the late nineteenth century when many aspects of America's earlier tradition of volunteerism were giving way to an increasing professionalization that relied not only on the leadership of ordained clergy, but also on an increasing array of religious "professionals" who often became identified with emerging centralized structures in many denominations and, by the early twentieth century, interdenominational organizations. This shift in emphasis was especially noticeable in several Protestant churches that became associated with the social gospel.

Many recent historians have viewed this professionalization of ministry as a symptom of institutional stagnation in American religion. In the case of American Protestantism, the increasing professionalization of ministries in centralized denominational headquarters and bureaucracies has been seen by some scholars as marking the decline of a lively religious volunteerism that led to the creation of an evangelical populism. Scholars who stress the evangelical-populist dimensions of American religion commonly see these histories in quantitative terms—focusing primarily on issues of church growth and decline. The sociologists Roger Finke and Rodney Stark observed that "unless the church is able to re-establish greater tension with its environment it will not be able to restore the rewards needed to maintain high levels of sacrifice by the religious."[35]

This book challenges readers to rethink the notion that institutionalization represents a sign of religious decay; in fact, ideas and themes associated with the social gospel were often disseminated by an expanding range of leaders and institutional networks. The late nineteenth- and early twentieth-century movement toward centralization in religious organizations paralleled wider movements occurring in other segments of American society, most especially in the growing efforts to expand the size and scope of the federal government in order to address social problems. The social gospel was part of a movement that increasingly advocated for expanded government solutions to social issues such as economic justice and racial equality.

On one hand, part of telling the story of the social gospel necessitates exploring the impact of influential ministers, many of whom served as the movement's primary theological voices. The social gospel arose at a time in the late nineteenth century when religious leaders, particularly Protestant ministers, often enjoyed enormous public status that extended beyond specific churches and denominations. Well into the twentieth century, clergy associated with the social gospel had their sermons published in numerous periodicals, and by the 1920s they reached even more listeners through mass media such as radio. However, to tell the story of the social gospel is not only to talk about the writings and activities of clergy—as important as they are to this narrative. It is also to show how a wide range of social gospel figures in the settlement house movement, women's home missions, the Protestant ecumenical movement, the Socialist Party, the YMCA/YWCA, the Fellowship of Reconciliation, and a wide range of caucuses and activist groups played a vital role in shaping and disseminating theological ideas. Examining the organizational networks that the social gospel helped to forge not only counters common arguments that its impact never extended beyond elite institutional leaders,[36] but also shows how some of the ideas coming from social gospel pioneers like Richard Ely, Washington Gladden, and especially Walter Rauschenbusch were reinterpreted in different contexts.

The social gospel has been critiqued for its lack of mass appeal, especially when compared to popular evangelicalism. However, to understand the impact of the social gospel in American religion, we need to examine how it was indeed a "movement" that played a critical role in forging a wider tradition of religious and political activism in twentieth-century America.

The Social Gospel Movement as Social Idealism

This book underscores the point that central to the broader development of the social gospel in American religion is the evolving character of its social idealism. Recent historians have been increasingly drawn to movements of American religion that have emerged outside formal religious institutions.[37] The historian Dan McKanan has observed the persistent presence of "radical religion" in American religious history, in which religious ideals are central to shaping movements of political radicalism such as abolitionism, women's rights, and the civil rights movement.[38] The social gospel as a movement of religious idealism reveals an ongoing tension between the imperative to work within pre-existent religious institutions and, at other moments, to push outside them. One reason that an earlier generation of scholars was quick to point to the demise of the social gospel after World War I is that they saw it mostly through established Protestant churches. Although this institutional history is critical to understanding the social gospel's development in the twentieth century, we must also look for ways that the key ideas and objectives of the movement had a wide impact outside explicitly religious institutions.

The first four chapters of the book deal with the period between 1880 and 1920, which many historians identify as the classic social gospel era in American religious history. Chapter 1 focuses on the shifting nineteenth-century historical context of American Protestantism that gave birth to the social gospel. Framed against the backdrop of an era in which many evangelical Protestants sought to "Christianize" America and the world, early social gospel pioneers such as Washington Gladden, Josiah Strong, and Frances Willard helped to shape the religious idealism that characterized the later social gospel. These leaders combined aspects of an earlier evangelical heritage with a liberal theology, articulating what figures like Gladden described as "social salvation"—a belief that central to Christianity's mission was the imperative to transform individuals as well as social structures.

Chapter 2 discusses how the social currents of the late nineteenth century contributed to the theological development of the social gospel. In particular, this chapter examines what was at times a symbiotic relationship between historical interpretations of Jesus and political socialism, a relationship fleshed out in American popular culture and in ecclesiastical and academic settings. This connection between Jesus and radical political action was made by a wide cross section of Protestant churches and had many parallels to developing traditions of social reform in Roman Catholicism and Judaism, which complemented and also challenged the assumptions of the dominant Protestant churches.

Chapter 3 investigates how the theology of the social gospel matured by the early twentieth century. While focusing on the impact of Walter Rauschenbusch, the chapter compares Rauschenbusch's classic iteration of the social gospel, epitomized in his 1907 book *Christianity and the Social Crisis*, with emerging views of religion and social reform coming from Reform Judaism and Roman Catholicism. The social gospel rose at a time when Protestant-Catholic tensions were running high and many of the classic Protestant social gospelers held discernible anti-Catholic views. Yet the ways certain Catholic leaders grafted a modernist view of social change upon a traditional theology represents a significant contrast to the approach taken by Protestant leaders, as does the work of figures within American Judaism who embraced many aspects of social gospel thinking. Jewish leaders like Emil Hirsch and Stephen Wise made frequent reference to works by leading Protestant social gospelers. However, leaders like Wise were clear that the American Jewish experience was unique and distinct from the dominant Protestant experience. Stephen Wise's legacy is critical not only because of his engagement with Rauschenbusch's work, but because he helped to define a template for religious-based social activism that would remain a prominent part of Judaism's legacy in twentieth-century American religion.

Chapter 4 examines the social gospel's institutional ascendency in American religion, specifically American Protestantism. The years from approximately 1908 to 1920 constituted an era in which the social gospel permeated the institutional fabric of numerous Protestant structures, transforming long-standing evangelical organizations like the YMCA and emerging bodies such as the Federal Council of Churches. On one hand, social gospel leaders like Rauschenbusch were confident of their institutional triumphs in American Protestantism. At the same time, developing theological and missional tensions within and outside these institutions created a rupture that affected the evolution of the social gospel tradition throughout the twentieth century. These tensions can be seen in the careers of two individuals: Harry F. Ward and Francis J. McConnell.

In the 1910s McConnell and Ward were two of the most prominent social gospel figures in American religion. As Methodists, they represented the largest Protestant denomination in the country, and both played critical roles in the institutionalization of the social gospel in

their denomination and in the Federal Council of Churches, an organization that until it merged with the National Council of Churches in
1950 symbolized many Protestant efforts to disseminate their theological and cultural worldview in America. By the early 1920s, however, the
works of both men reveal a growing tension with earlier views of social
gospel progressivism, and the chapter discusses an emerging conflict
between the social gospel's progressive and radical reform agendas. In
many ways, the deaths in 1918 of two social gospel stalwarts, Walter
Rauschenbusch and Washington Gladden, represent a symbolic transi-
tion for the movement, as much of its earlier progressive religious base
became increasingly fragmented in the decades that followed.

The final three chapters examine the development of the social gospel after World War I, arguing that this era of the long social gospel
culminated in the civil rights movement associated with the leadership
of Martin Luther King Jr.[39] Chapter 5 discusses the growth of the social gospel during the interwar period, from the early 1920s to the early
1940s. Part of the social gospel's legacy can be seen in the foundation
of organizations like the Fellowship of Reconciliation (FOR) and its
partnership with older Protestant organizations like the YMCA. With
leadership steeped in social gospel theology, the FOR and YMCA were
instrumental in promoting radical economic reform and increasingly
drawing attention to issues such as militarism, internationalism, pacifism, and racism. These organizations reflected a growing radicalism
among younger Americans, who while often alienated from institutionally based religion, were drawn to a wide range of religious youth movements that served as a model for later social activism in the twentieth
century.[40]

At the same time, the social gospel remained an active and formative impulse in American religious institutions. One key figure who embodied the ongoing institutional appeal of the social gospel after World
War I was Harry Emerson Fosdick. Fosdick was the most popular liberal
Protestant minister during the first half of the twentieth century, and
his career illustrates how Protestant social gospel commitments were
expanding in the interwar period to embrace a wider range of social
issues.[41] Additionally, the interwar period witnessed a significant turn
among many social gospel leaders to religious models outside North
America and Western Europe. The role of the Japanese Christian leader

Toyohiko Kagawa is especially important in illuminating how many social gospel leaders challenged earlier suppositions related to the dominant role of Western churches in mission, advocating for increasingly indigenous, non-Western leadership.[42]

Chapter 6 discusses the social gospel's impact on the civil rights movement and how it engaged emerging currents from the religious and political left in the 1960s and 1970s. While Martin Luther King Jr. is certainly the central figure in the story of the civil rights movement, King's success was undergirded by a range of leaders who subscribed to various aspects of the social gospel heritage. King's successes in nonviolent direct action represented a high-water mark for the social gospel in America; however, the years following his death witnessed a spate of theological critics of the social gospel. Just as some religious radicals in the 1920s and 1930s questioned many of the gradualist political suppositions of the social gospel, a range of Christian theologians raised issues about the extent to which the liberalism associated with the social gospel could be an effective instrument of social change in a postcolonial world.

At the same time that many leaders questioned the social gospel's liberal heritage as outdated, the churches and denominations most associated with the social gospel—the liberal religious mainline—suffered significant numerical losses. As these religious groups declined in the 1960s and 1970s, an eclectic assortment of Protestant and Catholic traditionalists disdained the political radicalism of churches influenced by the social gospel. The Vietnam War marked an end to an era dominated by ecumenically oriented Protestant churches, signaling a sharp decline in the social gospel movement's influence in American religion.

As mainline Protestant influence declined drastically in the 1970s, other groups sought to seize upon aspects of the social gospel legacy, even as they often differentiated themselves from these earlier liberal movements. Chapter 7 examines the rise of the Christian Right in the late twentieth century, analyzing how conservative evangelicals reinvigorated an older social gospel rhetoric of activism—from a politically conservative base. For many conservative evangelicals, the social gospel became a catchall phrase to describe how religion was co-opted by the perceived radicalism of the left. While the emergence of the Christian Right was a major development of the late twentieth century, the chapter also examines a movement commonly known as "progressive evangelicalism," which often defined itself against the political stands taken by the Christian Right. Both of these movements illustrate aspects of the earlier social gospel's agenda to "Christianize" America. Although these two evangelical groups cast themselves as angry prophets in the wilderness, they craved a greater public role for their religious traditions, not unlike the leaders of the original social gospel of the early twentieth century. In many ways, Ronald Reagan's election in 1980 was symbolic not only of the ascendency of groups like the Christian Right, but also of the institutional displacement of the religious left, associated with the heirs of the social gospel.

The book's conclusion reflects upon the social gospel's legacy in the early twenty-first century, providing a summation of its historical impact and its prospects in the twenty-first century. Early twenty-first-century survey data on American religion suggest a sharp downturn in the fortunes of American religious institutions—a decline that is especially evident in the more liberal religious movements that gave birth to the social gospel.[43] The conclusion takes up the question of whether the social gospel legacy can survive in a twenty-first-century era noted for being a time of religious pluralism but also an era of religious decline.

In my attempt to provide readers a comprehensive discussion of the topic, I have struggled to decide which individuals and groups to include in the narrative. The term "social gospel" was not widely used until the 1910s, even though the origins of the phrase date to the late nineteenth century,[44] and its use has most often described white Protestants. Yet to exclude the stories of Jewish, Catholic, and particularly African American religious reformers in this narrative would be to ignore the contributions of these nonwhite, non-Protestant groups on the broader history of religious-based social reform in American history. While I recognize the difficulty of using the term "social gospel" in discussing African American, Jewish, and Catholic reformers, it is important to note that figures like Reverdy Ransom, Stephen Wise, and John Ryan were quite cognizant of the ways their social thought contributed to the wider movement of religiously based social reform—what many Catholic, Jewish, and Protestant leaders in the early twentieth century called the "social awakening"—of which the predominantly white Protestant social gospel was part.

As this book discusses, the interactions between numerically dominant white Protestants and their African American, Catholic, and Jewish counterparts were often complex and contested, even as religious engagement among American Protestants concerning the place of the social gospel was also complex and contested. The figures in this book often discovered, sometimes painfully, the limits of their theological ideals to make permanent changes in the nation's social fabric. And yet the conversation about the public role of religion in America is just as vital today as it was during the lifetime of Walter Rauschenbusch. Quite simply, to understand the social gospel's impact is indispensable for any conversation about the larger importance of religion in American history.

1

"A Perfect Man in a Perfect Society"

The Emergence of the Social Gospel in Nineteenth-Century America

In 1876 the Congregational minister Washington Gladden published *Working People and Their Employers*, a contentious book on religion's role in an urban industrialized society. Gladden's analysis frequently returned to the theme that both labor and management needed to place the spirit of Christian love ahead of self-interest. For Gladden, infusing Christian principles into the social fabric of the industrial workplace would impart a "spirit that thinks less of personal power or gain or glory than of the common good. . . . Where this spirit abounds, there is always unity and fruitfulness; where this spirit is not, there is confusion and all kinds of evil."[1]

Many of Gladden's readers were not impressed by his conclusions. For several wealthy and prosperous Americans, his assertions about applying Christian teaching to the economic conditions of society reflected a movement away from the need for clergy to preach primarily about personal conversion. Likewise, leaders of the nascent labor movement found little solace in Gladden's musings, noting that his comments were typical of the detachment of the nation's churches from the workers' plight.[2]

Despite the book's mixed reception, Gladden had published what many scholars have identified as one of the first works associated with the rise of the social gospel in America.[3] In upcoming years, Gladden's name became synonymous with what was popularly known in the 1880s as social Christianity and by the early twentieth century as the social gospel. Gladden did not discount the importance of a personal conversion experience. Yet "conversion" needed to be defined in a way that encompassed how individuals contributed to a society, whereby social institutions would be structurally altered to conform to the teachings of

Jesus and the Gospel. As Gladden noted in the 1890s, "The end of Christianity is twofold, a perfect man in a perfect society. . . . These purposes are never separated; they cannot be separated."[4] Like many American Protestants of his time, Gladden insisted on the goal of "Christianizing" America through the moral suasion of its churches. Yet this process of Christianizing needed to prioritize the integration of the social ramifications of the gospel of Jesus into the social-economic structures of the nation. Washington Gladden's career was paradigmatic of an era when influential Protestant clergy, academics, and laity believed that their mission extended beyond the goal of traditional evangelism to save souls. Rather, Christianity's purpose was seen as the need to save society from the injustices created by nineteenth-century capitalism.

For Protestants like Washington Gladden, the need for churches to be invested in social reform was interconnected to the wider evangelical Protestant goal of "saving" America—that is, employing the practices of evangelism to convert Americans to Protestant Christianity. For Gladden and other Protestant leaders of his generation who were associated with what became known as the social gospel, reform went hand in hand with the churches' privileged position as the builders of a righteous nation.[5] This mission to build a "Christian America" was central to American Protestantism's institutional and theological mission—and to the rise of the social gospel. In examining the decades when Gladden came of age prior to and following the Civil War, one gains an understanding of the origins of the social gospel movement in America.

Antebellum Protestant Reform and the Origins of the Social Gospel

In many ways, the origins of the social gospel movement can be found in a tradition of American evangelicalism that took root before the Civil War.[6] The early decades of the nineteenth century were a time of spectacular growth in American Protestantism. Led by Baptist, Methodist, Presbyterian, and numerous other churches and sects coming out of what historians call the Second Great Awakening, these Protestants proclaimed the centrality of a personal conversion experience. By the same token, many Protestants believed that eradicating personal sin through conversion would create the conditions of a just society. For many evangelicals, their zeal in combining conversion and social reform was manifested in their opposition to slavery.

In the decades leading up to the Civil War, numerous churches were ripped apart by sectional divisions over slavery. While many denominations in the early nineteenth century tried to avoid debating the issue, seeing it as a political rather than religious question, a wide range of Protestant leaders increasingly were drawn to the abolitionist cause.[7] Paradigmatic of this spirit was the famed evangelist Charles G. Finney. Finney's primary purpose was to save sinners from the fires of hell. His revivals were punctured with calls for individuals to repent of their sins and accept faith in Christ. However, his support for the antislavery movement fed into a growing spirit of abolitionism in many parts of the North by the late 1830s.

Finney's theology came out of postmillennialism. As we have seen, postmillennialism is a movement that embraces a belief that conversion will lead to an increase in social righteousness, which in turn will serve as a precursor to the Second Coming of Christ. Evangelicals like Finney equated personal righteousness with the elimination of societal evils such as slavery. Finney's theology showed the influence of what has been called holiness theology. Often associated with the eighteenth-century founder of Methodism, John Wesley, holiness theology, or what has also been called sanctification or Christian perfection, taught that God has the power to purge humans of sin. Consequently, these evangelists believed that the more people converted to Christianity, the more righteous society would become.[8] Charles Finney preached a message that emphasized evangelicalism's role in transforming the world "to reform individuals, communities, and governments . . . until every form of iniquity shall be driven from the earth."[9]

By the 1850s, many holiness-influenced evangelicals were not only embracing the abolitionist message, but were engaging a wide range of reform efforts related to temperance, prison reform, and women's suffrage. This tradition of Christian perfection that influenced pre–Civil War evangelicals such as Finney and the Methodist revivalist Phoebe Palmer would also be picked up by a later generation of Protestant leaders who became associated with the social gospel.[10]

Antebellum evangelicalism placed a strong emphasis on the role of converted individuals in redeeming America from a variety of societal evils. However, the movement's strong emphasis on the innate sinfulness of humanity did not sit well with a small group of Protestant dissenters. These dissenters believed that God created individuals to be naturally capable of goodness, and they saw this goodness as a means to transform societal conditions. Thus, a second major influence on the eventual rise of the social gospel in America was the antebellum tradition of American theological liberalism.

The origins of American theological liberalism can be found chiefly in Unitarianism.[11] The Unitarian movement placed tremendous importance on human reason as a criterion for interpreting scripture. Unitarians came to question the doctrine of the Trinity as a nonbiblical fabrication of the early church. More importantly, this movement challenged evangelical Protestant notions of human sinfulness by affirming the natural goodness and rational nature of humanity. In New England, where Unitarianism primarily developed, the movement challenged the Calvinist theological suppositions of many of that region's churches. While Calvinism emphasized the chasm that existed between God and a sinful humanity, Unitarianism affirmed that God was accessible through human experience. Along with a populist-oriented movement called Universalism that developed in parts of New England, upstate New York, and the mid-Atlantic, Unitarianism elevated reason and human experience rather than historical doctrine as the primary mode for theological understanding. An important figure in the wider development of New England liberalism was Theodore Parker. From the mid-1840s until his death in 1860, Parker was one of America's most prominent abolitionist leaders, and his writings influenced future generations of American reformers, including those in the social gospel movement.[12]

Parker came out of a movement of New England liberalism referred to as Transcendentalism. This movement elevated the importance of individual experience while also repudiating most aspects of traditional Christian doctrine. Along with Ralph Waldo Emerson, Margaret Fuller, and Henry David Thoreau, Parker embraced a distinctive tradition of religious idealism that marked later iterations of theological liberalism. Although Parker's religious idealism moved way beyond the institutional parameters of early nineteenth-century Protestant evangelicalism, he emphasized that his religious idealism was rooted firmly in the teaching of Jesus and the New Testament. In one of his most famous sermons, Parker asserted that the timelessness of Jesus's teaching would survive the often outdated theological suppositions of a given era, revealing the power of Jesus's message in the face of transient doctrines: "Christianity is a simple thing. . . . It is absolute, pure Morality; absolute, pure Religion; the love of man; the love of God." Christianity was not about adherence to doctrine, "but rather a method of attaining oneness with God."[13] Parker's stress upon Christianity as the purest form of ethical religion would be critical to later proponents of the social gospel, especially his emphasis on the historical dimensions of Jesus's teachings.

Although theological liberalism in the early nineteenth century was largely confined to New England Unitarianism, by the 1840s and 1850s a small number of theological liberals emerged in more orthodox Protestant churches and denominations. The most prominent of these early liberals was Horace Bushnell, a Congregational minister in Hartford, Connecticut.

For the majority of his career, Bushnell saw his ministry as an effort to reinterpret an earlier tradition of New England Congregational theology.[14] He worried that Calvinism placed too much emphasis on fidelity to doctrine, at the expense of religious experience. At the same time, he disdained the way many evangelicals turned religious truth into an emotionally wrought conversion experience. For Bushnell, a critical idea in the development of the religious life was what he called "Christian nurture." Rather than stressing conversion as a singular event, Bushnell argued that faith was a constant process of growth and development. Conceding that Unitarians went too far in equating religion with ethics, he believed that the essence of the Christian life was understood as a process of constant personal development and growth. Although Bushnell's ideals were contentious among orthodox Christians, they increasingly found theological expression in American Protestantism by the late nineteenth century. In the years following his death in 1876, Bushnell's ideas of religious nurture impacted the thinking of a wide range of Protestant ministers, theologians, and church leaders who became associated with the social gospel.

Although they were vastly different traditions, postmillennial evangelicalism and the theological liberalism of Unitarianism both influenced the development of the social gospel in American Protestantism. Evangelicalism emphasized how personal conversion might lead to the building of a righteous society. Unitarian liberalism stressed the natural goodness of humanity and the ability of humans to change their personal and collective behavior. Both movements believed that central to Christianity's mission was a commitment to transforming societal conditions through righteous living. The belief that religion had a mission to transform individuals *and* social structures became a dominant theme in the social gospel after the Civil War.

Post–Civil War America and the Rise of Social Christianity

The North's victory in the Civil War provided occasions for many Protestant clergy to echo earlier millennial hopes that slavery's ending might usher in an era of righteousness in America. In the decades following the Civil War, however, this earlier evangelical confidence gave way to an increasing anxiety about the nation's future. For much of the nineteenth century, America was undergoing rapid social-economic transformations, which became more pronounced—and worrisome—for many Protestant leaders in the decades following the Civil War.

These social changes were exacerbated by continuous waves of immigration. By the mid-1880s, approximately 500,000 new immigrants per year were arriving to the United States, and that number rose exponentially by the early twentieth century.[15] While immigrant settlement impacted most regions of the country, it had a significant effect on many northern cities. For example, Chicago on the eve of the Great Fire of 1871 had a population just under 300,000. Less than twenty years later, that population was over a million.[16] Many of these new arrivals came to the country in abject poverty, and increasingly cities like Chicago, New York, Philadelphia, and Boston were filled with urban slums, comprised of recent waves of immigrants.

The massive numbers of immigrants, coupled with the development of industrial technologies, created the ideal conditions for new American industries. In the aftermath of the Civil War, industrialization hit the nation in full force, leading to the creation of massive economic monopolies in businesses such as oil, railroads, textiles, steel, and gas and electric. The so-called Gilded Age fostered for some a belief in America as a land of inexhaustible economic opportunities. Although some fraction of Americans did benefit from the growth of industrial capitalism, a large number were victimized by poverty. Conditions in urban tenements and slums worsened as they became more crowded, and the majority of the poor who were fortunate to find employment received substandard wages, with no limits on work hours or monitoring of workplace safety. There was no social safety net to protect workers if they became ill and could no longer work, nor any sort of social security or retirement benefits. Immigrant women and children frequently were employed in "sweatshops" working twelve-hour days in crowded, poorly ventilated spaces. At this time in American history, the idea that federal and state governments might pass laws to safeguard and protect workers did not exist.

Many political, business, and religious leaders saw social inequalities as simply a natural occurrence. The British philosopher Herbert Spencer believed that human progress depended on a struggle among individuals, whereby through physical strength and intelligence certain individuals and groups would gain wealth and prosperity. Often credited with coining the phrase "survival of the fittest," Spencer argued that human advancement and social advancement required personal freedom, and that government initiatives to regulate economic practices were misplaced.[17] While many American Protestant leaders did not necessarily embrace the intricacies of Spencer's social thought, they enthusiastically accepted the idea that religion and the accumulation of wealth went hand in hand. The historian Henry May noted that in the years following the Civil War, "many Protestant spokesmen delighted to point out that the road to success led through Christian living," whereby a just and benevolent society would emerge through the generosity of the wealthy.[18] Economic disparities went hand in hand with the freedom to work hard, earn wealth, and practice charitable giving. "The poor we have with us always; and this is not the greatest of our hardships, but the choicest of our blessings," one periodical noted in 1874. "If there is anything that a Christian may feel thankful for, it is the privilege of lifting a little of the load of some of his heavily-burdened neighbors."[19] This "gospel of wealth" found a hearing among an emerging generation of liberal Protestant preachers, including one of the best-known ministers in America, Henry Ward Beecher. The pastor of the Plymouth Congregational Church in Brooklyn, New York, Beecher was the model for the so-called pulpit princes of the late nineteenth-century who pastored large and often wealthy churches.[20] Although Beecher had been a supporter of the abolitionist movement, he often found it easy to equate scripture with making money. While he conceded that wealth could be abused, he asserted that a healthy (and Christian) society rested on the ability of hardworking men to become wealthy. "I thank God that there is a rising of men from the bottom of society toward the top. My heart goes with the men who are poor and ignorant and who are working for liberty to be larger and richer."[21]

Such sentiments by ministers like Beecher expressed a triumphant sense shared by many Protestant church leaders in the late nineteenth century. Although Protestantism comprised numerous denominations with varying doctrinal beliefs, these churches identified themselves broadly as "evangelicals."[22] Daniel Dorchester, a Methodist minister who wrote one of the major late nineteenth-century textbooks on the history of American Christianity, looked to a hopeful Protestant future in the twentieth century. While concerned about the "beastly" teachings of Mormonism and the "specter of Romanism," he believed that the numerical dominance of the evangelical churches would reform even the Roman Catholic Church "to the likeness of apostolic Christianity."[23]

However, the theological contours of evangelicalism were shifting. By the 1870s, increasing numbers of Protestants were moving away from earlier postmillennial beliefs that Christian conversion would lead to a righteous society. Instead, a new generation of Protestants embraced what has been called premillennialism. In juxtaposition to a belief that a righteous society could be built on earth, premillennialists, as we have seen, believed that social conditions would grow worse, in advance of the Second Coming. Building on the legacy of the Millerites, a group that in the late 1830s and early 1840s held to a precise date for the return of Christ, post–Civil War Protestants were increasingly drawn to a form of premillennialism called dispensationalism. Associated with a system devised by an Irish Protestant minister, John Nelson Darby, dispensationalists interpreted scripture in precise ways to show God's complete control of history. Darby's teachings centered on the "Rapture," a doctrine that held that true believers would be taken off the earth by God in sudden dramatic fashion (and unlike the Millerites, Darby's followers avoided precise dating). His teachings became the basis for many forms of popular evangelicalism that became prominent in the 1870s and 1880s.[24]

Protestants who embraced premillennialism felt that they had reason to be pessimistic about America's future. In addition to waves of non-Protestant immigrants coming to America, many American cities were beset with growing outbreaks of labor unrest in the 1870s and 1880s. A particular threat to Protestant missional hopes was the growing numerical dominance of the Roman Catholic Church. In the early nineteenth century, American Catholics were largely confined to a few scattered areas in the northeastern United States and the Eastern Seaboard. However, by the 1820s, Catholic immigrants started to come to America in massive numbers. Before the Civil War, most of these new Catholic immigrants were from Ireland and Germany. After the war, most Catholics arrived from eastern and southern Europe. By the early 1870s, the Roman Catholic Church became the largest religious group in the United States, and over the next twenty years the Catholic population doubled, rising from 3.5 million to 7 million.[25]

The question of how Christians should face the problems caused by immigration and industrialization *and* defend the nation from the menace of Catholicism and other apostate religions was central for Protestant leaders, including those who would embrace the social gospel. Since the founding of the first American colonies in the seventeenth century, American Protestants had displayed a fierce antagonism toward Catholicism. As Catholic immigration increased during the nineteenth century, so did Protestant animosity toward the Catholic Church. By the mid-1880s, a wide range of Protestants were beginning to call attention to the social-economic problems of the nation—as well as the problem of the Catholic menace to American society. The leader who most embodied this tension was Josiah Strong.

Strong's career is something of a paradox. Later scholars would see him as the worst embodiment of a white, ethnocentric (if not racist) vision of American Protestantism. Yet for a generation of Protestant leaders in the 1880s, Josiah Strong was a prophet who proclaimed a bold new direction for American Christianity that avoided the pessimism of premillennialism while proposing ways to reform the nation.[26] A Congregational minister, Strong had been involved in a number of Protestant missionary organizations that emerged prior to and following the Civil War. In 1885 he published his first major book, *Our Country: Its Possible Future and Its Present Crisis*. From the standpoint of other social gospel reformers who would emerge by the end of the nineteenth century, Strong was on the conservative end of the spectrum. However, as one historian noted, *Our Country* represented a sort of *Uncle Tom's Cabin* for urban mission and reform in the United States.[27] For many Protestants who came of age in the 1880s, Strong's book became an influential text in urban evangelicalism, selling over 100,000 copies in multiple editions.[28] He was aware that America's future was increasingly being defined by its industrial cities, and when he looked at urban America, he didn't like what he saw. Most especially, Strong was fearful of the rising presence of Roman Catholic immigrants. While he cited works by Protestant scholars like Daniel Dorchester to reassure his readers that Protestants were not losing numerical ground to Catholics, he conceded the growing presence of Catholicism, especially in urban working-class populations.

Strong joined a lengthy list of Protestants throughout the nineteenth century who saw in Catholic papal authority a danger to America's democratic heritage. He struck a theme that would be important to the development of the Protestant social gospel, maintaining the immutable connection between the history of Protestantism and American democracy:

> It is the theory of absolutism in the church, that man exists for the church. But in republicanism and Protestant America it is believed that church and state exist for man and are to be administered by him. Our fundamental ideas of society, therefore, are as radically opposed to Vaticanism as to Imperialism. And it is as inconsistent with our liberties for American citizens to yield allegiance to the Pope as to the Czar.[29]

Critics have castigated Strong for his ethnocentrism and cultural elitism, particularly his constant assertion of the cultural superiority of "Anglo-Saxon" Christianity.[30] Strong endorsed what seemed a "survival of the fittest" worldview of Herbert Spencer, coming precariously close to equating Anglo-Saxon cultural virtues with racial superiority. He dismissed political socialism as an immigrant ideology, seeing it as a menace to the teachings of Christianity. For Strong, socialism was synonymous with anarchism—both movements were associated in his mind with foreign immigrants who did not have the benefit of living in a democratic society.

Strong acknowledged that the nation's social-economic inequalities, and the human suffering they produced, made an appeal to socialist ideals inevitable. In his mind, it was imperative that Christianity address these inequalities from the pulpit and by concerted action. Just as importantly, however, Strong called upon Protestants to employ emerging disciplines of the social sciences, so that churches could more effectively engage systemically the social problems faced by the urban poor.

One of the works that Strong references in *Our Country* was an 1879 book by Henry George, *Progress and Poverty*. In the late nineteenth and early twentieth centuries, George's work became the basis for many reformers associated with the Progressive Era and the social gospel. Although Strong worried that aspects of George's theories could easily lead Americans to embrace socialism as a political panacea, he acknowledged that George understood how capitalism made it difficult for the poor to create a sustainable livelihood. George wrote, "In all the great American cities there is today as clearly defined a ruling class as in the most aristocratic countries in the world. Its members carry wards in their pockets, make up the slates for nominating conventions, distribute offices as they bargain together, and—though they toil not, neither do they spin—wear the best of raiment and spend money lavishly."[31] From Josiah Strong in the 1880s to Walter Rauschenbusch in the early 1900s, social gospelers stressed George's notion that unearned wealth was one of the greatest sins of modern capitalism. They believed that modern industrialization had created a society in which wealth came not through hard honest work, but rather through reckless economic speculation whereby the poor were always the most vulnerable. As a remedy to this parasitic tendency in capitalism, George proposed what he called the "single-tax." He envisioned this measure as a municipal tax that would force property owners to pay taxes on their lands, whereby the revenue would be used to promote public welfare initiatives, including the creation of parks and recreation facilities. While later social gospelers would see the single-tax as a somewhat naïve ideal, they frequently acknowledged the importance of George as an "apostle of a great truth."[32]

Although Strong appreciated aspects of George's witness, Strong's main purpose was to preach and encourage his audiences to live out a message that called for the redemption of America along Protestant cultural lines. He bequeathed to his generation a message that proclaimed a unified vision of Protestant America to which all Americans, regardless of background or religion, would subscribe. At the same time, Strong's success was indicative of how many Protestant leaders in the 1880s were increasingly seeking ways to apply religious beliefs to questions of social reform, including the man whom historians would later dub the "father of the social gospel" in America: Washington Gladden.

Washington Gladden and the Birth of the Social Gospel

As we have seen, Washington Gladden penned one of the first books associated with the rise of the social gospel in the United States. Decades later, as he neared retirement from his pastorate of the First Congregational Church of Columbus, Ohio, Gladden's pastoral successor told Gladden that he had two main interests—"liberal religious thought and a desire to see the Gospel of Christ applied in all the manifold relations of life." When Gladden heard this, he responded, "Well, what else *IS* there?"[33] By the time Gladden retired in 1912, he had established himself as perhaps the premier spokesperson in American Protestantism of what was increasingly being called the "social gospel." However, it took Gladden several years to develop his understanding of the social gospel.

Born in Pennsylvania in 1836 and raised in rural upstate New York, Gladden spent a good part of his young adulthood discerning his vocation. Ordained into the Congregational ministry, Gladden served churches in Pennsylvania and New York. In 1867 he became pastor of a Congregational church in North Adams, Massachusetts. A center for the textile industry, North Adams provided Gladden an early context in which he struggled to reconcile Christianity with the wealth disparities that he came across in the community. In some ways, Gladden's time in North Adams did not seem to produce an immediate social awakening. Many of his sermons dealt with the need for workers to develop healthy amusements, and one of his earliest publications was a travel guide that extoled the virtues of rural New England travel. However, Gladden's early theology revealed an emphasis on the dignity of a strong work ethic and the honor attached to manual labor. These themes would be fleshed out in subsequent years.[34]

Gladden's theological outlook owed much to his friendship with Horace Bushnell. Forced to resign his Hartford pastorate due to poor health,

Bushnell spent his final years writing on a range of topics, including the atonement. Unlike other evangelicals who saw Christ's death as a substitutionary or ransom sacrifice that provided believers with a supernatural infusion of salvific grace, Bushnell stressed that Jesus's self-sacrifice and death served humans as a model of Christian morality. Bushnell was not the first Christian leader to articulate what has been called a "moral influence" doctrine of the atonement, a position that dates from the medieval period. However, his arguments served many social gospelers like Gladden as a means to stress that the message of Jesus required Christians to live lives of Christlike morality and to practice high ethical standards in their public affairs.

Convinced that he could best utilize his talents as a writer outside a parish, in 1871 Gladden became an editor of the *Independent*, whose chief editor had once been Henry Ward Beecher. While at the *Independent* Gladden continued to extol the virtue of appropriate amusements as a necessary part of a Christian's development (and he held a deep fondness for a game that would be recognized by the end of the nineteenth century as America's national pastime, baseball). Although Gladden loved aspects of journalism, he increasingly felt constrained by the *Independent*'s editorial policy, which caused him to resign. In a letter to a colleague, Gladden noted that "of course I shall go back into the pulpit. Nothing else is left me."[35]

In 1875 Gladden's idealism took on new expression when he became pastor of the First Congregational Church in Springfield, Massachusetts. Initially, his support of the nascent American labor movement was tepid, stressing the power of the Golden Rule and Christ's love as the means to create a better society. Yet Gladden was one of the first major Protestant clergymen in the late nineteenth century to support labor unions, and his writings by the early 1880s reflected a more explicit endorsement of the labor movement. In 1882 he was called to the First Congregational Church in Columbus, Ohio, where he remained until his retirement in 1912.

Gladden's long-term Columbus pastorate was a model for many future social gospel leaders who would serve as ministers of large, urban, and wealthy churches. From his pulpit, Gladden gained national stature as a preacher; in many respects he became the preeminent Protestant clergy leader of the Progressive Era. His theology demonstrates a grafting of an earlier evangelical postmillennialism upon an emerging tradition of theological liberalism. Gladden's early years in Columbus were characterized by a myopic sense of optimism that social reform was achievable through a combination of moral suasion and progressive activism. Yet his message was one that would characterize much of the social gospel movement's development in the 1880s and 1890s: in order for Christianity to be effective, individuals needed to find ways to live out their faith ethically. Gladden's attitude toward traditional Christian doctrine was not as hostile as that of Theodore Parker. However, Parker's influence permeates Gladden's early theology. His sermons and writings repeatedly turned to the argument that the essence of Christian teaching needed to be translatable to the social realities faced by men and women living in a modern industrial society, and if doctrine could not hold up to that test, then it was suspect.

Gladden reinterpreted a theological concept that would become increasingly important for later proponents of the social gospel: the kingdom of God. Historically, the kingdom of God was a theological concept that many Christians believed embodied the culmination of human history, and a full manifestation of God's divine reign of peace and justice on earth. In many movements of Protestant theology, the kingdom of God often became synonymous with various understandings of the Second Coming of Christ. However, while many late nineteenth-century revivalists understood the kingdom of God as a catastrophic, apocalyptic end of human history, for liberals like Gladden, the kingdom of God was a concept synonymous with the ability of humans to live out God's will fully on earth. For those who became associated with the social gospel movement, this meant that the kingdom of God was an updated interpretation of a deep-seated American Protestant vision of building a righteous society in America.

Gladden's view of the kingdom of God concept exemplifies what came to be called social salvation, whereby a righteous society would be built not merely by personal conversion, but also by a transformation of the social fabric of modern society: "The law of the kingdom requires us to love the Lord with all our hearts, and our neighbors as ourselves. . . . It insists that the spirit of this commandment must rule in every transaction between man and man, on week days as well as Sundays, in the market as well as in the home." By the end of the nineteenth century, Gladden's evolving social outlook moved him more boldly to embrace the cause of organized labor, including the right of workers to form unions, to engage in collective bargaining, and to participate in revenue-sharing enterprises with their employers. Yet one could hear in his sermons echoes of an earlier evangelical Protestant vision that placed individuals under divine judgment for their failure to live their lives in accordance with God's will:

> [Christ's] law must be preached as the law of all life—must be preached till it produces conviction of sin. A great many of the people in the pews need to be convicted. . . . A thorough preaching of the law of Christ in its application to the shop and mart and the mine and the kitchen and the office and the senate and the forum, would be very disquieting, no doubt. Many would be pricked to the heart by such a presentation; not a few would stop their ears and say: "Away with this fellow who profanes the pulpit with secularities!" But some would listen; we might hope to hear them crying, "Men and brethren, what shall we do?"[36]

By the mid-1880s, a small but influential group of Protestant clergy, like Washington Gladden and Josiah Strong, expressed alarm at the growing complexities of American industrialization and called on the nation's Protestant churches to come together to address these social problems. "The duty of the church with respect to the public institutions for the care of the poor and the unfortunate is, therefore, to see that they are purely and humanely governed—that the law of Christ is the life of their administration." For Gladden, what Protestantism needed was concerted action on the part of its churches to unite in a common mission to engage the social problems of the nation—and the world. "The churches of any Christian land can secure this result if they unite to demand it; and until they have done it an essential part of their work is left undone."[37]

While Gladden was a peripatetic speaker who became a well-known national lecturer, his understanding of "social salvation" included serving the pastoral care needs of his wealthy congregation, a model that would be used effectively by later generations of prominent social gospel clergy leaders. Rather than engage social issues in his Sunday morning sermons, Gladden was more apt to hold church discussion on social

issues on Sunday evening and at weeknight forums.[38] Further, his social networks included some of the most powerful political figures in
America, most notably Theodore Roosevelt. As Gary Dorrien noted,
"Gladden was never dangerous. He spoke the language of moral progress, cooperation, and peace to the end of his life."[39] Gladden's ministry
would prove highly influential, inspiring many religious leaders to use
the power of moral suasion to change hearts and minds toward a new
understanding of faith and a converted life. His view that one of the
chief aims of religion was to engage the injustices of society and serve
as a major catalyst of systemic social change was a major theme of the
social gospel that extended into the twentieth century. At the same time
that Gladden's view of social salvation was maturing in the 1880s, a large
number of Protestant laywomen were seeking ways to live out their understanding of this concept in several North American urban areas.

"Do Everything" Women

As a young girl growing up outside Chicago, Frances Willard had
dreams of a life that extended beyond conventional norms of marriage and motherhood. As she wrote in her journal in 1861, "I feel that
in the future there is something waiting for me—what, I can not tell,
that will break in upon this quietness."[40] In her early twenties she was
engaged to marry a young seminarian at nearby Garrett Biblical Institute and contemplated a future as a minister's wife. Willard's decision
to break off the engagement led her to pursue a remarkable career that
made her one of the best-known public figures of the late nineteenth
century. After serving as president of the Northwestern Woman's College (later merged with Northwestern University) and as an organizer
for the urban revivalist Dwight L. Moody, in 1879 Willard was elected
president of the Woman's Christian Temperance Union (WCTU). The
WCTU was founded in 1874 for the purpose of promoting temperance
reform. During Willard's presidency the WCTU continued to emphasize
the importance of the "pledge," whereby Americans would vow not to
consume alcohol.

However, Willard's agenda went beyond promoting temperance. A
lifelong Methodist, she advocated for the right of women to preach
and be leaders in the church. In 1888 she was denied a seat at the

northern Methodist church's governing general conference, despite the fact that she was elected by her regional annual conference in Chicago. Increasingly, Willard advocated for the rights of women not only in the church, but in society. Throughout the 1880s and 1890s, Willard pushed the WCTU to throw its support behind women's suffrage as well as economic reform. Willard defined her philosophy of social activism as a "do everything" agenda. While many rank-and-file members of the WCTU often defined their organization's mission as the passage of prohibition laws, Willard's views on economic justice grew more radical in the 1880s and 1890s. Heavily influenced by the egalitarianism of Fabian socialism coming from Great Britain, Willard increasingly connected the economic oppression of the poor with the societal oppression of women.

Women who shared Frances Willard's vision of social reform had to negotiate a predominant nineteenth-century ideology of "separate spheres." According to this view, women's primary purpose was to raise Christian families and provide nurturing homes, leaving it to men to be responsible for working outside the home. However, Willard used this gender conservatism to her advantage. She spoke of her work with the WCTU as "organized mother-love," whereby she affirmed the separate spheres ideology that women should use their innate gifts as nurturers to heal the social wounds of the country.[41] Willard, who remained single throughout her life, served as a model for a younger generation of American women to take up a wide range of work in American Protestantism, including what became known as the home mission movement.

The home mission movement had deep-seated roots in American Protestantism. In the early nineteenth century, many Protestant churches mobilized their mission through what were called voluntary societies. Largely functioning as groups with little or no national structure and staffing, some of these organizations were more symbolic than practical. At the end of the Civil War, however, many Protestant churches turned their attention to developing professional denominational boards, staffed with personnel and financial resources for mission.[42] The American Missionary Association was at the vanguard of these changes. Founded in 1846 and largely supported by New England Congregationalist leaders, the AMA strongly embraced abolitionism.

In the decades following the Civil War, it was instrumental in ministering to freed African Americans in the South and became a major catalyst behind the founding of several historically black colleges in the United States.[43]

The efforts of organizations like the AMA were part of a trend among many of the larger Protestant denominations in America to develop more centralized institutions. By the 1870s, Protestant foreign missions were beginning to display greater movement toward consolidating resources on a national level (although in many cases foreign missionaries were still responsible for raising monies to support their efforts). At the same time, several Protestant women were at the forefront of organizing a variety of home missions, or deaconess societies.

The deaconess model was embraced by a disparate cross section of women who wanted to emulate the early church mandate to be in service to the poor. In the 1830s and 1840s, deaconess societies developed in German Lutheranism that stressed these biblical models, especially around caregiving roles, particularly nursing. Women in the United States and Canada supported the involvement of these deaconess societies in nursing and health care, but they often envisioned a broader mission field for their work.

The drive to create deaconess, or home mission, societies, was originally evident in northern denominations, but soon spread to the South as well.[44] Starting with the founding of home mission "training schools" in Chicago (Baptists in 1881 and Methodists in 1885), these schools became essential to the development of the deaconess movement—and a women-led social gospel—in American Protestantism.

By the early 1900s, young single women found themselves able to enter fields of urban missions in Protestant training schools throughout major North American cities like Chicago, New York, and Toronto. Oftentimes, wearing a distinctive garb that resembled a nun's habit, deaconess women not only took up door-to-door evangelism, but had responsibility for establishing residences in poor immigrant neighborhoods. Paralleling the late nineteenth-century rise of the settlement house movement associated with Jane Addams and Hull House in Chicago, deaconess women developed a wide range of outreaches toward the urban poor. Their deaconess houses became places where immigrants could come for spiritual care and practical instruction on a number of domestic tasks such as sanitary food preparation, as well as basic lessons in citizenry, personal finances, and the English language.

The women's home mission movement often used the separate spheres language of leaders like Frances Willard. However, home missionaries and deaconesses often possessed a radical social praxis. Lucy Rider Meyer, the founder of the Methodist-affiliated Chicago Training School in 1885, asserted that to be a deaconess was not to be "a goody-goody kind of woman." Rather, it was a means by which a young single woman could engage the fullness of Christian womanhood in America: "Her field is as large as the work of woman, and the need of that work. In deaconess ranks today may be found physicians, editors, stenographers, teachers, nurses, bookkeepers, superintendents of hospitals and orphanages, kitchen-gardeners and kindergartners."[45]

For Meyer, deaconess women embodied Frances Willard's "do-everything" agenda of integrating religion and social reform. This philosophy carried over into the education curriculum of many deaconess training schools. These schools offered courses not only in Bible and theology, but also in emerging social science disciplines like sociology, which influenced much of the missionary work accomplished by these women.

One of the most important influences on the theological and social outlook of the women's home mission movement, and many other proponents of the social gospel, was the economist Richard T. Ely. A graduate of Dartmouth College, Ely was part of a generation of late nineteenth-century Americans to do graduate work in Germany, receiving his Ph.D. in economics from the University of Heidelberg in 1880. A professor at Johns Hopkins University and later the University of Wisconsin, Ely provided a social scientific foundation that a variety of social gospel leaders built upon. While echoing aspects of Henry George's work, Ely made the explicit connection between Christianity and economic reform. His 1889 book *The Social Aspects of Christianity* was called by one scholar "the first attempt in America to bring technical economic science to bear on the understanding of the Christian faith."[46]

Ely's theology was typical of many late nineteenth-century liberals in that he tended to interpret Christian theology through the prism of the historical Jesus, as opposed to an apocalyptic or eschatological reading of scripture. Yet Ely's lasting contribution was that he called on Americans to understand the relationship between Christianity and modern economic problems, recognizing the social ramifications of Christianity. "We must devote ourselves long and carefully to the study of the science of human happiness, social science. This second branch of the gospel of Christ, so long neglected, ought to be pursued with equal earnestness, with equal diligence, by Christians, with theology."[47]

Richard Ely's importance lay not only in his integration of progressive economic theory into Christianity. His writings were part of an emergent social gospel's effort to challenge a predominant social and political conservatism that characterized a wide spectrum of American Protestant churches. Ely helped to popularize the notion that inherent to Jesus's life and teaching was an idealism that modeled the equality of all persons—and the right of all individuals to have access to a sustainable economic livelihood.

By the early 1890s, the varied ministries of women deaconesses, theorists like Richard Ely, and ministers like Gladden and Strong were part of a growing network of American Protestants associated with social Christianity. These Protestants often integrated the social sciences into a liberal theological orientation, largely derived from theologians like Horace Bushnell, that increasingly led many Protestants to question the evangelical Protestant stress upon a dramatic conversion experience. The emerging conviction that individuals were social beings who needed to find ways to adapt their faith to the social realities of the modern world played into a growing movement of religious education. By the end of the nineteenth century, most of the major Protestant churches saw the Sunday school not primarily as a form of outreach to the poor (as it was initially conceived by many eighteenth-century evangelicals), but as a means to raise up youth for service to the church and the nation.

In 1874 a Methodist minister named John Vincent helped to establish a new educational institution, Chautauqua. Located in a bucolic rural setting in western New York, Chautauqua provided a forum for many middle-class Americans to gather for recreation and educational programs. While initially designed as a means of promoting educational renewal within Methodism, by the 1890s the summer institutes held at Chautauqua featured some of America's most influential politicians, religious leaders, and social reformers. These gatherings exposed many middle-class Americans to a range of religiously motivated reformers, like Richard Ely, who emphasized the social ramifications of Christianity. By the early 1900s, the Chautauqua model served as a template for the development of regional Chautauquas that became especially popular in the Midwest and the South. From the late nineteenth century through the 1920s, the Chautauqua movement represented one of the major platforms by which social gospel leaders reached large middle-class audiences.

The late nineteenth-century rise of national lecture forums like Chautauqua illustrated how Protestants sought to articulate a religiously motivated vision of social reform, but also demonstrates how the major proponents of Protestant social Christianity believed that their religious heritage was essential to "perfecting" American democracy. While later generations of Protestant social gospel leaders refuted many aspects of Josiah Strong's ethnocentrism, they stressed the interrelationship between the historical values of Protestantism and the role of American democracy to create the conditions of freedom and justice for Americans. At the same time that American Protestant leaders like Strong and Gladden manifested hope in Protestant expansion and social reform, a marginalized segment of Protestant churches developed a nuanced version of this vision.

African American Social Christianity

In his 1903 book *Souls of Black Folk*, W. E. B. Du Bois reflected on what he called the "double consciousness" of African Americans, who on one hand found themselves judged by the standards of white Americans, while also striving to develop a self-identity as African Americans. One of the leading American intellectuals of the twentieth century, Du Bois represented a direct challenge to the self-help model of African American social advancement espoused by Booker T. Washington's Tuskegee Institute. Rather than advocating African American economic advancement through the industrial education that Washington believed over time would convince white Americans of their equal role as productive citizens, Du Bois noted that problems of racial justice cut deeper. Specifically, African Americans needed to understand the permanent wounds of slavery and how white America created a social system that made it almost impossible for people of color to achieve equality. "The history of the American Negro is the history of this strife," Du Bois argued, "the longing to attain self-conscious manhood, to merge his double self into a better and truer self."[48] Among those who grappled with Du Bois's argument was Washington Gladden. In a review of Du Bois's book he referred to it as "pathetic and appealing," calling it a work that all Americans needed to read. "I want you all to read it. It will give you, I think, a deeper insight into the real human elements of the race problem than anything that has yet been written." For Gladden, the book represented an important insight into the psychology of race prejudice in America; he reflected "that our first business is to do what we can to purify the atmosphere which [African Americans] breathe."[49] What Gladden didn't necessary fully realize, however, was that many African American religious leaders were already attempting to redefine the terms for American racial justice.

The late nineteenth century was a period when many African Americans were organizing independent churches and creating new denominations and political organizations. Their efforts at social amelioration and urban outreach paralleled those of predominantly white Protestant churches. However, the focus of African American social Christianity was always on race. In the aftermath of the Civil War, white northern evangelicals were influential in planting churches and colleges in the South that became the focal point for African American institutional growth in the late nineteenth century. Many African American institutions founded in the 1880s and 1890s echoed Booker T. Washington's self-help philosophy. African Americans needed to build structures that would enable them to be economically self-sufficient, while not antagonizing southern whites. At the same time, Du Bois emphasized the need for African Americans to develop institutions that promoted the development of an elite group of educated African American leaders. In many ways, the formation of black churches in the South became important to this vision. As the historian Evelyn Brooks Higginbotham observes, black churches became "mediating structures" that allowed segments of the African American community to strive for economic and political power.[50] Higginbotham notes that African American religious institutions developed out of the intersection between conservatism and radicalism, "the nexus between respectability and protest."[51] Black churches were dedicated to implementing Du Bois's concept of the "talented tenth," whereby African American communities raised up educated men and women who would serve as the primary leaders and change agents for the black community (hence the idea of the top ten percent). By the late nineteenth century, many African American men and women coming out of historically black churches made up a disproportionally large number of the "talented tenth," as well as representing the historical vanguard of what has been called the Black Social Gospel.

One especially noteworthy example of this tradition was the Atlanta-based ministry of Henry Hugh Proctor. Proctor was the longtime minister of the First Congregational Church of Atlanta, Georgia. First Congregational Church was established after the Civil War by the American Missionary Association. When Proctor became its pastor in 1894, he was the first African American minister of the church, and his preaching made him popular with both black and white audiences. Washington Gladden, who visited First Congregational Church on several occasions, observed that Proctor possessed "the dignity and self-command of the true orator; it is easy to understand the hold he maintains over this large congregation."[52]

Amid the harsh realities of segregated Atlanta, Proctor not only preached racial tolerance but also developed a wide range of ministries that empowered African Americans. Proctor created what has often been called an "institutional church" model. His congregation fostered a range of ministries that included numerous men's and women's groups, a Christian Endeavor Society (a popular Protestant youth movement of that era), recreation facilities, classroom space, and a temperance society. One commentator noted that First Church "was the most progressive and best organized church I saw in the South," with a social impact that exceeded much larger congregations.[53]

At a time in American history that scholars have identified as the nadir for African American civil rights, Proctor was a strong advocate for racial justice, equipping the black community in Atlanta with the practical tools to survive and thrive in the segregated South. His story also reflects a wider history of interracial cooperation in the American South that became vital to the future success of the civil rights movement in the twentieth century.

Although Methodists and, to a much lesser extent, Congregationalists had a presence in the South among African Americans, the fastest-growing Protestant church among African Americans was the Baptist, culminating in 1895 with the founding of the National Baptist Convention. The National Baptist Convention soon became the largest African American denomination in the United States and by 1916 was the third largest religious body in the country.[54] Closely paralleling developments in the wider home mission movement, the Woman's Convention of the National Baptist Convention, founded in 1900, engaged in a variety of social ministries that employed many of the same strategies used by white churches. Its longtime president, Nannie Helen Burroughs, was one of the most visible forces in the National Baptist Convention, staying active in that church until her death in 1967. Burroughs also served as the founding president of the NBC's National Training School in 1909, designed to provide vocational training for African American women. Like many white women in the home mission movement, Burroughs frequently walked a fine line between social conservatism and social radicalism—the desire to support black churches and institutions while also vigorously attacking racism and other social problems faced by African American communities. These women's groups in the NBC also provided space for an emerging social gospel liberalism to take root within their churches. Like women in predominately white churches, home missionaries like Burroughs supported the institutional missions of their denomination, and, like their white counterparts, often staved off efforts by male colleagues to take control of women's boards. However, African American women created an institutional power base that over time allowed these women to reach out to white women, in ways that anticipated later reform coalitions in the twentieth century. By the 1920s, many white and African American women's groups coming out of the churches would be at the forefront of a nascent civil rights movement.[55]

Many scholars have noted the failure of white social gospelers to acknowledge what W. E. B. Du Bois identified as America's "color line" that kept white and black Americans at arm's length. An example of this separation can be seen in the reluctance of white reformers to condemn an upturn in lynchings of African Americans during the 1890s. In that decade Ida B. Wells, an African American writer and journalist, chronicled the silence of white Americans on this issue, singling out high-profile reformers like Frances Willard for their failure to engage issues such as lynching. Although Willard championed the right of women to vote, she largely ignored issues facing African Americans—a fact that drew the ire of leaders like Wells. She asserted that "no crime however heinous can excuse the commission of any act of cruelty or the taking of any human life without due course of law."[56] Wells's journalistic crusade drew international attention, and culminated with her undertaking a tour of England in 1894 to raise awareness of lynching in the United States.

Despite the efforts of figures like Wells, the majority of white social gospelers in the late nineteenth century held tepid, if not indifferent, views on issues of racial justice. Some leaders, notably Washington Gladden, did decry lynching and advocated for civil rights. However, these pleas were usually diluted by a tendency to see issues of racism through an economic prism, in which economic advancement of poor workers would ultimately benefit African Americans. At the same time, late nineteenth-century African American leaders helped to lay an institutional foundation within black churches that would be critical to the development of the social gospel movement into the twentieth century.

Conclusion

In November 1893 a young African American minister, Reverdy Ransom, gave an address at the Mt. Zion Congregational Church in Cleveland, Ohio, reflecting upon the recently concluded Columbia Exposition in Chicago. Ransom reported favorably not only on the exposition, but also on the World Parliament of Religions held in conjunction with the fair. With representatives from a variety of religious traditions—Protestant, Catholic, Jewish, Hindu, and Muslim included—Ransom couldn't help but see the hand of God involved as America reached the end of the nineteenth century: "The Parliament of Religions has wrought mightily in preparing the hearts of men for the coming of the kingdom of the Son of God. When the light of the future ages shall reveal the causes that have shared for real the destiny of mankind, the Parliament of Religions at Chicago will be named the mightiest."[57] Ransom devoted a significant portion of his Mt. Zion address to the plight of African Americans who struggled to overcome racism and achieve social equality. While "the night of the Negro's suffering and trial has been long and dismal," Ransom affirmed that the years ahead would create unprecedented opportunities for African Americans. "This land of the Negro's suffering must yet bear witness to his triumph. Here, under the same stars where he was despised and fettered, he must yet be honored and free."[58] Ransom would emerge as one of the most prophetic African American religious leaders in the early twentieth century for his attacks against racism and his advocacy of African American equality. Yet his optimistic sentiments about the future would have fit the hopeful spirit shared by several American Protestant leaders of his era. Later social gospel leaders would characterize the end of the nineteenth century as a time when prophets of social Christianity cried out "in the wilderness." In actuality, however, Protestants were institutionally creating networks through ministers, deaconess societies, institutional churches, and settlement houses that allowed the social gospel to develop into the twentieth century.

By 1900, some figures associated with this early phase of the social gospel shifted their focus. Richard Ely remained a prominent voice advocating for progressive economic reform, but increasingly his work moved away from his earlier discussion of religion to focus more on urban planning. While settlement houses and deaconess societies continued to develop in the early twentieth century, many Protestant women's groups struggled to resist efforts to place their work under the control of male-dominated denominational boards. Further, the death of important Christian feminists like Frances Willard in 1898 shifted groups like the WCTU toward a more single-issue focus on temperance reform than on Willard's wide ranging social reform agenda.

At the same time, the work of late nineteenth-century pioneers of social Christianity had already altered the religious landscape of American Protestantism. These early reformers helped to establish the social gospel's institutional foundation within Protestant churches; through their efforts, the social gospel was well on its way to developing a popular and intellectual foundation in American religion. While these Protestant groups continued to explore the practical implications for understanding the meaning of "social salvation," other religious groups were engaging in similar efforts in developing the social aspects of their traditions. If anything, the efforts of religious leaders to flesh out the practical implications of Washington Gladden's faith in creating "a perfect man in a perfect society" were only just beginning.

2

Interpreting the "Golden Rule"

Turn-of-the-Century Protestant, Catholic, and Jewish Reformers

In late 1894 William Carwardine, a Chicago-area Methodist minister, published his account of the Pullman Palace Car Company strike that had occurred earlier in the year. George Pullman, the founder of the Pullman Company, boasted that he had created the ideal environment for his workers, many of whom lived in his model company town of Pullmantown, Illinois, where Carwardine was a minister. The majority of Chicago church leaders largely embraced Pullman's assessment that his company provided workers the equivalent of heaven on earth, despite the fact that Pullman repeatedly raised property rents in Pullmantown while cutting employee wages. While many Chicago clergy spoke of the dignity of labor from their pulpits, most stood firmly behind Pullman, seeing the strike as a result of immigrant radicalism that threatened to undermine American democratic institutions—including churches.[1] The stage was set for a major strike that ultimately resulted in President Grover Cleveland sending in federal troops to quell violence between police and strikers.

Carwardine represented a small faction of Chicago clergy who had taken a leadership role in supporting the strikers, and asserted in his book that religious leaders had a moral obligation to stand up for worker rights:

> I contend now that in the discussing of this theme I am preaching the gospel of applied Christianity—applied to humanity—the gospel of mutual recognition, of co-operation, of the "brotherhood of humanity." The relation existing between a man's body and his soul are such that you can make very little headway appealing to the soul of a thoroughly live and healthy man if he be starving for food.[2]

Carwardine's support of the Pullman strike demonstrates that several Protestant reformers who embraced what Richard Ely and other leaders often called "applied Christianity" were convinced of the need to harness religious faith as a means to address the pressing social problems of the era. Yet by the end of the nineteenth century, many religious leaders struggled to decide how to interpret these convictions—theologically and practically. While many religious leaders talked about the Golden Rule of loving one's neighbor in their sermons, speeches, and publications, how did this translate into specific political models and strategies? At the close of the nineteenth century, many religious voices—Protestant, Jewish, and Catholic—offered a range of perspectives on the biblical question, "Who is my neighbor?" For many of these leaders, the question of loving one's neighbor had implications for how they began to embrace various models of socialism.

"What Would Jesus Do?"

In the early 1890s Charles Sheldon, a midwestern Congregational minister, wrestled with how to address Christianity's relationship to social problems in his Topeka, Kansas, church. Sheldon had some sympathy with aspects of theological liberalism. However, he was more passionate about temperance reform and, like other Protestant evangelicals, believed in the redemptive power of Christianity—that is, Protestant Christianity—to promote mission and evangelicalism, as well as to stave off movements of political radicalism. Throughout the 1890s, Sheldon developed a number of adult classes in his church that revolved around fictional narratives he wrote to boost church attendance and to propagate his views on religion and reform. His early publications were only moderately successful, but in 1897 he published the book that would cement his fame: *In His Steps*.

In His Steps became a huge best-seller, and it remains an immensely popular book into the twentieth-first century. The book tells the story of a young minister who challenges his congregation to walk in the footsteps of Jesus for one year, basing individual actions on the simple criterion of whether Jesus would engage in particular activities. Central to the book's narrative is a question that galvanized many people to embrace aspects of the social gospel: What would Jesus do?

W.W. J.D

In the late twentieth century, the abbreviation WWJD? became a widely marketed slogan among evangelicals. Few who took this slogan to heart, however, recognized its historical origins. On one hand, Sheldon's book espoused a revised evangelical view of postmillennial salvation, manifested in the power of Christian conversion to create a better world. On the other hand, *In His Steps* espoused a theological orientation that resonated strongly with aspects of liberal theology. For Sheldon, walking in Jesus's footsteps required the individual to suffer as Christ suffered. This belief that one needed to follow in Christ's footsteps might lead the disciple to experience worldly rejection, persecution, and even death. However, Sheldon believed, as did other "evangelical liberals" in the social gospel tradition, that one's willingness to make these sacrifices would have redemptive consequences for humankind.

Sheldon's model of Christianity took a page from William Stead's 1894 book *If Christ Came to Chicago!* A prominent British journalist, Stead had spent several months living in Chicago as the city hosted the World's Columbian Exposition in 1893. Coinciding with the four hundredth anniversary of Columbus's "discovery" of America, the Columbian Exposition was seen by its organizers as an occasion to showcase American wealth and technological sophistication, and (accentuated by the design of the exposition's buildings and attractions) to serve as a celebration of America's rising political and cultural stature on a world stage. Stead's book uncovered Chicago's massive poverty, analyzing the city's economic, political, and moral corruption, particularly focusing on areas of the city that were notorious for crime and prostitution. The book echoes themes found in Jacob Riis's highly influential 1890 work *How the Other Half Lives*, which drew attention to the massive wealth disparities that separated the rich and the poor in New York City. Stead's concern was to show readers that Jesus would not tolerate the poverty and vice of urban America, and to chastise Chicago's churches for not using their moral forces to redeem the city. Like Sheldon, Stead insisted that churches needed to set aside doctrinal differences and mobilize their faith resources in a concerted effort to redeem the nation from the sins of wealth and moral vice. "The old forms having served their turn and done their work are passing away. They hinder where they ought to help, and fail to interpret the full orbed revelation of the will of God toward us in all its bearings upon the social, political and national life of man."[3]

Stead and Sheldon asserted that Christlike suffering offered the pos-sibility of redeeming society. In Sheldon's fiction, this redemption oc-curs not only when an individual experiences a personal conversion, but also when communities come to understand that the achievement of a righteous society requires personal sacrifice. A few years before Sheldon published *In His Steps*, he authored a modestly successful 1894 novel, *The Crucifixion of Philip Strong*. In this novel, Philip Strong is an ide-alistic young minister who soon encounters rejection and persecution from members of his congregation because of his insistence on preach-ing about social issues. He challenges members of his congregation who represent questionable economic practices (including those from the "li-quor industry") with his insistence that Christians need to live morally virtuous lives dedicated to the poor. The congregation's hostility toward Strong leads to physical abuse and, at the novel's climax, his death as he preaches—dying upon the church altar in the shape of a crucifix. How-ever, "redemption" occurs for the congregation when they take to heart their late minister's mission to live as Christ lived. Before Philip dies, he dramatically quotes an early nineteenth-century hymn. The lyrics expressed many social gospelers' romanticized view of personal sacrifice as analogous to Christ's own death on the cross:

"In the Cross of Christ, I glory,
Towering o'er the wrecks of time;
All the light of sacred story
Gathered round—"[4]

Later at Philip's funeral, his grieving wife remarks, "He was very young to die," in which a parishioner remarks tersely, "So was Christ."[5]

The popular Christianity represented by Charles Sheldon, as well as other so-called social gospel novelists, highlighted ideas that would be developed by later social gospelers with an increasing level of sophistica-tion.[6] While figures like Sheldon, Josiah Strong, and Washington Glad-den fervently saw themselves connected to an evangelical Protestant worldview, their theological outlook stood in opposition to the increas-ingly popular premillennialism and any understanding of Christianity that separated personal conversion from the redemption of society. For these figures, and for many social gospelers, the idea of Christlike sacrifice had potentially wide-ranging ramifications for the redemption of the social order. However, at the same time that Sheldon's question "What would Jesus do?" was gaining popularity, other leaders of social Christianity believed that a more rigorous engagement with social-political ideologies was necessary. The 1890s was a decade marked by economic instability, with high unemployment and numerous strikes, in which the Pullman strike was only one example. The absence of any government regulation of the nation's financial sector had created a condition of unregulated financial speculation, ultimately causing an international monetary crisis that led to several bank failures early in the decade. In the aftermath of the Chicago World's Fair, thousands of unemployed workers, many of whom helped to build the so-called White City, now lived in the abandoned buildings of the fair's exhibits. In the face of these conditions, religious leaders looked to integrate Christian teachings into emerging political models that contained a more vigorous critique of American capitalism. These critiques led many religious leaders to embrace aspects of a political ideology that ministers like Charles Sheldon feared: socialism.

The Rise of Christian Socialism

In the 1880s Richard Ely helped to inaugurate the American social gospel through his integration of an ethical interpretation of Jesus's teachings into economic and political structures. In the wake of Ely's success, a spate of Protestant leaders sought to engage the questions he raised by probing how American political institutions should embody the social teachings of Jesus. While these reformers saw themselves as defenders of American democratic values, many became fascinated with following Ely's lead in integrating Christian teaching into emerging theories of socialism. When the Socialist Party of America was formed in 1901, it represented the coming together of disparate political streams of the socialist movement, with numerous currents expressing hostility toward religion. Several socialists embraced Karl Marx's belief that religion was the "opiate of the people," and saw religious leaders as the caretakers of an ideological worldview that was hostile to the interests of American workers. However, socialist language of solidarity with the poor, its indictment of wealth, and its vision of a just society paralleled many of the social gospel visions of the kingdom of God as an earthly ideal. As the historian Jacob Dorn notes, Protestant leaders were drawn to socialism not so much out of a commitment to dogmatic theory, but "by its appeal to a sense of justice, its historical sweep, or a desire for human solidarity."[7] Thus many social gospel figures were committed to what was often called Christian socialism.

Christian socialism's roots can be traced to the Church of England in the early and mid-nineteenth century. Influential Anglican clergy such as Frederick Robertson and Frederick Denison Maurice established residential communities in poor working-class areas in urban England. These communities lived and worked among the urban poor, and were precursors to the settlement house movement, beginning with the founding in 1884 of Toynbee Hall in London. By the 1880s and 1890s, the theological and social ideals surrounding these earlier nineteenth-century British Christian socialists increasingly had an impact on American clergy and laity, especially in the Episcopal Church. Many Episcopal leaders supported the development of institutional churches that stressed themes of "applied Christianity." These churches contained not only sanctuaries for worship, but also classroom space and gymnasiums. They offered a wide range of "social service" programs, including vocational training, daycare for children, and recreational activities that closely paralleled the outreach of settlement houses.

One of the major figures in the Episcopal Church who embraced the model of British Christian socialism was William Dwight Porter Bliss. In 1889 Bliss founded a small group of similar-minded Episcopalians, the Society of Christian Socialists, and in 1890 he organized in Boston a short-lived community, the Church of the Carpenter, a congregation that sought to live out the urban reform vision represented by Robertson and Maurice. Many in this community were idealistic intellectuals and academics, including a Wellesley College English instructor, Vida Dutton Scudder. Reflecting years later, Scudder noted the impact on her faith journey of Bliss's idealism and the "true agape" generated by the group when they worshiped and prayed together for an "imminent revolution" in America.[8]

In the 1890s Vida Scudder and a wide range of Protestant leaders saw Christian socialism as an identity that manifested the potential of Jesus's words to create a just society. The personal politics of these "socialists" often varied. Many were devotees of Henry George's single tax, while others gravitated toward the utopianism associated with Edward Bellamy, whose 1888 novel *Looking Backward* provided an idealistic vision of the year 2000. *Looking Backward* reflected a future rid of poverty, where society was geared toward an equal sharing of economic resources and a motivation to serve the greater public good. Christian socialists like Bliss argued that Christianity needed more than faith in the Golden Rule to change society. "Those sentimental Christians who say that all that is necessary is for individuals to obey Christ are in danger of saying, 'Lord, Lord,' without showing what the Lord would have us do."[9] For Bliss, true Christians needed to support legislation to protect the rights of workers, including laws to limit work to an eight-hour day. "It would reduce the hours of labor in factory and in shop, that men may have longer hours of labor in the home, the library, and the church."[10]

For some Protestants, however, the idealism of Christian socialism didn't go far enough. What Christianity needed was to embrace concrete socialist solutions that called for more direct government regulation of businesses and the protection of worker rights, especially the right to unionize. The vast majority of social gospelers rejected more stringent political solutions of socialism, particularly the economic determinism of Karl Marx. At the same time, some leaders took the themes of Richard Ely further by asserting that Jesus's example could be integrated into emerging traditions of late nineteenth-century democratic socialism. Two distinctive examples of Protestant ministers who combined Christianity and socialism in unique ways during the 1890s were Reverdy Ransom and George Herron.

Born in Ohio just before the beginning of the Civil War in 1861, Reverdy Ransom grew up in a post-Reconstruction America that witnessed the growth of new forms of racism, in both the North and South. Ransom was a member of the African Methodist Episcopal (AME) Church. Founded in 1816 by Richard Allen, the African Methodist Episcopal Church was a denomination that emphasized Methodist themes of social holiness while striving to create social-economic opportunities for African Americans despite the barriers of institutional racism. Early in his life, Ransom was attracted to the leadership models of two prominent AME bishops, Daniel Payne and Henry McNeal Turner. In addition to founding numerous AME churches, Payne advocated for the creation of colleges that would educate an emerging generation of young African Americans, including Wilberforce University in Ohio, which Ransom entered in 1881.

On the other hand, Henry McNeal Turner exemplified a leadership model that also engaged Ransom. Turner modeled an American tradition of black nationalism associated later in the twentieth century with Marcus Garvey and Malcolm X. While Turner initially believed that racial integration was desirable, by the end of the nineteenth century he became strident in his calls for African Americans to leave the United States and establish colonies in Africa. Although Ransom did not embrace the "back to Africa" movement, his ministry was largely defined by the desire to push an agenda that sought to empower black communities and challenge the suppositions of American racism. One of Ransom's encounters with racism occurred when he transferred to Oberlin College. Oberlin had been founded as a school that advocated evangelical perfectionism, abolitionism, and women's rights. However, by the 1880s its student facilities were segregated, and Ransom perceived that the "outward friendliness" of students and faculty masked the college's segregationist practices. After he protested the segregation of the college's dining hall, Ransom's scholarship was revoked, forcing him to leave Oberlin and return to Wilberforce.[11]

Yet Ransom's reform efforts were also firmly rooted in the tradition of the wider Protestant social gospel. Initially influenced by Washington Gladden and Richard Ely, Ransom carried into his ministry a commitment to integrate economic reform into the imperative for racial justice. After his ordination in the AME Church in 1888, and serving a series of pastorates, in 1896 Ransom became pastor of Bethel AME Church in Chicago, and in 1900 he established in that city the Institutional Church and Social Settlement House, the first institutional church founded by the AME. During his years in Chicago, he developed friendships with prominent reformers in the settlement house movement, including Jane Addams, Mary McDowell, and Graham Taylor.[12] Like other social gospel leaders, Ransom believed that institutional reform required an engagement with the social sciences, and he supported a range of programs designed to provide vocational and cultural uplift. Yet Ransom's ministry was committed to a tradition within the AME, and within the wider black church in America, to empower African Americans economically and politically.

Like white social gospel leaders of his time, Ransom drew on an eclectic range of influences, including the Russian author and ascetic Leo Tolstoy, Henry George, and the British social critic John Ruskin. Their ideas helped to shape his views on socialism. Ransom saw socialism as a realistic political option for African Americans to achieve economic power, serving as a remedy to the problems of poverty and class in America. "There are more than a million Negro toilers in this land. . . . Their destiny is bound up with the destiny of the Republic, with the destiny of man."[13] As he used Jesus as an example of social equality, Ransom challenged African Americans to critique practices that excluded them from membership from most of the nation's labor unions. For Ransom, without a vigorous labor movement, African Americans would continue to be cast in a subservient role in society. "When millions of toilers are degraded, labor is degraded, man is degraded," he wrote in 1896. "That the Negro will enthusiastically espouse the cause of socialism we cannot doubt. Social and industrial oppression have been his portion for centuries. When he comes to realize that socialism offers him freedom of opportunity to cooperate with all men upon terms of equality in every avenue of life, he will not be slow to accept his social emancipation."[14] Ransom's support of "biblical socialism" and the institutional church movement continued to be a feature in his subsequent ministry. After leaving Chicago, he became pastor of the Charles Street AME Church in Boston and in 1907 of the Bethel AME Church in Harlem.

Ransom was typical of many social gospel leaders who often equated an embrace of socialism with a religious perfecting of American democracy:

> Under the influence of Christianity, the general diffusion of knowledge, and the growth of democratic ideas in the state, both in Europe and America, the more advanced members of society are trying to lift the lower, if not to the political, industrial, and social heights whereon they stand, at least to a higher plane of life.[15]

While Ransom sought to fuse aspects of Christianity and political socialism, his contemporary George Herron took aspects of this synthesis further.

The meteoric career of George Herron shows how religious liberalism and political socialism came together at the end of the nineteenth century. Herron was born in 1862 and spent his early life searching for a vocation that would enable him to rise above his family's meager economic status. After studying for a time at Ripon College in Wisconsin, Herron entered the Congregational ministry, serving short stints pastoring churches in Ohio, Wisconsin, Minnesota, and Iowa. What Herron lacked in formal theological training he made up for in his skills as an orator. In 1893, thanks to the support of a benefactor, Herron became a professor of applied Christianity at Iowa (later Grinnell) College.

Herron's position at Iowa College gave him an institutional base from which to reach a wide audience through public speaking and writing. The Progressive Era journalist William Allen White noted that Herron was "one of God's pedestal dwellers, always moving about in bronze or marble."[16] Herron belonged to a broader tradition of political populism that characterized many parts of the Midwest and Great Plains. The people of these regions tended to be suspicious of what they perceived as the elitist economic policies of urban "robber barons" who exploited farmers and craftsman outside the nation's biggest cities. Yet Herron's message took this populism further. In many ways, Herron came across as apocalyptic as he castigated wealthy Americans for the social-economic inequalities in the nation, arguing that only a radical commitment to Jesus's teachings would save America. "The kingdom is coming in the world, whether we and our age want it or not," he noted in 1894. "If we receive the kingdom, it may come without observation; but if we resent its coming, it will grind us to powder in the fury of revolutions."[17] Although many of his critics claimed that Herron was advocating violent revolution, his main interest was in promoting a reform vision that integrated Christianity into a model of democratic socialism. He was especially influenced by Giuseppe Mazzini, an Italian politician who was a central figure in Italy's birth as a modern nation in the 1860s and 1870s.[18] Mazzini's rhetoric mixed themes from Christianity and democratic socialism in a way that would appeal to a range of social gospelers, including Herron and later Walter Rauschenbusch.

Herron's sense that the kingdom of God would create the conditions of social equality was both conservative and radical. His orations castigated the church's moral failure to embrace the full power of Jesus's ethics for improving economic relationships between the rich and poor. Like Charles Sheldon, Herron often espoused a liberal postmillennialism that saw Christianity as promoting a love ethic that would create a just society, as more individuals followed Jesus. On the other hand, Herron saw modern capitalism as devoid of any redeeming qualities. "The kingdom of God is a political economy," Herron asserted. "It is the good housekeeping and divine thrift of the state. It is the regulation of production and distribution through communion with God." For Herron, the essence of Christianity was Christlike service toward one's neighbors. Jesus's spirit in modern society provided seekers "a natural law which commands us to seek first the kingdom of God and his righteousness. . . . All gain through selfish ways is everlasting waste, and only the righteousness of the kingdom is eternally profitable. Every man who loses something for Christ's right's sake enriches the life of the humanity of which he is a part."[19]

By 1900, the major public phase of George Herron's ministry was over. After becoming involved in an affair with the daughter of his primary benefactor at Iowa College, Herron resigned his faculty appointment. After a period in which he worked on behalf of the American Socialist Party, Herron's political vision shifted more to the center. He became an early supporter of American intervention in World War I and was an advisor to Woodrow Wilson during the Versailles Peace Conference in the war's aftermath. However, Herron left a strong impact on the social gospel, including at Grinnell College. Over the next two decades, Grinnell was strongly associated with the social gospel. Several of its graduates went on to careers in public service, including Harry Hopkins, who served as one of the principal architects of Franklin Roosevelt's New Deal administration in the 1930s.[20]

Conversely, many mainstream social gospel leaders at the turn of the century had little use for Herron. Washington Gladden complained that Herron's political interpretation of Christianity seemed to bypass any connection to organized Christian churches. While conceding that churches had "very imperfectly understood the teachings of Christ," Gladden believed that churches could serve as conduits for God's ongoing "revelation through incarnation" in society.[21] Another critic of Herron was Francis Greenwood Peabody, professor of applied Christian ethics at Harvard Divinity School, who noted that Herron's identification of Jesus with modern social-economic systems distorted the type of "primitive" community described in the New Testament: "Jesus does not shut it within the limits of any single social scheme, still less of a programme which can have no important place in the organization of the modern world."[22]

While several contemporaries dismissed him, Herron set the stage for a broader debate among many religious leaders pertaining to how one could apply religious teachings, especially coming out of the Bible, to concrete political-economic models. Herron's successes demonstrated the ongoing appeal among many Protestants who labeled themselves Christian socialists. Yet Herron's radicalism highlighted a growing debate among Protestant leaders about the extent to which one could establish a biblical basis for political engagement. If one dismissed Herron's argument that equated the kingdom of God with modern economics, then how should the social teachings of Jesus be used responsibly to change society? Increasingly, this question led many social gospel leaders to look to Germany for answers.

The Kingdom of God in Germany

In 1873 Borden Parker Bowne, a recent graduate of New York University, traveled to Germany, where he planned to study at the Universities of Göttingen and Halle. The son of a Methodist minister, Bowne was attracted to aspects of that tradition's religious pietism, but felt that it lacked any sort of coherent philosophical substance to sustain it in the modern world. Like many young men of his generation who grew up in the pietistic world of American evangelism, Bowne was in search of a religious faith that made sense to him in the context of a world dominated by new developments in religion and the natural sciences. He found that faith in Germany.

Since the early nineteenth century, philosophical and theological ideas from Germany had elicited a range of responses from numerous religious leaders, who often saw in German philosophy and theology a threat to centuries of religious tradition. Nevertheless, during the second half of the nineteenth century, Germany produced many of the most influential scholars who shaped the wider contours of Protestant liberalism. Largely associated with the philosophy of Immanuel Kant in the late eighteenth century and, in particular, the writings of the theologian Friedrich Schleiermacher in the early nineteenth century, German liberalism elevated religious experience, as opposed to doctrinal tradition, as a means for understanding God's nature and purpose.

At first, German liberalism gradually found its way into American theological circles, impacting some of the leaders of New England Transcendentalism such as Theodore Parker. However, the full impact of German liberalism would be most felt after the Civil War, when increasing numbers of Americans traveled to study theology at leading German universities like Halle, Marburg, and especially the University of Berlin. As with any theological tradition, German liberal theology produced numerous currents. However, when one looks at the development of the social gospel in the United States by the end of the nineteenth century, common themes of German liberalism are evident.

First, American social gospelers were exposed to German traditions of biblical higher criticism. German liberalism's stress on the historical Jesus expanded on wider questions related to the Bible's structure that had been explored by earlier leaders in Unitarianism and Transcendentalism. Many German scholars increasingly delved into the life setting of the scriptures, employing social science methodology to flesh out the historical context of the ancient world. Not only did these developments challenge earlier notions of religious supernaturalism, but they forged a mentality that the scriptures needed to be approached from the standpoint of modern intellectual inquiry. Critical study of the Bible impacted a range of liberal Protestants, including many, like Bowne, who were not necessarily connected to the social gospel. At the same time, the German emphasis on the historical development of scripture would be translated by American religious leaders in ways that fleshed out the ethical implications of Judaism and Christianity. For many German liberals, the most important aspect of the biblical record was not predicated on whether Moses authored the first five books of the Hebrew Scriptures or whether the physical resurrection of Jesus actually happened. The issue was how the Bible, represented by the prophets of the Hebrew Scriptures and the teachings of Jesus, had wider ethical ramifications for the social transformation of societies.

Second, German liberalism elevated the importance of church history, seeing a symbiotic relationship between theology and the study of Christianity's doctrinal development. For centuries, church historians frequently stressed the providential nature of Christianity. Historical events such as the Protestant Reformation were seen mostly in the context of divine providence. By the mid-nineteenth century, however, German historians like Johann August Neander were seeking to explain church history as the result not of divine intervention, but of ongoing debates by faith communities over the interpretation of doctrine and theology. By the 1860s, a Swiss immigrant to America and former student of Neander's, Philip Schaff, was establishing himself as the preeminent church historian in the United States. Originally teaching at a small German Reformed seminary in Mercersburg, Pennsylvania, Schaff ultimately moved to the faculty of Union Theological Seminary in New York City. Schaff become a major figure in the academic study of religious history, and prefigured the importance that many social gospel leaders assigned to the critical study of the church's past, as a means to fully understand the role of theology in the present.

Perhaps the two most important German scholars who influenced the development of the social gospel in the early twentieth century were Albrecht Ritschl and Adolf von Harnack. A professor of systematic theology at Gottingen, Ritschl built on many of the intellectual suppositions of Friedrich Schleiermacher. While Schleiermacher was orthodox in some respects, he stressed the importance of religious experience as a means to fully grasp the divine nature and even to reinterpret religious doctrines. One particular concept that would increasingly fascinate American Protestants was Ritschl's stress on the kingdom of God as a means of understanding the historical mission of Christianity as a religious movement. Von Harnack, a professor at the University of Berlin, not only built on Ritschl's work but also helped to shape one of the dominant historical interpretations of the early Christian church that would carry well into the twentieth century. Like many liberal historians of his generation, von Harnack sought to understand what he considered to be the essential truths of early Christianity, expressed in the teachings of Jesus, and separate these from later social influences, particularly what he saw as the overreliance of the Western church on the teachings of the Apostle Paul. For von Harnack, as with many of the German idealists who followed him, understanding Jesus in his historical context was essential for interpreting the true nature and character of Christianity. Both Ritschl and von Harnack's understanding of Christianity shifted the interpretation of the New Testament away from an otherworldly understanding of Jesus's message, instead emphasizing the significance of his teachings to the realization of a new kingdom in this world. Almost without exception, the major social gospel leaders who emerged by the early twentieth century incorporated some aspect of this theological understanding into their worldview.

Finally, and of particular importance to Borden Parker Bowne, German philosophy and theology understood God as an immanent being. Traditionally, Protestant doctrine taught that God was transcendent, completely separated from the world. For many German theologians and philosophers influenced by Kant, the idea of God's transcendence negated the ability of humans to experience God's redeeming actions in the world. At Göttingen, Bowne studied with Hermann Lotze, a philosopher who expanded on the idealism of Kant and argued that God's nature could be understood through the attributes of human personhood. When Bowne returned to the United States, he accepted a position at recently founded Boston University as professor of philosophy. From 1876 until his death in 1910, Bowne helped establish a philosophical movement known as Boston Personalism. While he did not show much interest in questions of social reform, Bowne's philosophy fostered numerous generations of individuals who shaped a significant tradition of social gospel idealism, including Francis McConnell, Georgia Harkness, and most especially, Martin Luther King Jr.

In the face of widespread labor unrest in North American cities, by the early 1900s a wide range of Protestant leaders wrestled with the extent to which Jesus's religious teaching were translatable to contemporary social-economic models. For the most part, these leaders rejected what they perceived to be the lack of historical and theological sophistication in George Herron's writings. At the same time, several figures engaged the question that was central for Herron: How can the life of Jesus relate to contemporary questions of social reform? This question was central to the intellectual quest of a young Baptist minister turned professor, Shailer Mathews.

Born in 1863, Mathews grew up in a pietistic Baptist home in rural Maine. After graduating from Colby College and Newton Theological Seminary, Mathews served a brief pastorate before returning to teach at Colby. After studying in Berlin for a year, in 1892 he followed his mentor at Colby, the sociologist Albion Small, to the newly founded University of Chicago, where he became a professor of New Testament studies.[23] Chicago presented a relatively new model for an American research university. Its first president, William Rainey Harper, took seriously the modernist direction of religion modeled by German research universities and consequently hired many faculty who had received graduate training in Germany.

The University of Chicago was significant not simply because it focused on the emerging disciplines of the social sciences, but also because Harper wanted the university's students to study and apply the social sciences to a range of institutions, including settlement houses, churches, and synagogues. Even though Mathews never earned a research doctorate, he fit the ethos of the new university. Like his mentor Albion Small, Mathews approached the study of the New Testament from the perspective of what was called "Christian sociology." He helped found the *American Journal of Sociology*, which in its early years published numerous articles on how religion might effectively address contemporary social problems—what Mathews and others often referred to as "social service." Like George Herron, Mathews wanted to recover the Jesus of the New Testament. However, in keeping with the tone of German critical scholarship, he wanted to present a careful reconstruction of Jesus's first-century social context. This discernment led to the publication in 1897 of Mathews's first—and in some ways most influential—book, *The Social Teaching of Jesus*.

Mathews was quick to dismiss the idea that Jesus's social teachings could be equated with contemporary models of social-economic reform, such as capitalism or socialism. However, his conclusion was clear: one could not interpret Jesus's message without understanding that it was rooted in an idealistic vision to transform society. With judicious citations from the New Testament running throughout the book, Mathews noted that Jesus expressed a social vision that saw the possibility of a future reign of God on earth: the kingdom of God. By this kingdom "Jesus meant *an ideal* (though progressively approximated) *social order in which the relation of men to God is that of sons, and* (therefore) *to each other, that of brothers.*" [24]

Invoking the arguments of Adolf von Harnack, the book served as an influential template for many social gospel leaders in the early twentieth century. Mathews dismissed any interpretations of the New Testament that depicted Jesus's message in an apocalyptic fashion. In the first-century context, Jesus was an idealist who hoped to change the way people lived as a society. "Jesus trusts the inherent powers and capacities of the race," Mathews noted. "The ideal he portrays was not intended for creatures less or more human than the men with whom he associated and out of whom he hoped to form his kingdom. Individual and social regeneration is possible because man and society are inherently salvable."[25]

For a later generation of "crisis theologians" such as Reinhold Niebuhr, these assertions by Mathews were evidence that liberals were hopelessly naïve, creating a watered-down Christianity that lacked an adequate understanding of human sin and evil. Yet a large part of Mathews's scholarly motivation was to reclaim Christian tradition from those who saw it primarily as an otherworldly faith, particularly given the rising popularity of premillennialism. Mathews was quick to point out that the Bible did not give any sort of blueprint on how a just social order could be constructed. Jesus "is neither a champion nor an opponent of *laissez faire*; he neither forbids trades [*sic*] unions, strikes and lock-outs, nor advises them; he was neither socialist nor individualist."[26] Yet

> his denunciation is unsparing of those men who make wealth at the expense of souls; who find in capital no incentive to further fraternity; who endeavor so to use wealth as to make themselves independent of social obligations and to grow fat with that which should be shared with society;—for those men who are gaining the world but are letting their neighbors fall among thieves and Lazarus rot among their dogs.[27]

Aspects of Shailer Mathews's arguments were incorporated by other Protestant leaders. Francis Greenwood Peabody's 1900 book *Jesus Christ and the Social Question* was later described by Mathews as "one of the most comprehensive and sanest treatments" of the applicability of Jesus's social teachings to the modern era.[28] Peabody echoed Mathews by insisting that Jesus was "not primarily an agitator with a plan, but an idealist with a vision."[29] Peabody was likely critiquing radicals like Herron when he noted that "instead of regeneration by organization, Jesus offers regeneration by inspiration. He was not primarily the deviser of a social system, but the quickener of single lives."[30]

The interpretations of Jesus by Mathews and Peabody were on one hand fairly conservative. Each worried that fusing together Christianity and political socialism represented a misreading of the New Testament, and in the case of Herron, the product of poor biblical interpretation. Yet Mathews and Peabody were not simply engaging in an abstract quest for the historical Jesus, echoing the title of a book by Albert Schweitzer in 1905. They believed that the true mission of Christianity—to create a "cooperative commonwealth"—had become obscured by the Hellenistic tradition of St. Paul, which had turned the church toward belief in the afterlife, at the expense of reforming society.

Although the tradition of German liberalism would come under heavy theological scrutiny after World War I, the movement was indispensable to the rise of the social gospel. Its idealistic view of the individual corresponded with the perspective that individuals could change the course of history, working in creative partnership with God. This idealism would become indispensable to the social gospel's development well into the twentieth century.

However, many Protestants who embraced German liberalism at the end of the nineteenth century often were slow to recognize some of the less savory aspects of these traditions. German Protestants tended to express a discernible hostility toward Roman Catholicism, and contributed toward a prejudice shared by many American Protestants that the Catholic Church was responsible for a lost theological vitality. Equally troubling was the fact that German liberalism often had anti-Jewish and ant-Semitic tendencies. Pioneer figures of German liberalism such as Kant, G. W. F. Hegel, and Schleiermacher all believed that Judaism represented a form of primitive religion that was superseded by the superior qualities of Christianity, with Kant going as far as arguing that Judaism had no historical connection to Christianity. While later German philosophers and theologians did not go as far as Kant, the tradition repeatedly affirmed that Christianity (in its Protestant forms) epitomized religious faith in its highest form. Schleiermacher himself noted, "Only a sick soul . . . would abandon [Christianity] for one of its rivals."[31] Ironically, while many aspects of German biblical and theological scholarship displayed these anti-Semitic tendencies, the tradition's stress upon historicity appealed to many American Jewish leaders. In particular, the insistence that religion's chief purpose was ethical rather than doctrinal impacted the late nineteenth-century development of Reform Judaism, a tradition that would play its own unique role in the rise of the social gospel.

Judaism and Social Reform

Although Jewish communities existed in America during the colonial era, it wasn't until the mid-nineteenth century that Jews began to develop more defined institutional networks in America.[32] In many ways, the organization of synagogues closely followed patterns of American Protestantism, as Jews often emulated models of local congregational autonomy practiced by many churches/denominations. Likewise, as the nineteenth century progressed, many Jews, like their Christian neighbors, grappled with the question of whether and how to preserve older traditions and faith practices. By the mid-nineteenth century, it appeared that this modern side of Judaism had gained the upper hand in America.

The movement commonly referred to as Reform Judaism largely had its origins among a small group of German rabbis in the late eighteenth and early nineteenth centuries. Heavily influenced by German Enlightenment traditions, these rabbis attempted to reinterpret Judaism in the context of Enlightenment theory and Jewish tradition. One of the pioneers of the German Reform movement was Samuel Holdheim, an example of the influence wielded by German Jewry on the later development of the American Reform movement. As a rabbi in both Frankfurt and Berlin, Holdheim taught that scripture needed to be seen in light of contemporary society. For Holdheim, Judaism "was not a matter of ritual deeds at all, but of beliefs, sentiments, and moral commitments." Holdheim's stress on personal experience and religion as ethics echoed themes found in liberal Protestant theology.[33] Perhaps the most influential German rabbi, in terms of shaping the contours of what became Reform Judaism, was Abraham Geiger. By the mid-1800s, Geiger articulated a vision of Judaism that integrated classical themes from the Bible and Talmud in ways that explored the social ramifications of Judaism in the modern world. The historian Michael Meyer observes that Geiger saw the message of the Hebrew prophets as "the most viable and important component of Judaism. The Prophets' concern for the poor and downtrodden, their contempt for ritual acts unaccompanied by social morality, and their vision of peace for all humanity" was the essence of Judaism's message to modern society.[34]

While Holdheim and Geiger were part of a coterie of German rabbis who wanted to reinterpret Judaism in a modern framework, they found it difficult to establish and sustain synagogues in Germany's strict state-controlled context (whereby taxes were collected to support either Catholic or Lutheran churches, depending on the territory in which one lived). By the mid-nineteenth century, several of these Reform rabbis and intellectuals immigrated to the United States. In the context of American religious volunteerism, the Reform movement began to gain traction, producing several influential leaders including Isaac Wise, considered the chief founder of the Reform movement in America, David Einhorn, Kaufmann Kohler, and Emil Hirsch.

In many ways, Emil Hirsch stands out as the primary late nineteenth-century example of what could be seen as a "social gospel" tradition in American Judaism. Born in Luxembourg in 1851, Hirsch was brought up in Germany until his father moved his family to the United States when Hirsch was fifteen. After studying at the University of Pennsylvania, Hirsch returned to Germany to complete graduate studies at the Universities of Berlin and Leipzig. After a series of short-term pastorates, in 1880 Hirsch became rabbi of Temple Sinai in Chicago, one of the most prominent congregations in the American Reform movement. His tenure at Sinai surpassed Gladden's in Columbus, as he stayed on as rabbi until his death in 1923.

Temple Sinai had been pastored by Kaufmann Kohler, one of the major theologians in American Reform Judaism and a figure who epitomized the strong assimilationist movement in the early Reform movement (he was also Hirsch's brother-in-law). In 1873 Kohler drew the ire of many critics by initiating Sunday Sabbath services in addition to the traditional Saturday Sabbath. While the Sunday Sabbath movement did not catch on in many other American Reform temples, it demonstrated the pressure that several American Jews felt to assimilate into the work cycle largely defined by Protestants. Despite Kohler's intellectual stature in American Judaism, attendance at Temple Sinai fell off until he resigned in 1879 (he would eventually become president of the Hebrew Union College in Cincinnati, the founding American seminary of Reform Judaism).

Hirsch fared better in his tenure at Temple Sinai. For the next two decades he drew large crowds, including many Protestants, to Sinai and lectured extensively throughout the country. One example of Hirsch's broader influence was his role in drafting the 1885 Pittsburgh Platform, a defining statement of principles for the Reform movement. The eighth principle of the platform was written by Hirsch: "In full accordance with the spirit of the Mosaic legislation, which strives to regulate the relation between the rich and poor, we deem it our duty to participate in the great task of modern times, to solve, on the basis of justice and righteousness, the problems presented by contrasts and evils of the present organization of society."[35] Hirsch's outlook shared a great deal in common with that of Felix Adler, a former Reform rabbi who left Judaism to found the Ethical Culture Movement, stressing the belief that all great religious truth was contained within its ethical application, rather than tradition. In his sermons, however, Hirsch returned to the theme that Jews had a responsibility to apply their faith to the great social problems of the modern era. He noted that Judaism in the future "will be impatient of men who claim that they have the right to be saved . . . while not stirring a foot or lifting a hand to redeem brother men from hunger and wretchedness."[36]

Like Washington Gladden, Hirsch pastored a large and wealthy congregation. During the early years of his ministry at Temple Sinai, Chicago, like other American cities, received a large number of Jewish immigrants from Eastern Europe, the majority escaping pogroms from Russia. With an accelerating rate of new immigrants arriving into the city, Hirsch was instrumental in supporting the founding in 1888 of the Jewish Training School. A year before Jane Addams and Ellen Gates Starr established Hull House, the Jewish Training School was created in an effort to provide free education and social services to poor immigrant Jewish youth. In addition to the rudiments of a primary school education, the Training School supported a variety of programs in "Americanization," including English instruction, vocational training, and education on hygiene and home economics.[37]

Ultimately, Hirsch's view of modern American Judaism would not be embraced by the majority of American Jews, including those in the Reform movement. Outside Temple Sinai, few Reform synagogues embraced Sunday Sabbath practices. Yet Hirsch represented a strong current within the Reform movement that sought to apply theological idealism to the major social problems of the day. Like his predecessor at Temple Sinai, Kaufmann Kohler, Hirsch saw the primary value of religion in its embodiment of ethical conduct. As Kohler noted, Judaism "looks to the *deed* . . . not to the empty creed and the blind belief. . . . Only in devotion to his fellows is man made to realize his own god-like nature."[38] Reform Judaism shared with Protestant social gospelers a belief that religion's ultimate purpose was to critique the contemporary social-political order. Some representatives of Reform Judaism even went so far as to acknowledge the ways Jesus illustrated the vision of a transformed society described by the prophets in the Hebrew Scriptures. Despite the parallels between Reform Judaism and liberal Protestantism in a shared belief in "social salvation," the relationship between the two traditions in many ways remained strained. While Reform Judaism was similar to liberal Protestantism in its efforts to create a thoroughly modern form of religious expression, American Catholics often resisted these movements to embrace modernity, while at the same time selectively incorporating liberal critiques in their own evolving views of social questions.

American Catholicism and the Legacy of *Rerum Novarum*

Throughout the nineteenth and into the twentieth century, the anti-Catholic attitudes of leaders like Josiah Strong were engrained in the fabric of American Protestantism. By the same token, American Catholics, like Protestants, were vigorously debating questions related to the church and modernity, specifically, the church's wider engagement with social issues. With the vast majority of immigrants to the United States coming from predominantly Catholic nations, many American Catholic leaders engaged questions of how their religious tradition should reach out to these immigrants, while also grappling with the wider social-economic abuses of industrial capitalism. For centuries, Catholics stressed the role of papal encyclicals, whereby popes interpreted matters of church doctrine and practice toward a range of theological, ethical, and, as the nineteenth century evolved, political issues.

During the late nineteenth century the Catholic Church faced numerous challenges to its ecclesiastical and political authority. Political revolutions in France, Germany, and Italy disrupted taken-for-granted assumptions of religious establishment, whereby the Catholic Church derived income from government-supported taxation. Increasingly, Catholic leaders were facing not only the theological challenges of rival Protestant churches but also rising political movements, such as socialism, that often perceived the church as a dangerous political rival. Since the mid-sixteenth-century Council of Trent, Catholic teaching had relied heavily on the theology of Thomas Aquinas. Aquinas's teaching placed tremendous stress on what has been called natural law philosophy. While emphasizing the inherent sinfulness of humanity, Aquinas believed that humans represented the highest order of God's creation, possessed with innate characteristics that made life purposeful, including the ability to receive the grace of God through the ministrations of the church. The theological suppositions of Aquinas's thought, rooted heavily in the philosophy of Aristotle and traditions of Catholic medieval theology, provided Catholicism a grounding that enabled the Church to claim a sense of united theological identity amid diverse Catholic communities worldwide. While many individual American Catholics were attracted to aspects of political socialism, officially the Catholic Church saw socialism as part of the sins of the modern world. It was a secular movement whose ideology was seen as hostile to the church.

With growing Catholic populations in cities such as New York, Boston, and Chicago, by the mid-nineteenth century, a variety of Catholic benevolent orders and relief societies were established whose mission was geared toward alleviating the suffering of poor immigrants. Some organizations, like the Society of St. Vincent de Paul, opened industrial schools and orphanages that provided youth vocational schooling. Other orders, like the Sisters of St. Joseph, based in Rochester, New York, had the mission "to educate young girls, destitute of parents, friends and employment, in some useful trade for which they seemed qualified."[39] These Catholic initiatives echoed a wide range of Protestant reform efforts to alleviate personal suffering, while also displaying a degree of suspicion toward organized labor as a movement dominated by socialists and anarchists.

However, since so many immigrants to the United States were coming from predominantly Catholic countries, several American Catholic leaders were sympathetic to many aspects of the burgeoning labor movement. In Boston, a city that by the 1880s had a firm Irish-Catholic majority, the diocesan newspaper *Boston Pilot* published frequently on behalf of labor rights. In 1885 a labor correspondent for the *Pilot*, under the pseudonym Phineas, called for the support of the fledging labor union the Knights of Labor, noting that imbalances of wealth made labor organization essential: "The consolidation of huge blocks of capital has rendered possible . . . the subjection of millions of workmen. And it is by counter-organization . . . that the latter can regain the lost ground."[40]

The *Pilot*'s commentary echoed a growing debate among Catholic leaders over the extent to which their church should embrace nineteenth-century intellectual currents, especially related to movements of political socialism. In the 1880s and 1890s, many immigrants debated a broad range of radical political options, including Marxism, anarchism (the belief that capitalism and centralized governments symbiotically caused a suppression of workers' rights), and syndicalism (a system that stressed a network of workers' cooperatives that could create worker ownership). The vast majority of American Catholics shared Protestant suspicion of socialist-leaning economic and political models. Condé Pallen, a late nineteenth-century Catholic journalist and editor, repeatedly attacked socialism as an affront to Church teaching. Reflecting Catholic natural law beliefs, Pallen castigated those who believed it possible to create a secular society rooted in justice and equality:

> To have a perfect society, we must have the perfect individual, and only then will we arrive at the perfect State. It is, therefore, in the regeneration of the individual that social perfection is to be sought, and in Christianity only is that regeneration to be found, as only in Christianity are the essential means to be found of bringing it about.[41]

Pallen's perspective resonated with a segment of American Catholics who were opposed to secular ideologies and worried that their tradition would be overwhelmed by the apostate teachings of Protestant church leaders. Conversely, many late nineteenth-century Catholics read and embraced the ideas coming from popular social theorists like Richard Ely and Henry George. One such Catholic figure was a New York City priest, Edward McGlynn. In the 1880s and 1890s, McGlynn developed a reputation as a reforming priest as well as popular public orator. He became a strong proponent of the single-tax theories of Henry George, and was a major supporter of George's 1886 campaign for New York City mayor. As McGlynn stumped for George, he not only proclaimed the economic wisdom of the single tax, but also asserted that this proposal encapsulated the timeless truths of Christianity. He noted in an address in 1887,

> Christ tells us that at the very peril of our souls we must look after the bodies of these little ones; we must feed the hungry; we must comfort and, as far as we can, heal the sick; we must provide shelter for the homeless; we must look after the weak, the blind. . . . It is because of the proper care of the bodies of men, of the proper feeding of those bodies, of the proper sheltering of them, that we make it possible for human nature to expand as a beautiful flower . . . and to feel that God the Father has not been entirely unmindful of the wants of the child.[42]

Edward McGlynn had a strong influence on a wide range of social reformers, both within and outside churches. His labor advocacy, modeled on Jesus's example, anticipated broader appeals by leaders like Charles Sheldon and William Stead to popular portrayals of Jesus as an individual who, if he lived in the late nineteenth century, would stand on the side of the dispossessed workers of the nation. While McGlynn was considered far outside the mainstream of the Catholic Church (ultimately being censored by the church in 1891), his ministry paralleled efforts of prominent "Americanizing" Catholic bishops, like James Cardinal Gibbons, to support worker rights to unionize. In 1889 Gibbons's influence helped galvanize a Catholic congress for laity that not only took a stand in support of organized labor, but also sought ways to cooperate with Protestants in solving the economic problems of the nation.

The efforts of reforming priests like McGlynn and bishops like Gibbons were significant steps in developing a Catholic response to late nineteenth-century industrialization. However, many American Catholic leaders worried that if the church followed radicals like McGlynn, it was merely mimicking apostate Protestants and secular socialists. In some way, the most important development in the wider history of Catholic social teaching was Pope Leo XIII's 1891 papal encyclical *Rerum Novarum* ("of revolutionary change"). *Rerum Novarum* expressed a long-standing papal wariness toward modern democratic movements, associating these movements with secularist political trends. Yet *Rerum Novarum* argued that conditions of modern industrialization required Catholics to move beyond personal morality; they needed to use their faith tradition to create broader political changes. *Rerum Novarum* restated the Catholic Church's condemnation of political socialism, seeing it as a negation of the individual's rights to private property and personal welfare. The encyclical's stress on natural law theory emphasized the imperative that the state had a moral as well as legal obligation to protect the rights of the poor. Although *Rerum Novarum* emphasized that the state did not have the right to infringe upon the individual's rights to wealth, the state did have an obligation to "watch over" the economic practices of society, in order that workers "who contribute so largely to the advantage of the community may themselves share in the benefits which they create—that being housed, clothed, and bodily fit, they may find their life less hard and more endurable."[43]

The encyclical was clear that a critical aspect of preserving an individual's freedom from state coercion was to protect persons' rights to exercise their faith, which included having time for worship, personal devotion, and caring for one's family (including procreation). By the end of the 1890s, Pope Leo indicated to American Catholics that his intentions to create reform needed to fall within certain parameters. His 1899 encyclical *Testem Benevolentiae* unequivocally stated that church teachings took precedence over the politics of the secular state, with Leo condemning the position of those in the American Catholic Church who wished to accommodate their faith to the precepts of American democratic society. Leo's pronouncement against the so-called Americanists in the Catholic Church seemed to corroborate Protestant fears that Catholicism was inherently undemocratic. Yet in the decades ahead, *Rerum Novarum* would serve as an indispensable model for the development of Catholic social teaching that would include a range of Catholic reformers including Dorothy Day and Pope Francis I.

By the 1890s, Protestants and Catholics were articulating a shared message of social reform, asserting that their religious traditions could be applied to the larger social fabric of society. Although both traditions stressed the power of moral suasion to change hearts and minds, a noticeable difference emerged between the two traditions. As members of a tradition that saw itself at the center of the nation's religious life, Protestants saw Christianity as a way to improve the quality of life by Christianizing America. They believed that the key tenets of their faith could infuse and transform key societal institutions in the nation, including government, business, and even the nuclear family. Although Catholics didn't disagree with this vision of Christianizing the nation per se, the tradition of reform crafted by *Rerum Novarum* stressed the indispensable role of the Catholic Church in shaping a moral vision that would protect individual rights while, in theory, making sure that the state guaranteed these rights—including most importantly one's right to follow the teachings of the Catholic faith. As the twentieth century developed, both traditions would often mingle and merge with one another to create a critical component of wider movements of religiously based social reform.

Conclusion

In December 1899 Dwight Lyman Moody, perhaps the most prominent evangelical revivalist in the Western world, died at the age of sixty-two. While Moody was a staunch premillennialist who was trying to save as many people as possible out of a fallen, sinful world, Moody's friends and associates included some of the most prominent figures associated with the rise of the social gospel in America, including the pastor/journalist Lyman Abbott (editor of the magazine the *Outlook*, and Henry Ward Beecher's successor at Plymouth Congregational Church), Frances Willard, and Washington Gladden.

In many ways, Moody's career drew to a close an era in which a disparate range of Protestants could still embrace the label "evangelical" and, to a degree, claim that they shared a common Protestant mission to evangelize the nation and the world. Moody's career helped to galvanize new organizational movements like the Student Volunteer Movement. Founded in 1888, the SVM embodied late nineteenth-century Protestant missional hopes for world evangelism through its motto, "Jesus Christ for This Generation." Late nineteenth-century Protestant hymns like "We've a Story to Tell to the Nations" reflected an evangelical postmillennial hope that the world was literally on the verge of experiencing the transformative power of Protestantism:

> For the darkness shall turn to dawning,
> and the dawning to noonday bright,
> and Christ's great kingdom shall come on earth,
> the kingdom of love and light.[44]

Yet, even as a wide range of Protestants could enthusiastically sing this hymn, the shared belief in missional unity was being undercut by a range of theological divisions. By the early 1900s, the optimistic missionary hope of globally spreading Christianity was offset by an increasing wariness among evangelicals that the church was losing sight of Moody's concern that the primary purpose of Christianity was to save sinners from the evils of a fallen world. While many evangelicals conceded the belief that Christians needed to show compassion and care for the poor and the destitute, the primary means to do this was to preach conversion. Increasingly, many of these same evangelicals were drawn to ideas of "Bible prophecy" that embraced dispensationalist beliefs in the imminent return of Christ. By the early twentieth century, the contours of what would later be known as fundamentalism were forming in northern denominations such as the Presbyterian and Baptist Churches, with many adherents emphasizing biblical inerrancy and premillennialism.[45]

It was in this context of theological uncertainty that the social gospel matured as a movement. As the twentieth century began, an increasing number of articles and books on social Christianity were published by well-established figures like Washington Gladden as well as newer voices. One of these emerging voices was a Baptist minister, Walter Rauschenbusch. He spent his early career as the pastor of a small German-Baptist immigrant church near the Hell's Kitchen section of New York City. Amid the city's tenement poverty, Rauschenbusch called on his church to resist the pessimism that looked to the imminent Second Coming of Christ. In an 1896 article critiquing the popularity of premillennialism, he observed that instead of believing in an otherworldly Christianity, people needed to see God's spirit challenging Christians to make the world a more righteous place. "The question is, which will do more to make our lives spiritual and to release us from the tyranny of the world, the thought that we may at any moment enter into the presence of the Lord, or the thought that every moment we are in the presence of the Lord?"[46] In 1904 Rauschenbusch elaborated on his vision in an article entitled "The New Evangelism" in the *Independent* magazine. The article echoed earlier nineteenth-century Protestant themes, but in a way that seemed to be signaling a new direction for twentieth-century evangelicalism. Lamenting the fact that much of the style and rhetoric of evangelicalism was not reaching the masses of Americans, Rauschenbusch called on churches to revision evangelicalism in ways that acknowledged that God's spirit was doing something new and radical in the modern world. "We must open our minds to the Spirit of Jesus in its primitive, uncorrupted and still unexhausted power. The Spirit is the fountain of youth for the church. . . . By the decay of the old, God himself is forcing us on to seek the new and higher."[47]

In some ways, the prediction that the Holy Spirit would do something new in America was fulfilled two years later, in 1906, when an African American holiness preacher named William Seymour helped to inaugurate what has been considered the birth of modern pentecostalism in a series of revivals at Azusa Street in Los Angeles. Emerging out of the late nineteenth-century holiness movement, pentecostalism stressed the gifts of the Holy Spirit and, at least at its inception, saw speaking in tongues as a gift that united believers, regardless of race, gender, and ethnicity, into a common purpose amid the last days on earth.

The theological changes hoped for by Walter Rauschenbusch were not as emotionally dramatic as those experienced by William Seymour at the Azusa Street revivals. However, Rauschenbusch's vision that religion was poised to do something radical at the dawn of the twentieth century set the context for the maturity of the social gospel and, in its own way, defined the tradition's broader significance as a movement of American religious idealism.

Kingdom Coming

The Social Gospel and the "Social Awakening" in the Early Twentieth Century

In 1914 Eugene Lyman, a professor of Christian ethics at Oberlin Theological Seminary, reflected on the interconnection between the message of the biblical prophets and the social conditions of the modern world. As Lyman discussed the unfolding of this prophetic tradition in the Hebrew Scriptures and the ministry of Jesus, he provided a succinct summary of the theological worldview that characterized the early twentieth-century social gospel in American Protestantism: The "fundamental constructive purpose of the prophet finds full expression in the great ideal which he gave to the world—the ideal of the kingdom of God. . . . By it the Christian faith was cradled. Through it the best spirit of our modern time finds expression." For Lyman, Jesus was the "climax of Hebrew prophetic religion" and "in him we find eternal expression of the motives for social progress. If then we are to appreciate the full value of prophetic religion as a social force, we must turn to Jesus' thought of the kingdom of God."[1] Lyman's assertion picks up on the ideas of many late nineteenth-century Protestant leaders like Washington Gladden, in identifying the kingdom of God as a concept that embodies Jesus's social teachings for the modern age. Yet in many ways Lyman's tone was more urgent than that of earlier social gospel leaders, as Lyman noted the inseparable connection between one's personal faith and the struggle for social justice: "The direct, inward, intimate relation of the soul to God is one of religion's supreme achievements, gained at the cost of great struggles with dogmatic authority, with the deadness of the letter, with formalism in worship and morals; an achievement never again to be lost so long as the Son of Man finds faith upon the earth."[2]

Lyman's observation was written at a time when the social gospel had gained an increasing level of acceptance in many religious institutions and in the wider culture. In 1910 Ray Stannard Baker, one of the most prominent journalists of the Progressive Era, noted that religious faith would play an essential role in galvanizing various measures of progressive political reform—what Baker and others referred to as the "social awakening" occurring in many parts of the nation. In particular, he singled out Walter Rauschenbusch's 1907 book *Christianity and the Social Crisis,* a book that "leaves the reader inspired with a new faith in the power of religion to meet and solve the most complex of problems of the day."[3]

Between 1907 and his death in 1918, Walter Rauschenbusch was the most influential proponent of the social gospel movement in America, and his theology had a major impact on a disparate range of religious leaders in the decades following his death. In the 1940s Henry Pitney Van Dusen, president of Union Theological Seminary, observed that Rauschenbusch had "the greatest single personal influence on the life and thought of the American church" of any figure in his generation.[4] However, Rauschenbusch's was not the only perspective on religion and social reform that emerged in this era. In the early years of the twentieth century, Protestant, Jewish, and Catholic leaders agreed that their faith traditions needed to engage questions of economic justice and social inequality in America. Yet many individuals connected with the so-called social awakening often had vastly different ideas on how religion translated into specific political models. As leaders like Walter Rauschenbusch strove to articulate their theological understanding of what by the early 1910s was being called the "social gospel," they were fundamentally transforming the way many Americans were viewing the relationship between religion and social reform.

Walter Rauschenbusch's Coming Kingdom

In early 1907 Walter Rauschenbusch was preparing to leave for Europe, on sabbatical from his teaching position at Rochester Theological Seminary. A few weeks before his departure, *Christianity and the Social Crisis* was published. At year's end, Rauschenbusch was aware that it had become one of the most talked-about books on religion in America. By 1910, it had sold over fifty thousand copies and had been reprinted multiple times. For Rauschenbusch the task of Christianity was nothing short of rooting out sin from the social fabric of the nation. Behind Rauschenbusch's faith was an optimism that men and women were capable of changing the course of history, and that a prophetic Christianity was an essential component of the effort to galvanize wider social-economic changes in America. "Religion is not dying. It is only molting its feathers, as every winged thing must at times." For Rauschenbusch, this molting went hand in hand with his belief that God was actively involved in leading believers to engage the social-economic struggles of the early twentieth century. "All history becomes the unfolding of the purpose of the immanent God who is working in the race toward the commonwealth of spiritual liberty and righteousness."[5]

Walter Rauschenbusch's emergence as the preeminent figure of the social gospel was a culmination of numerous theological currents coming out of the late nineteenth century. His stress on God's immanence and the belief that religion's primary mission was to translate its teachings into sustained work for social reform was being embraced by a wide range of religious leaders in the early twentieth century, as was his tendency to equate the historical essence of Christianity with various models of democratic socialism.

Rauschenbusch was born in 1861. His father, August, was a fifth-generation Lutheran minister in Germany who immigrated to the United States in the 1840s. Caught up in many of the revivalist currents that characterized antebellum evangelicalism, August Rauschenbusch converted to the Baptists and became one of the leaders among burgeoning German Baptist immigrant communities in the Northeast and Midwest. By the start of his own ministry in the 1880s, Walter Rauschenbusch's theology had moved far away from his father's. However, he preserved much of his father's religious pietism, as many of Rauschenbusch's writings reflect a discernible stress on personal piety, even as he challenged much of the historical and theological foundations of more traditional Protestant orthodoxy.

Rauschenbusch lived during a time of great historical and theological changes occurring in American religion—especially American Protestantism—in the late nineteenth and early twentieth centuries.[6] After studying at a German gymnasium school for four years, essentially the equivalent of a college preparatory academy, Rauschenbusch returned to his hometown of Rochester, New York, where he attended the University of Rochester and Rochester Theological Seminary. His father headed the seminary's German department, designed to train German-immigrant pastors for ministry in America. The seminary's president was Augustus Hopkins Strong, a stalwart conservative who greatly enhanced the seminary's prestige both through its financial donors (one of the school's main benefactors was one of Strong's former parishioners, John D. Rockefeller) and through the seminary's mission to train ministers for service in pastoral ministry and foreign mission. Although the school's professors resisted liberalism, many students, including Rauschenbusch, read the work of theologians like Horace Bushnell. In fact, some faculty worried that Rauschenbusch was becoming too enamored with Bushnell's theology. As he prepared to graduate from seminary, Rauschenbusch was in line to receive an appointment to become president of a Baptist seminary in India. However, his budding liberalism caused one of Rauschenbusch's seminary professors to write a negative recommendation to Baptist foreign missionary officials, costing Rauschenbusch the position.[7]

In 1886 Rauschenbusch was called to serve a small German immigrant parish in the Hell's Kitchen section of New York, one of the poorest areas of the city. For the next eleven years, he spent his time ministering to his congregation and searching for ways to engage the social-economic inequalities in the city. Initially influenced by Henry George, Rauschenbusch read a variety of social reformers. He was drawn to the Christian socialism of Frederick Denison Maurice and Frederick Robertson, as well as various theories of democratic socialism. He read Marx and Frederick Engels and, while conceding the appeal of radical socialism, he distrusted the antireligious foundation and ideological dogmatism of Marxism. He was also well versed in many aspects of German theology.

Early in his ministry, Rauschenbusch wrestled with how to address the poverty that enslaved his congregants. Although his sermons often displayed an orthodox theological bent, he struggled with the suffering of his parishioners, and agonized at presiding over the funerals of children who died from contagious diseases contracted in crowded tenements. Part of Rauschenbusch's personal breakthrough occurred early in his New York ministry during the fall of 1886, when he heard Father Edward McGlynn give a speech in support of the mayoral candidacy of Henry George. Rauschenbusch was taken by McGlynn's fusing together of a vision of a coming kingdom of God on earth and George's single-tax proposals. From this initial encounter Rauschenbusch delved into social reform efforts in his parish, at times meeting fierce resistance. With his health breaking and after he had become almost completely deaf, Rauschenbusch's congregation granted him a sabbatical in 1891 to travel and study in Germany. When he returned to America the following year, he established a small fellowship, primarily of like-minded Baptist ministers, called the Brotherhood of the Kingdom.[8]

Rauschenbusch's association with the Brotherhood of the Kingdom helped him to refine many of his theological ideas. Central for him was his understanding of the kingdom of God that required "a growing perfection in the collective life of humanity, in our laws in the customs of society, in the institutions for education, . . . and in our readiness to give our life as a ransom for others."[9] Yet Rauschenbusch repeatedly turned to the idea that collective responsibility for societal change needed to emerge out of a deep-seated pietism. As he noted in an article from 1897, not long after he returned to Rochester Theological Seminary as a professor,

> But the main thing is to have God; to live in him; to have him live in us; to think his thoughts; to love what he loves and hate what he hates; to realize his presence; to feel his holiness and to be holy because he is holy, to feel goodness in every blessing of our life and even in its tribulations; to be happy and trustful; to join in the great purposes of God and to be lifted to greatness of vision and faith and hope with him—that is the blessed life.[10]

Even though Rauschenbusch developed a reputation as a religious radical, his pietism connected him to aspects of an earlier evangelical heritage, in ways absent from the works of Herron, Mathews, and Peabody. While still in New York, he collaborated with Ira Sankey, Dwight L. Moody's musical partner, in translating Sankey's revival hymns into German. Yet he shared with other Protestant liberals a wariness toward premillennialism, and lamented that many of the revivalists coming out of the Moody tradition made dispensationalism a litmus test of faith. These doctrines circumvented the social message of Jesus, who "was neither ascetic nor other-worldly. . . . He believed in a life after death, but it was not the dominant element in his teaching."[11]

The manuscript that ultimately became *Christianity and the Social Crisis* had a gestation period of over fifteen years. He had written a book-length manuscript while in Germany in 1891, and several of his colleagues in the Brotherhood of the Kingdom urged him to refine his ideas.[12] The first sentence of this unpublished manuscript reflected Rauschenbusch's growing conviction that "Christianity is in its nature revolutionary."[13] Looking to the witness of the Hebrew prophets and to Jesus's ministry, Rauschenbusch asserted that these prophets were not interested merely in a "slight amelioration" of social problems,

> but a change so radical that they dared to represent it as a repealing of the ancient and hollowed covenant and the construction of a new one. A proposal to abolish the Constitution of the United States would not seem so revolutionary to us as this proposal must have seemed to the contemporaries of the prophets.[14]

Rauschenbusch underscored many aspects of Jesus's social radicalism as he reworked his earlier manuscript. When *Christianity and the Social Crisis* was finally published in 1907, Rauschenbusch did not expect it to receive many accolades and was preparing to turn his research primarily to church history. However, national and international praise for the book came from a wide range of religious and secular leaders, shaping the contours of his future writing and his public ministry for the rest of his life.

Christianity and the Social Crisis emphasized God's actions in history and the work of individuals acting in partnership with God for social change. While his interpretation of Christianity's development relied heavily on the interpretations of Albrecht Ritschl and Adolf von Harnack, his rhetorical style balanced a combination of crisis and opportunity for Americans. His book laid out a basic theme that he would return to in his future writings, namely, that historical Christianity had lost touch with its initial ethic focused on radical social change. Jesus "nourished within his soul the ideal of a common life so radically different from the present that it involved a reversal of values, a revolutionary displacement of existing relations."[15] After centuries when Christian communities were governed by theological ideals that stressed otherworldliness at the expense of worldly engagement, churches at the dawn of the twentieth century now were becoming increasingly aware of the power of Jesus's social teachings to change society.

Central to Rauschenbusch's vision was his belief in democratic socialism. While critics saw socialism as a curtailment of individual and
collective freedom, Rauschenbusch believed that socialism was a political system that allowed for the perfection of American democracy. It
"should be hailed with joy by every patriot and Christian, for it would
put a stop to our industrial war, drain off the miasmatic swamp of unde-
served poverty, save our political democracy, and lift the great working
class to an altogether different footing of comfort, intelligence, security
and moral strength."[16] Rauschenbusch emphasized that one of the grav-
est abuses of capitalism was that the resulting wealth inequality generated a wider spiritual crisis for Americans. As he summarized,

> It is the function of religion to teach the individual to value his soul more
> than his body, and his moral integrity more than his income. In the same
> way it is the function of religion to teach society to value human life more
> than property, and to value property only in so far as it forms the material
> basis for the higher development of human life. When life and property
> are in apparent collision, life must take precedence.[17]

Rauschenbusch was clear that "history laughs at the optimistic illusion
that 'nothing can stand in the way of human progress.'"[18] He concluded
Christianity and the Social Crisis with an assertion that religion could
never make possible a perfect social order:

> In asking for faith in the possibility of a new social order, we ask for no
> Utopian delusion. We know well that there is no perfection for man in
> this life: there is only growth toward perfection. . . . At best there is always
> but an approximation to a perfect social order. The kingdom of God is
> always but coming.[19]

In 1927, reflecting on the rise of the social gospel, Shailer Mathews
noted the ways that *Christianity and the Social Crisis* was unique, during a period when many academics and church leaders were publishing
books on the church and social problems. Rauschenbusch "possessed a
style of singular brilliancy, and his criticism of the economic practices of
capitalistic organizations was scathing."[20] Yet in many ways, Rauschenbusch's socialism was tempered by his pietism and a desire to address

people of power in a charitable fashion. For years he enjoyed a close friendship with John Rockefeller, a Baptist layman, and saw no conflict between his own social evangelism and Rockefeller's wealth. In the aftermath of the success of *Christianity and the Social Crisis*, Rauschenbusch was approached by John Phillips, the editor of the *American Magazine*, to write a series of prayers that could be used for various public occasions. After these prayers were serialized in the *American Magazine*, they appeared in book form in 1910 under the title *Prayers of the Social Awakening*. Rauschenbusch noted in the volume's preface that public prayer was a necessary social response to redeem society. In prayer, "we feel the vanity and shamefulness of much that society calls proper and necessary. If we had more prayer in common on the sins of modern society, there would be more social repentance and less angry resistance to the demands of justice and mercy."[21]

Rauschenbusch's next major book, *Christianizing the Social Order*, was published in 1912. As he discussed the meaning of the book's title, Rauschenbusch was clear that he did not want to make membership in the church compulsory, in any sort of theocratic way. Christianizing America meant bringing society "into harmony" with the ethical convictions of Jesus, in a fashion that would create a just social order. Rauschenbusch took for granted that Jesus exemplified "the perfect expression of the will of God for humanity" that served as a standard for all Americans to follow, regardless of religious background. He looked hopefully at the fact that "an increasing portion of our Jewish fellow-citizens, will still consent that in Jesus our race has reached one of its highest points, if not its crowning summit thus far, so that Jesus Christ is a prophecy of the future glory of humanity, the type of Man as he is to be. Christianizing means humanizing in the highest sense."[22] Throughout his ministry, Rauschenbusch vigorously attacked anti-Semitism. At the same time, he illustrates many aspects of the cultural imperialism characteristic of a wide spectrum of late nineteenth-century Protestants. Like other social gospelers of his generation, Rauschenbusch believed that the nation's Protestant churches needed to play a unique role in upholding American democratic institutions. As he noted, "Democracy has been best led in Protestant countries where a free type of religion ranged men of distinctively Christian character on the side of popular liberty."[23] At the same time, leaders like Rauschenbusch took for granted that finding ways to incorporate Jesus's teachings into the institutional fabric of American life was necessary to preserve democracy. In this regard, the idealistic language of socialism merged well with the social gospel's understanding of Jesus.

The historian Sydney Ahlstrom probably had Rauschenbusch in mind when he referred to the social gospel as "the praying wing of Progressivism."[24] In the context of his greatest public visibility between 1907 and 1918, Rauschenbusch's mix of a progressive theology and religious pietism was at the center of the idealism that drove much of the social gospel movement in America. Through his writings and lectures at universities, lyceum halls, and churches, he displayed a tension between wanting to preserve the institutional stability of middle-class American Protestant churches and challenging churches to embrace the revolutionary social teachings of Jesus. Part of this tension can be seen in the fact that although he regularly voted for the Socialist Party presidential candidate, Eugene Debs, he never joined the Socialist Party. Rauschenbusch's work was not the only creative synthesis being made in the early twentieth century related to religion and politics, nor was his vision necessarily the most radical. However, in the years between *Christianity and the Social Crisis*'s initial publication in 1907 and the beginning of World War I in 1914, Rauschenbusch benefited from a wider sense that America's churches were finally embracing their rightful role in creating a cooperative commonwealth in America. This vision was especially pronounced in the nation's largest Protestant denomination, the Methodist Episcopal Church. By 1910, that church increasingly led American Protestantism in the incorporation of social gospel themes in its denominational institutions.

Harry Ward, the Methodist Federation for Social Service, and the Birth of the Social Creed

Harry Ward was motivated by one task: advocating for the poor. In turn-of-the-century Chicago, first through his work in the settlement house movement and then as a pastor of impoverished churches on the city's South Side, Ward accentuated the "What Would Jesus Do?" vision espoused in Charles Sheldon's fiction. However, Ward's view of social reform, even early in his ministry, was far more radical than those of Sheldon and many of his colleagues in the social gospel movement.

Born in England in 1873, Ward grew up outside London in a family of strict Methodists. Like his father, Ward became a Methodist lay preacher and had occasion to preach in several Methodist chapels in and around London. Even though Ward sought to push beyond his working-class background, aspects of his British Methodist heritage would always be part of his ministry. While scholars note the important role played by Anglicanism in the development of the social gospel in the United Kingdom, British Methodism embodied its own unique tradition of social action. The most prominent figure to come out of British Methodism in the late nineteenth century was Hugh Price Hughes. Hughes was a major leader in the Forward Movement, a renewal movement within Methodism that supported ecumenical cooperation and the creation of networks among British churches to engage social problems. Like Washington Gladden, late nineteenth-century British Methodists ministers such as Hughes and his colleague Samuel Keeble argued for a reinterpretation of Christianity rooted in evangelical pietism that engaged social problems associated with industrialization.[25] Ward was rooted in this heritage, even as he developed it in different ways.

With the goal of pursuing a college education, Ward emigrated to the United States in 1891. He eventually earned degrees at Northwestern University and Harvard University, where he served as Francis Greenwood Peabody's research assistant. At Northwestern, Ward met the person who became his intellectual mentor and, later in life, his closest friend, George Albert Coe. An undergraduate classmate of Walter Rauschenbusch's at the University of Rochester, by the early twentieth century, Coe was a leading figure in the religious education movement, and would later teach at Union Theological Seminary and Columbia Teachers College.

Ward was a good student; however, his interests were more practical than scholarly. As he matured, he reflected many aspects of his Methodist upbringing as a staunch supporter of temperance reform. At the same time, the moralism that came out of his Methodist background quickly translated into a maverick view of activism. He returned to Chicago from Harvard in 1898 and served as head resident of the Northwestern University Settlement House, a position that he lost in 1900 due to his authoritative leadership style and charges that he was too radical. Ward then pastored a small parish adjacent to the Chicago stockyards, made up primarily of employees in the meatpacking industry.

Chicago's infamous "Back-of-the-Yards" would be immortalized in Upton Sinclair's 1906 novel *The Jungle*. In microcosm, Chicago's meat-packing industry became a symbol of the urban squalor and industrial abuses that social gospelers like Ward were fighting against. The meat-packing industry was notoriously hazardous. Many laborers, mostly poor immigrants, lost limbs in machinery and endured twelve-hour workdays, seven days a week. One historian noted how this area of Chicago, commonly called "Packingtown," had a visceral effect on first-time visitors:

> The unique yards smell—a mixture of decaying blood, hair, and organic tissue; fertilizer dust; smoke; and other ingredients—permeated the air of the surrounding neighborhoods. . . . To the white-collar worker or university student passing through on a streetcar, Packingtown's very appearance and physical isolation must have enhanced its image as a world apart.[26]

In his years as a Methodist minister in Packingtown, Ward's health suffered tremendously. At five feet five, Ward came across to many who met him as a frail and sickly man, yet much like Methodism's founder, John Wesley (who approximated Ward's height), Ward was filled with an uncompromising zeal that would characterize his lengthy public career as an individual who was either admired as a visionary prophet or loathed as a dangerous radical. Employing a technique used by English Methodist ministers like Hugh Price Hughes, Ward took his message outside his church, preaching on street corners near the stockyards. These sermons drew attention to the wealth disparities that separated the city's rich and poor, calling his hearers to renewed moral and ethical standards to care for the poor. In many ways, this behavior characterized Ward's career, as he "maintained the social ethics of the street preacher who saw modern American society, at least at some moments, as Babylon."[27] He also lectured widely throughout Chicago and preached sermons castigating the idea that poverty was somehow preordained: "But if you say that some must always roll in luxury and some must starve in squalor, I refuse to believe it, because I believe in a God of justice who has called himself the God of the poor."[28] Ward's ministerial career in Packingtown paralleled Walter Rauschenbusch's ministry in Hell's Kitchen. More than Rauschenbusch, however, Ward was an effective organizer who built alliances with a range of progressive reformers in

Chicago, including Jane Addams, who referred to Ward as "my little minister," and fellow Methodist Mary McDowell, head resident of the University of Chicago settlement house.[29]

Even as he built social reform connections in Chicago, Ward forged links with like-minded religious leaders across the country. Early in his ministry, he became active in the Open and Industrial Church League. Established in 1894, this organization was an important precursor to the modern ecumenical movement, serving as an opportunity for Protestant leaders to explore ways to engage in applied Christianity for "the alleviation of human suffering, the elevation of man, and the betterment of the world."[30] Additionally, Ward increasingly developed relationships with other national Methodist leaders interested in social reform, most especially Frank Mason North.

North had spent the majority of his career in ministries designed to build outreach networks between churches and secular organizations and leaders. As head of New York City's League of Church Extension, North had been a longtime proponent in northern Methodism of adopting policy statements on social issues. In 1903 North wrote the lyrics to what would become the best-known hymn to come out of the social gospel era, "Where Cross the Crowded Ways of Life." The lyrics of this hymn echoed many of the themes of early twentieth-century reformers who saw the amelioration of injustice coming from those who walked in Christ's footsteps:

> Till all the world shall learn your love
> And follow where your feet have trod,
> Till, glorious from your heaven above,
> Shall come the city of our God![31]

In December 1907 Ward, North, and a small coterie of Methodist clergy traveled to Washington, D.C., and founded what some historians have considered the first modern caucus group in an American Protestant denomination: the Methodist Federation for Social Service (MFSS).[32] As a caucus within the Methodist Episcopal Church, the MFSS had a mission "to stimulate a wide study of social questions by the Church, side by side with practical social service, and to bring the Church into touch with neglected social groups."[33] North and Ward possessed very different personalities, and ultimately their specific reform agendas would move them in different directions. However, they succeeded in bringing to Washington an influential group of Methodist leaders who formed the MFSS, including Worth Tippy, a prominent Cleveland minister, and Herbert Welch, president of Ohio Wesleyan University and future Methodist bishop. At the conclusion of the caucus's first meeting, President Theodore Roosevelt hosted a reception for the group at the White House, affirming favorably a statement on social principles that the new organization had adopted. In order to create a working template, the MFSS created what it called a social creed—a model that ultimately would be embraced by a wide range of Protestant churches:

> The Methodist Episcopal Church stands—
> For equal rights and complete justice for all men in all stations of life.
> For the principles of conciliation and arbitration in industrial dissensions.
> For the protection of the worker from dangerous machinery, occupational diseases, injuries, and mortality.
> For the abolition of child labor.
> For such regulation of the conditions of labor for women as shall safeguard the physical and moral health of the community.
> For the suppression of the "sweating system."
> For the gradual and reasonable reduction of the hours of labor to the lowest practical point, with work for all; and for that degree of leisure for all which is the condition of the highest human life.
> For a release from employment one day in seven.
> For a living wage in every industry.
> For the highest wage that each industry can afford, and for the most equitable division of the products of industry that can ultimately be devised.
> For the recognition of the Golden Rule and the mind of Christ as the supreme law of society and the sure remedy of all social ills.[34]

Although Frank Mason North often received credit for writing the social creed, the primary author was Harry Ward. Containing little theological language besides the emphasis on the Golden Rule, the social creed laid out a list of principles related to workers' rights, including minimum wage protection, limits on worker hours, workplace safety, and the right to unionize. In the spring of 1908 the Methodist Episcopal Church approved this social creed as an official policy statement, and between 1908 and 1916 most of the largest American Protestant churches adopted similar social creeds based on the Methodist version.

The fact that Protestant denominations like the Methodists were able to pass social creeds was seen by leaders like North as a sign that churches were institutionally committed to social reform. However, groups like the MFSS carefully avoided aligning themselves with specific social-economic models like socialism, preferring to advocate for more general ideals. Herbert Welch noted that the MFFS's original purpose was "to be irenic rather than controversial. Its charter membership contained men of widely variant views, bound together not by opinions but by certain ideals and loyalties."[35] Indeed, the MFSS reflected the mindset of many social gospel leaders of that time. Although these Methodist reformers were motivated by the proposals of social reform advanced by figures like Walter Rauschenbusch, they were also interested in building alliances between churches, businesses, and organized labor.

In the years following the establishment of the MFSS, Harry Ward's primary focus revolved around MFSS membership recruitment. Even after he was appointed pastor of a church in the affluent Chicago suburb of Oak Park, Illinois, Ward spent much of his time traveling across the country, seeking to build local MFSS chapters and forge alliances between the church and organized labor. While Walter Rauschenbusch may have been the most prominent Protestant social gospel leader in the early 1910s, Ward's work was indicative of a spirit of grassroots activism that characterized many social gospel leaders. This vision was by no means confined to leaders in American Protestantism.

Stephen Wise's Progressive Idealism

In May 1908 Stephen Wise, rabbi of the Free Synagogue of New York City, was invited to speak to the third annual meeting of the Christian Socialist Fellowship on the theme of the "social message of the prophets." At thirty-three, Wise already was well established as a leader in Reform Judaism. A year earlier, he had founded the Free Synagogue in part out of a desire to foster an uninhibited discussion on the relationship between modern Judaism and social reform. Yet Wise was quick to point out to his Christian colleagues that the use of the term "Christian socialism" was nothing short of "odious." The Christian Socialist Fellowship was founded in 1906 out of its members' desire to directly connect Christian teaching with membership in the Socialist Party of America. Wise reminded his colleagues that for American Jews the term had connotations with the Christian Socialist Party in Germany—a party noted for its anti-Semitism. "I have come to feel . . . that I could not speak upon your platform unless the anti-Semitic attitude of the Christian Socialist party in Europe were clearly and vigorously repudiated by you, not only because it is not a part of your own creed but because you believe it to be, as I do, anti-Christian and anti-social."[36]

Wise's misgivings about lending his support to this event reflect the tension felt by Jewish leaders who, while generally supportive of the Protestant social gospel, worried about some of its anti-Jewish themes. Although Emil Hirsch was often referred to as the "Jewish ambassador to the Gentile world,"[37] in many ways Wise epitomized that role. He was born in Budapest, Hungary, in 1874, and came to the United States the following year when his father, Aaron, became rabbi of Congregation Rodeph Shalom in New York City. From an early age, Wise imbibed the liberal spirit of the Reform movement, and his education included degrees from Columbia University and rabbinical studies at Oxford University and with Adolph Jellinek, Chief Rabbi of Vienna. In 1900 Wise became rabbi of Temple Beth Israel in Portland, Oregon, where he developed a reputation for his outspokenness on labor rights. In 1907 he founded the Free Synagogue in New York City, where he would remain until his death in 1949.[38]

In many ways, the foundation of the Free Synagogue reflected a strong Protestant ethos, especially in its congregational emphasis on freedom of conscience and a free pulpit. The bylaws of the synagogue affirmed these values:

> Believing that the power of the synagogue for good depends, in part, upon the inherent right of the pulpit to freedom of thought and speech, the founders of the Free Synagogue resolve that its pulpit shall be free to preach on behalf of truth and righteousness in the spirit and after the pattern of the prophets of Israel.[39]

Wise's New York congregation paralleled an eclectic assortment of Protestant urban-based "People's Churches" that had been founded in many American cities during the early twentieth century, primarily as a means to reach out to the labor movement. One of the more popular examples of this model was the Presbyterian Labor Temple in New York, pastored by Charles Stelzle. Stelzle sought to integrate modern marketing techniques into an approach that was geared specifically to working-class groups in the city. While Wise respected Stelzle's efforts, his closest colleague in New York was a Unitarian minister, John Haynes Holmes. As minister of what became known as the Community Church of New York, Holmes created a ministry that was firmly rooted in the theology of the social gospel, and over the years both men developed close professional relationships with Walter Rauschenbusch.

While Wise embodied many aspects of Reform Judaism in the early twentieth century, he parted company with his comrades in the Reform movement on one issue: he was a strong Zionist. When Reform Judaism was codified by the Pittsburgh Platform in 1885, it had renounced the ideal of a Jewish homeland. While studying in Europe in the 1890s, Wise had had the opportunity to meet Theodor Herzl, the major supporter for the Zionist cause of creating a Jewish homeland. In 1898 Wise attended the Second Zionist Congress in Basel, Switzerland, where Herzl appointed him American secretary of the world Zionist movement. Part of the paradox of Wise's ministry is that while he would often liberally quote Jesus in his sermons, he also reflected a passionate commitment to Zionism, at a time when support for this movement was at a nadir among Reform Jews. He was also very clear about the fact that the Free Synagogue would not serve as a sort of gateway for the congregation to become liberal Protestants. As he stated in his first address to the new congregation in January 1907,

The Free Synagogue is not to be an indirect or circuitous avenue of approach to Unitarianism; it is not to be a society for the gradual conversion of Jewish men or women to any form of Christianity. We mean to be vitally, intensely, unequivocally Jewish. Jews who would not be Jews, will find no place in the Free Synagogue, for we, its founders, wish to be not less Jewish but more Jewish in the highest and noblest sense of the term.[40]

A major aspect of Wise's ministry was reaching out to a wide range of progressive reformers, locally and nationally. In addition to Rauschenbusch and Holmes, Wise formed friendships with labor advocates such as the union leader Samuel Gompers, the attorney Clarence Darrow, and the prominent Boston lawyer and future Supreme Court Justice Louis Brandeis. Wise noted,

As long as labor organizations are denied a hearing . . . ; as long as they are treated with scorn and contumely; as long as they are cast out and denied, it is not to be wondered at that the leaders, finding themselves and their organizations outlawed, should in turn be guilty of outlawry; that being cast out, they should resort to the weapon of the outcast; that being denied a hearing after the manner of orderly and reasoning friends, they should make themselves heard after the manner of destructive and unreasoning foes.[41]

In the aftermath of New York's Triangle Shirtwaist Fire in 1911, which killed 146 workers, a large number of whom were Jewish immigrants, Wise called for a public investigation into the conditions of the factory. He served on a committee that increased public awareness of the lack of adequate safety provisions in the Triangle factory.

Wise's activism also embraced a commitment to racial justice. In 1909 W. E. B. Du Bois galvanized the establishment of the National Association for the Advancement of Colored People. Among the cofounders of the NAACP were Emil Hirsch, Reverdy Ransom, Jane Addams, John Haynes Holmes, and Stephen Wise. In his advocacy for African American rights, Wise lamented the economic subjugation of labor and the exclusion of African Americans from the labor movement. "Few tendencies in American life today are more menacing than the shutting out of the Negro toiler from the ranks of organized labor," he observed to a labor gathering. "I would ask the American workingman not to commit the injustice of color discrimination." Like other social gospel leaders, Wise noted that employers often hired African Americans as "scab" workers or strike breakers. He compared the use of African Americans as strike breakers to the militarized Cossacks in Russia and Ukraine: "Make the Negro a Cossack and his end will be tragic, but no less tragic will be the consequences to the American industrial democracy which will have wrought this deadly evil and terrible injustice to two races."[42]

Although Wise formed strong friendships with many Protestant social gospel leaders, he was cognizant of the fact that as a Jew he remained an outsider in America. In 1911 he was invited to speak to a conference of social reformers in Lake Mohonk, New York. Lake Mohonk had long hosted a range of gatherings for Progressive Era and social gospel leaders.[43] Yet Wise refused to attend the event, reflecting on the irony that the conference hotel epitomized America's "gateless ghetto," in that it did not normally house Jews. "Ordinarily, the Lake Mohonk Hotel gives the Jews no quarters, so I turned around and gave them no quarter."[44] Incidents like these only reaffirmed Wise's belief that Jews needed to strive for their own homeland, an advocacy that would grow stronger after World War I.

Wise always insisted that the Free Synagogue was a community open to all social classes, but like many of his Protestant colleagues, he often courted the favor of people who were part of the political mainstream. Unlike his friend John Holmes, who supported the Socialist Party, Wise formed friendships with many Democratic Party leaders, like New Jersey governor Woodrow Wilson. Yet Wise also became a frequent lecturer at numerous forums and symposiums that featured an array of religious reformers who advocated a wide range of progressive and socialist political solutions. In addition to the Chautauqua movement, one of the most prominent public lectureships in the early twentieth century was Boston's Ford Hall Forum. Established in 1908 by a Baptist layman, George Coleman, Ford Hall strove to create an open public forum that would enable Bostonians to hear addresses from a wide range of contemporary intellectuals. Initially inspired by Rauschenbusch's *Christianity and the Social Crisis*, Coleman saw Ford Hall as an opportunity for "the striking of mind upon mind," whereby audiences would be able to engage speakers in direct conversation on public issues. Between its founding in 1908 and over the next ten years, Ford Hall regularly featured lectures on topics related to religion and social problems. Like Chautauqua, the "open forum" model of Ford Hall would be replicated in other parts of the country in the early decades of the twentieth century.[45] In addition to Rauschenbusch and Wise, its lecturers included religious reformers such as John Haynes Holmes, Shailer Mathews, Samuel Schumann, another activist New York Reform rabbi, and a Roman Catholic priest who offered an alternative perspective on the amelioration of American economic problems, John Ryan.

John Ryan and a "Living Wage"

Despite the fact that Walter Rauschenbusch viewed with fondness individual Catholic leaders, he largely followed the pattern of previous generations of Protestants by seeing Catholicism as un-American, noting to a colleague, "In spite of the fine Americanism of many of its members and leaders, this Church is an isolated and foreign body in the midst of our national life."[46] *Rerum Novarum* made clear that government involvement in the economic sector was a necessary consequence of preserving the sanctity of human life, including the ability of Catholics to raise families and earn a living wage—a wage sufficient to live a holistic life and contribute to the larger well-being of the family, the church, and society. This encyclical was a template for a disparate range of religious arguments for social justice that would extend into the twentieth century, and the most important interpreter of the implications of *Rerum Novarum* for American economic life was a Midwestern priest, John Ryan.

Ryan grew up poor in rural Minnesota and came of age at a time when the American Catholic hierarchy was contesting issues related to Americanization.[47] Even as Ryan imbibed the teachings of Thomas Aquinas and the Council of Trent, he was drawn to the writings of reformers like Henry George and, in particular, Richard Ely. Throughout his career Ryan expressed distrust of various models of socialism. However, he embraced many of Ely's arguments in favor of a government-regulated economy, and believed that economic justice was derived from deep-seated moral-ethical duty. While he did not dispute the important contributions of reformers like Ely who saw social reform embodied in the historical Jesus, Ryan believed that societal reform was primarily grounded in the Catholic doctrinal teachings of *Rerum Novarum*. After his ordination to the priesthood in 1898, Ryan began doctoral studies at the Catholic University in Washington, D.C. In 1906 Macmillan Press, the same press that a year later published Walter Rauschenbusch's *Christianity and the Social Crisis*, published Ryan's first major book, a revision of his doctoral dissertation entitled *A Living Wage*. With its foreword written by Ely, *A Living Wage* laid out many of the arguments that Ryan would reiterate throughout his career. While the book stressed the need for government regulation of the private sector, Ryan did not share Rauschenbusch's belief in the need to create a "Christianized" socialism; rather, he emphasized the potential power of Catholic teachings to reform political-economic structures.

Ryan's analysis revealed his familiarity with the arguments used by many social gospel Protestants, who often relied on German idealists such as Kant and Hegel as the basis for their social idealism. At the outset of *A Living Wage*, however, Ryan made clear that he was trying to create a middle path between "semi-anarchism" based on economic individualism and "state absolutism," associated with many types of socialism.[48] With a theological grounding in Thomist theology and *Rerum Novarum*, Ryan asserted that the natural rights of individuals went beyond mere existence or service to society: "they exist and are sacred and inviolable because the welfare of the person exists—as a fact of the ideal order—and is a sacred and inviolable thing."[49] State intervention to provide workers a "living wage" did not result from a desire to "Christianize" society in the same sense used by Protestants. Rather, the right to a living wage emerges out of the moral grounding that a person is "a being endowed with certain indestructible rights," including the right to earn a fair wage that would safeguard the worker's rights as well as the rights of the worker's family.[50] While Walter Rauschenbusch saw social reform as a means to make government model the ideals of the kingdom of God, Ryan's analysis focused on the regulation of the economy as a way to elevate an individual's rights, both personally and collectively. According to Ryan,

> The individual is endowed by nature, or rather, by God, with the rights that are requisite to a reasonable development of his personality, and . . . these rights are, within due limits, sacred against the power even of the State; but . . . no individual's rights extend so far as to prevent the State from adjusting the conflicting claims of individuals and safeguarding the just welfare of all its citizens.[51]

Ryan was clear that workers "are not equal in all respects, nor is it reasonable that they should possess equal amounts of property. But they are equal as persons, and as such have equal rights to a certain reasonable minimum of property—the means of a decent livelihood."[52]

A *Living Wage* enabled Ryan to develop a wider platform as a significant voice tying together religion and social reform. While he taught theology at St. Paul's Seminary in Minnesota, he also had many opportunities to speak to wide-ranging audiences throughout the country. In 1914 Ryan received an offer to teach political science at the Catholic University in Washington, D.C., and in 1916 he published his follow-up book, *Distributive Justice*. Like Rauschenbusch's *Christianizing the Social Order*, *Distributive Justice* allowed Ryan to flesh out in greater detail the ways that his view of a living wage might translate into contemporary economic and political practices. Scorning both socialism and Henry George's single-tax ideas, Ryan was clear that capitalist owners had a natural right to earn wealth, while at the same time safeguarding the rights of workers. Yet in his conclusion, Ryan conceded, "neither just distribution, nor increased production, nor both combined, will insure a stable and satisfactory social order without considerable change in human hearts and ideas." For Ryan such a state of affairs could not be accomplished without "a revival of genuine religion."[53] The best means of assuring that government and business safeguarded worker rights was to apply Catholic teaching to the industrial order.

Walter Rauschenbusch and John Ryan are examples of the divergent perspectives on economic reform coming out of the early twentieth-century social gospel tradition. For Rauschenbusch, the issue was largely seen from the perspective of how the social teachings of Christianity laid an economic foundation that focused on the government's role in redistributing economic wealth into the hands of workers (modeled best by democratic socialism). For Ryan, the central issue was how Catholic social teaching created a template for understanding the fundamental rights of all individuals to own private property, in which government, if necessary, might be called upon to regulate the fair distribution of wealth to protect the poor (modeled by what we would call today liberal capitalism). As the social gospel moved into the period after World War I, both of these currents of reform would increasingly intermingle.

The historian Jay Dolan observed that John Ryan galvanized a tradition of American social ethics "that was both very Catholic and very American."[54] Ryan's somewhat traditional views of Catholic theology were grafted onto the social gospel critiques of wealth advocated by figures like Richard Ely. With his stress on Catholic natural law tradition, Ryan believed that Christianity, embodied by the Roman Catholic Church, could create the conditions of justice for individuals and societies. While government intervention and regulation might be necessary to ensure the benefits of a just society, Ryan viewed the political ends of socialism to be at odds with those of Christianity, even as he sought common cause with other religious progressives to advocate for minimum wage protection, the reduction of workers' hours, and labor union rights. Ryan's advocacy repeatedly got him into trouble with various leaders of the Catholic Church, even while he argued that his work was an effort to develop a model for Catholic social teachings based on *Rerum Novarum*.

Despite important differences, John Ryan's Catholic social liberalism would often be compared with the teachings of Protestant social gospelers like Walter Rauschenbusch. While Ryan attempted to make the case for how historical Catholic theological traditions could be applied to the social conditions of the modern world, another emerging social gospel figure made her own unique synthesis of Christian tradition to address social injustices.

Interweaving Threads: The Social Christian Vision of Vida Dutton Scudder

Writing in her 1937 autobiography, Vida Dutton Scudder noted that her life hadn't moved along in a smooth, predictable fashion. Her journey was mostly "an interweaving of threads; and the threads put in my hands by the Fates, along which my fingers moved so blindly; were intricate to handle. Sometimes they knotted, sometimes they interfered with one another."[55] Scudder's remark alludes to her numerous interests and involvements, as well as the ways that she challenged the social conventions of her era. As we noted in the last chapter, she embraced the Christian socialism associated with W. D. P. Bliss, but her understanding of that tradition stemmed from a deep-seated connection to historical streams of Christian doctrine.

Scudder was born in Madura, India, in 1861. Within a year of her birth, Scudder's father, a Congregational missionary, died in a drowning accident. Scudder was brought up in her mother's family home in suburban Boston, ultimately receiving bachelor's and master's degrees from Smith College. She discovered the Episcopal Church as a young girl and was confirmed by Phillips Brooks, well-known rector of Trinity Church, Boston. As she was completing her undergraduate work at Smith, Scudder had the opportunity to study at Oxford University in 1884–1885, an experience that dramatically changed her life. Scudder's time in Oxford helped to clarify her goals, vocationally and in terms of her religious commitments. At Oxford she came to realize "the plethora of privilege" that surrounded her life and upbringing.[56] At one point, she even contemplated joining the Salvation Army. However, the person who helped Scudder realize her larger calling was John Ruskin, a figure who influenced many social gospel leaders, including Reverdy Ransom.

For much of his career, Ruskin was known as an art critic and social theorist whose work increasingly cast light on the industrial problems of nineteenth-century England. Writing in 1900, Scudder recalled the first time she heard Ruskin lecture at Oxford and how the combination of his intelligence and moral insight aided her social awakening. Ruskin called for an "aesthetic revival" to counter the impact of industrialization on the urban landscape.[57] In the face of urbanization, industrialization, and, in particular, a growing gap between the rich and poor, how might the artist play a role in redeeming society? "New questions began to form in his hearers' minds," she wrote. "Were political economy and art so far separated, after all? . . . Could a nation play beautifully that did not work healthfully?"[58]

Scudder's artistic sensitivity, reflected in her passion for teaching literature, combined with a unique faith perspective. Her love for the Episcopal tradition was evident in her growing connection to the themes of Anglo-Catholicism, fusing together personal piety, church liturgy, and social action.[59] Upon her return to the United States, Scudder sought ways to integrate her faith into a vision of social change. In 1887 she became a professor of English literature at Wellesley College, where she remained until her retirement in 1927. At the same time Scudder taught and wrote on literature, she was strongly motivated to find ways to equip young people, especially women, with the passion to engage social injustice.

One model for Scudder was the settlement house movement, epitomized by Jane Addams. Addams insisted that Hull House would not sponsor any religious services, but at the same time, she vigorously sought support from a network of influential Protestant and Jewish leaders in Chicago, including Emil Hirsch, Reverdy Ransom, and Harry F. Ward.[60] In 1889, the same year that Addams founded Hull House, Scudder played a significant role in the establishment of the College Settlements Association, which sponsored a range of settlement houses in New York, Boston, and Philadelphia.[61]

Scudder shared Jane Addams's belief that what made the settlement house movement meaningful was not simply its impact on the urban poor. Rather, Scudder drew attention to how the settlements transformed those who worked with the poor. The mission statement of the College Settlements Association noted that "you have a vision of brotherhood wherein no man lives unto himself; of a neighborhood where no man may fall among thieves; of a house wherein are many mansions and no dark rooms; of a freedom that is perfect service."[62]

This faith-based language was also evoked in Scudder's decision to join the Society of the Companions of the Holy Cross, a women's lay organization in the Episcopal Church. After the death of one of her closest friends at Wellesley, Scudder found solace in the Companions, a group that gave her regular opportunities for sustained fellowship among like-minded women. In her autobiography, Scudder spoke of the importance that this community had for her in developing a discipline of intercessory prayer:

> All true prayer calls for initial silence in the Presence of the Most Holy. . . . Petition for personal ends is natural to the childlike spirit; meditation rising perhaps into contemplation ensures vitality, peace and growth; . . . But intersection unites most perfectly our love for God and for our neighbor; it is here that the last danger of spiritual self-culture is overcome, and that the Self is merged in oneness with redeeming love.[63]

Scudder's theology and social witness echoed aspects of the pietism that characterized Walter Rauschenbusch, who became her close friend. However, Scudder was deeply impacted by her study of the early and medieval church, particularly the examples of Christian mystics like

Catherine of Siena. She returned repeatedly to her belief that the most vital social activism emerged from the interconnection of deep piety and prayer. Despite her high regard for and friendship with Rauschenbusch, Scudder always insisted that he and other Protestants ignored the role that church tradition played in shaping radical social action. While Rauschenbusch followed in line with many Protestant social gospelers by largely discounting the role of the late patristic and medieval churches, for Scudder these traditions were living waters.

In 1911 Scudder experienced what she described as another conversion experience by joining the Socialist Party. After years of wrestling with the issue of the compatibility of Christianity and socialism, she decided that her religious faith and her political commitments went hand in hand. In March 1912 Scudder supported striking textile workers in Lawrence, Massachusetts. The Lawrence strike represented a cross section of labor leaders and organizers, including members of the International Workers of the World, a group with ties to numerous radical political movements. For the majority of social gospel leaders, the IWW epitomized the worst excesses of the labor movement, in terms of its rejection of organized religion. Yet when Scudder went to Lawrence, she was invited to speak to a workers' gathering. Invoking Jesus's Beatitudes ("Blessed are ye when men shall revile you and persecute you"), Scudder praised the strikers' cause as just and believed that "on every man and woman there had flashed the vision of a just society, based on fair reward to labor and on fraternal peace."[64]

Scudder's support of the Lawrence strikers nearly cost her her teaching position at Wellesley and strained her relationship with some professional colleagues. At the same time, she was one of a small number of social gospel leaders in the early twentieth century who actually took the step of joining the Socialist Party. For the next several years, Scudder lobbied in vain to get Rauschenbusch to join the party. She assured him that membership would help "vindicate the honor of Christianity" among workers who still harbored suspicions about organized religion's support of the labor movement. "Nothing but party-membership convinces those men that one is in earnest. I covet you for the party. My being in it doesn't count except to myself. Yours would. It would draw many, & we could get a political socialism of a better type."[65]

Another way that Scudder differed from Rauschenbusch, and from other male social gospel leaders, was the position she took toward the public role of women. Although social gospel leaders like Rauschenbusch favored women's suffrage, their views on the issue tended to be formulated around a late Victorian sentiment that women's nature would make politics more humane by bringing feminine attributes of nurture and motherhood to the public square.[66] Rauschenbusch and other male social gospel leaders constantly worried about the "feminization" of American religion, supporting what many have termed muscular Christianity. Muscular Christianity was a late nineteenth-century movement that emphasized the interconnection between religion (usually in the form of Protestant Christianity) and masculinity. Positing Jesus as a model not only of social reform, but also of alleged masculine virtues such as physical strength and courage, proponents of this movement sought to reinterpret Christianity in order to attract men into the nation's churches. In 1911–1912 numerous Protestant churches supported what was known as the Men and Religion Forward Movement, an interdenominational effort that staged a series of national rallies to promote male church membership. Numerous crusades and rallies were held throughout the nation, and a wide range of social gospel figures like Rauschenbusch, Washington Gladden, and Charles Stelzle took an active role in supporting this crusade.[67]

Social gospel leaders like Rauschenbusch believed that the Men and Religion Forward Movement did more "to lodge the social gospel in the common mind of the Church" than any other movement.[68] However, this crusade reflects the ambivalence of many male social gospel leaders about the public role of women. Men like Rauschenbusch were willing to support women's suffrage, relying to a degree on Victorian sentiment that women's voting might aid in the "Christianizing" of society. However, these men worried about the "feminizing" effects of too many women in leadership roles. Scudder remained unmoved by such arguments. The "advancing freedom of women" was one of her life goals, and her career was dedicated to ensuring that women could pursue broader vocations in the church and society rather than being confined to marriage and raising children. "Not only for their economic independence, . . . but for their liberty to find untrammeled self-realization, such as I think women have never before found, in the arts and professions, in business life, even in marriage."[69]

Vida Scudder was significant not only because she was a model for women in the church, but because her writings connected the work of social justice to Christian spiritual disciplines. While Protestant social gospel leaders often spoke of the power of Christianity as a societal force outside the realm of the church, Scudder's social vision constantly returned to her hope that the historical tradition of the Church universal "with its supernatural power to disturb" would not disappear from the contemporary social context.[70] In the decades ahead, many figures associated with the social gospel would follow Scudder's path in exploring traditions of Christian mysticism and tying these traditions to the transformation of society.

For all of their differences, figures like Walter Rauschenbusch, Harry Ward, Stephen Wise, John Ryan, and Vida Scudder emphasized the belief that systemic social change needed to be accompanied by dramatic spiritual changes within the individual. Frequently, these leaders used the term "personality" to speak of how God's love was making it possible for believers to acquire the God-given resources necessary to change society. As the historian Eugene McCarraher observes, the concept of personality "denoted the highest achievement of humanity: sensitivity of feeling, rationality of judgment, and capacity for spiritual insight, all nurtured in a supportive community setting."[71] The social gospel concept of personality implied God's care for the individual and also the interconnection between the perfectibility of the individual and the perfectibility of society. In subsequent years, this concept would represent one of the social gospel's core theological themes.

Conclusion

In 1909 Emil Hirsch noted the fundamental connection between a person's religious faith and the moral-ethical need to serve the world:

> Religion alone unfolds the worthwhileness of the moral life . . . because it assures me that the Universe is so ordered as to express a moral purpose and serve a moral plan. . . . [The individual] is created to be a co-

worker with God. And the forces of the universe are so constituted as to co-operate with him in his endeavor to work with God.[72]

In many ways, Hirsch's assertion parallels the Protestant Eugene Lyman's observations on the intricate connection between personal and social religion:

> Social progress then needs the service of personal religion. . . . With the constant enrichment and complexity of our ideals must go the renewal and the broadening and deepening of our spiritual powers. Here again is a great need for religious faith. And as for social causes themselves, though they often are dealing with conditions and institutions rather than directly with men, which of them does not gain new meaning from the thought of the infinite worth of the soul, from the sense of the immanent God actively working out his will in this present world, and from the application of Christ's law that only he who loses his life for a great end shall find it?[73]

The two statements express a critical principle of the early twentieth-century social gospel as it matured theologically: one's personal faith went hand in hand with one's desire to embrace a social faith committed to the transformation of society.

By the time that Lyman made these comments in 1914, the social gospel had evolved considerably as a theological tradition from its late nineteenth-century origins. In *Christianizing the Social Order*, published in 1912, Walter Rauschenbusch described Christianity's contribution to the spirit of the "social awakening" in society. While he acknowledged that many factors had led to the social awakening in America, it was clear to him that churches were the driving engine of change: "Those who come after us will judge how well or ill we played our part, but whenever men hereafter write the story of how Christendom became Christian, they will have to begin a new chapter at the years in which we are now living."[74]

On the eve of World War I, numerous social gospel leaders believed that the nation was in the midst of a "great spiritual movement" in which Americans, regardless of religious affiliation, embraced this social awakening. "Outside of the churches the social awakening is remarkable for the religious spirit which it creates in men who thought they were done with religion," Rauschenbusch observed. Americans "show all the evidences of religion,—love, tenderness, longings mysterious to themselves, a glad willingness to sacrifice time and money for the salvation of their fellows. What is this but religion?"[75]

Yet Rauschenbusch also had his worries about the future. For all the ways that he believed the Christian church was at an important historical crossroads, he conceded that numerous aspects of Christianity worked against social change. When it came to religion, "we need a great faith to serve as a spiritual basis for the tremendous social task before us, and the working creed of our religion, in the form in which it has come down to us, has none." With centuries of church tradition stressing the role of individual salvation, there was little within the fabric of everyday religion that opened the doors to the social awakening. "Its hymns, its ritual, its prayers, its books of devotion, are so devoid of social thought that the most thrilling passions of our generation lie in us half stifled for lack of religious utterance."[76]

In particular, Rauschenbusch worried about the popularity of premillennialism. With its pessimistic theology and belief that any form of social amelioration was doomed to fail, premillennialism seemed antithetical to the spirit of the modern age. "The apocalyptic hope has always contained ingredients of religious force and value," Rauschenbusch conceded, "but its trail through history is strange and troubled reading. It has been of absorbing fascination to some Christian minds, but it has led them into labyrinths from which some never emerged."[77] Rauschenbusch observed that the ongoing appeal of various forms of apocalyptic theology was a major reason why the "kingdom hope" of the social gospel had not caught on at a popular level in America. Another prominent social gospel cleric noted tersely, "To condemn the pre-millenarian movement as the activity of literally minded fanatics gets us nowhere."[78]

Many social gospel leaders entered the second decade of the twentieth century confident that they were part of a wider movement that was transforming religion's ability to engage the nation's social-economic problems. These leaders also recognized that they needed to look for concrete signs that their ideas were making a significant impact on American religious and secular organizations. While they could point to numerous publications, a growing network of women's organizations, settlement houses, institutional churches, and various religious agencies and caucuses, they also yearned for a united base to bring the nation's religious forces together in concerted action. Many Protestant leaders found the grounds for this hope in the emergence of the ecumenical movement.

4

"The Church Stands For . . ."

Institutionalizing the Social Gospel

In December 1908 the Federal Council of Churches in Christ was founded. Representing an initial membership of thirty-three Protestant denominations, the FCC did not aim to create organic mergers among member churches. Rather, it envisioned a model of federation in which denominations could act in tandem with the Federal Council in the goal of Christianizing America.[1] At the culmination of the FCC's founding meeting in Philadelphia, Eugene Russell Hendrix, bishop of the Methodist Episcopal Church, South, and the inaugural president of the FCC, gave a lengthy oration that noted the historical milestone in bringing the nation's Protestant churches together. He proclaimed triumphantly that "when the standards of the Gospel shall have become the rule of society, His Kingdom will be here when His Spirit shall have conquered and sanctified the individual life, His will will be done."[2] Hendrix's remarks were typical of the addresses given at the Federal Council's founding, combining earlier Protestant hopes for evangelicalism with the reform themes of the social gospel.[3]

One of many supporters of this developing model of ecumenical cooperation was Harry Ward, who as we have seen was a principal founder of the Methodist Federation for Social Service and the primary author of its social creed. Ward and other Protestant leaders hoped that the institutional mobilization of groups like the Federal Council would give Protestants a platform by which they could engage the moral conscience of the nation. Charles Macfarland, an important early leader of the Federal Council, asserted that the strength of the FCC was how it manifested the power of God to bring disparate parts of the church together into unified mission. "God has put into our human order the mingling together of unity and diversity. . . . I believe that the movement of which the Federal Council of the Churches of Christ in America is the most concrete expression is an illustration of this principle of progress."[4]

The formation of the Federal Council was a milestone in the development of the modern ecumenical movement. Well into the twentieth century, the ecumenical movement came to symbolize a level of cultural prestige for church leaders associated with what scholars have called the "Protestant establishment": a network of church leaders and influential figures in the worlds of academia, business, and, in particular, government. Over the next several decades, many social gospel leaders connected to the ecumenical movement enjoyed a high level of public influence, with access to a range of national leaders including American presidents. Although by and large Protestant leaders continued to advocate measures of moral suasion in hopes that they might sway the consciences of various political and economic interests, they also desired a central role in helping to shape the institutional contours of the nation.

However, the social reform zeal of leaders like Walter Rauschenbusch increasingly raised a critical question for many social gospel Protestants: was the goal of the social gospel to reform the nation's social-economic system or was it to create radical alternatives to replace these older structures? American entry into World War I and the social chaos that accompanied the war's aftermath disrupted much of the social gospel's Progressive Era optimism and influenced the movement's development in the 1920s and 1930s.

The Social Gospel and the Federal Council of Churches

When the Federal Council of Churches in Christ was founded in December 1908, it adopted a modified version of the MFSS social creed and issued a report entitled "The Church and Modern Industry," written by Frank Mason North. An updated version of this report in 1912 concluded by reiterating social gospel principles—for example, that the church had a mission centered on "redemption of the individual in the world, and through him of the world itself, and there is no redemption of either without the redemption of the other."[5]

The Federal Council's constitution was clear that it had no authority to dictate the doctrinal standards of member churches, other than that churches needed to acknowledge Jesus Christ as "Divine Lord and

Saviour."[6] The FCC emphasized that its mission was centered on the cooperation of churches in order "to secure a larger combined influence for the churches of Christ in all matters affecting the moral and social conditions of the people, so as to promote the application of the law of Christ in every relation of human life."[7] North captured the worldview of many founding FCC leaders by observing that "the strength of the Church is not in a program but in a spirit." Churches were seen as playing the central role in promoting broader "ethical and practical values" that would make social reform possible.[8]

Although the Federal Council boasted of its large membership, throughout its history its administrative leadership and chief financial support came from a relatively small number of churches. Over the next several decades, the FCC's major institutional clout emerged from denominations that historians have often labeled the "seven sister" churches: Methodists, northern Baptists, Episcopalians, Congregationalists, Presbyterians, Disciples of Christ, and, later in the twentieth century, certain Lutheran denominations.[9] Although Federal Council leaders stressed that this body spoke in a united voice for American Protestants, in its early years the FCC struggled to establish a clear mandate for its mission. For much of its operating budget it depended on funding from member denominations, but many rank-and-file members of those churches expressed concern about the social gospel leanings of the organization. The FCC's continuity with earlier Protestant missional objectives was reflected in the creation of a Commission on Evangelism and a Commission on Temperance. However, much of the FCC's public notoriety revolved around the Commission on the Church and Social Service. This commission was chiefly responsible for the FCC's adoption in 1912 of the "Social Creed of the Churches," an expanded version of the FCC's social creed of 1908. This commission was designed to serve as "a connecting link between the churches and the various social movements, thus increasing the social spirit among the churches and infusing the social movements with the Christian spirit."[10] The Federal Council embodied an "irenic" progressivism that sought to elevate certain reform ideals, as opposed to advocating specific political methods, such as socialism. In many ways, the FCC held to an earlier vision of social gospel leaders like Josiah Strong and Washington Gladden, whereby, in the words of one scholar, "the church should not supplant other agencies of reform so much as dominate them through the power of its moral appeal and example."[11]

This optimistic spirit of Protestant reform was reflected in an exposition on the Federal Council's social creed written by Harry Ward in 1914. Intending his work to be used as a study guide for pastors and church laity, Ward discussed major provisions of the social creed, followed by questions and suggested readings, including John Ryan's *A Living Wage* and several books by Walter Rauschenbusch. While noting the appeal of certain socialist principles as economic remedies, Ward made clear that "the churches are not committed to any propaganda save that of principles." The task of organizations like the FCC was "to fire men with the passion for distributive justice until they shall become pioneers in social discovery and inventors of social methods."[12] Ward's book echoed the wider strategy of the FCC, in that it did not endorse specific social-economic models of reform, instead providing individuals with the moral inspiration to create social change.

Even though its pronouncements were nonbinding on member churches, the FCC achieved a level of public success due to its growing symbolic role in American Protestantism. Of particular importance to the FCC was the financial backing that it received from wealthy patrons, as well as the fact that many influential politicians looked to the FCC as the "voice" of American Protestantism. Over several years, the organization would expand institutionally; by the 1930s the FCC had administrative headquarters in New York, Chicago, and Washington, D.C.

Just prior to the outbreak of World War I there were clear signs that not all Protestant leaders embraced the social stands of the FCC. Laypersons in many Protestant denominations stressed that Christian faith was fundamentally concerned with individual salvation and not social reform. Even as social gospelers dismissed movements like premillennialism, belief in doctrines such as the Rapture and an imminent Second Coming of Christ animated many rank-and-file Protestants. Beginning in 1910, a wealthy California businessman promoted the publication of a series of pamphlets designed to address a range of questions on Christianity's relationship to the modern world. In this series, which ultimately appeared under the title *The Fundamentals*, a disparate coalition of ministers, evangelists, and missionaries asserted their faith in scriptural inerrancy—that is, the literal truth of the Bible—as well as the heretical nature of modernist interpretations of scripture.

Although Harry Ward strongly supported the work of the Federal Council, increasingly his primary interest was to cultivate working alliances between churches and labor activists. In 1913 he left Chicago to accept a part-time teaching appointment at Boston University as professor of social service, splitting his time between his teaching and his work on behalf of the Methodist Federation for Social Service. One of Ward's Boston students was a southern Californian, G. Bromley Oxnam. Oxnam wanted to emulate Ward in his own ministry, applying much of the social idealism that he learned from Ward to his early parish work in Los Angeles. Years later, when Oxnam became a Methodist bishop and one of the most influential public figures in American Protestantism, his views of Ward would not be as favorable.

Despite its initial problems garnering grassroots support, by 1914 the Federal Council was well established. Its leaders included many prominent social gospel clergy as well as lay supporters. By the mid-1910s, institutional support for the social gospel ran high among a wide range of Protestant institutions, including denominational boards and agencies, missionary organizations, and theological seminaries. Also, the FCC's vision of social reform was consistent with the mainstream of the social gospel movement in its desire to promote ideals leading to reform, as opposed to embracing specific social-economic solutions such as socialism. At the same time, organizations like the Federal Council of Churches were attracting the attention of important politicians, including American presidents.

Making the World Safe for Democracy: The Social Gospel and World War I

On December 15, 1915, Woodrow Wilson became the first American president to speak before the Federal Council of Churches. Wilson's task was to address the topic of the rural church in America. What the delegates mostly heard, however, was a speech that emphasized the important role that American Christianity needed to play in creating a righteous nation, formulated along politically progressive lines.

When Wilson was elected president in 1912, he seemed to represent the triumph of certain social gospel ideals in the public arena. He was involved in a fiercely contested presidential campaign against two other political progressives, the incumbent William Howard Taft and former president Theodore Roosevelt, who ran as a third-party candidate of the newly formed Progressive Party. Many social gospel leaders were drawn to Roosevelt's campaign, while others threw their support behind the Socialist Party candidate, Eugene Debs. Wilson, a former president of Princeton University and governor of New Jersey, was a relative political novice. However, he proved capable of winning the trust of many influential progressive leaders, including those in the social gospel movement. One of Wilson's major supporters was Stephen Wise, who vigorously lobbied for Wilson's election and came to regard him as a leader who would be "bracketed with the names of Washington and Lincoln equal to the genius of the spirit of America and worthy to become the champion and servant of humanity."[13] Many progressive leaders felt ambivalent about the candidates, but Wise enthusiastically stumped for his friend Wilson. He noted to Jane Addams that Wilson was "absolutely dependable as a Progressive," and noted that a wide range of social reformers would be pleased by the outcome of a Wilson presidency.[14]

Theologically, Wilson was more traditional in his beliefs, having grown up in the South as the son of a Presbyterian minister. However, he epitomized the aspirations of many social gospel Protestants who believed that social reform went hand in hand with creating a righteous nation.[15] Although Wilson's FCC address was full of references to the church as a builder of personal character, his message also encapsulated many social gospel themes. For Wilson, the essence of Christianity lay not in doctrine but in the development of unselfish individuals who were committed to the task of building a better world:

> Christianity is not important to us because it is a valid body of conceptions regarding God and man, but because it is a vital body of conceptions which can be translated into life for us—life in this world and a life still greater in the next. Except as Christianity changes and inspires life, it has failed of its mission. That is what Christ came into the world for, to save our spirits, and you cannot have your spirit altered without having your life altered.[16]

Wilson concluded his address by asserting that American history showed the inherent link between patriotism and Christianity and how the two were tied together through unselfish service. His comments undoubtedly resonated with many listeners in the audience:

> All the transforming influences in the world are unselfish. There is not a single selfish force in the world that is not touched with sinister power, and the church is the only embodiment of the things that are entirely unselfish—the principles of self-sacrifice and devotion. . . . America is great in the world, not as she is a successful government merely, but as she is the successful embodiment of a great ideal of unselfish citizenship.[17]

Wilson's rhetoric resonated with the social gospel belief that Christianity had a critical mission in democratizing Western civilization. Wilson would play on this sentiment when America entered World War I in 1917.

In the buildup to the U.S. declaration of war, some social gospel leaders expressed a staunch commitment to nonintervention. John Haynes Holmes noted in 1916 that America could halt German aggression by the strength of the nation's "faith in brotherhood and democracy," which was stronger than "the sword and shield."[18] However, these sentiments were swept away by many social gospelers who came to view the war as nothing short of a holy crusade. Woodrow Wilson provided influential Protestant social gospelers the wedge they needed to support American intervention in Europe, enabling them to see the war as a conflict in which the future of Christianity was at stake. His declaration of war speech before Congress in April 1917 included the notable assertion, "the world must be made safe for democracy." Wilson shared the belief of many social gospel leaders that religion and democracy were inseparable.

Even though America did not enter World War I until 1917, public opinion moved in support of the Allies during the years leading up to U.S. entry. In 1914 reports of German war crimes against civilians in neutral Belgium immediately led to strong condemnation of Germany from American religious leaders. The sinking of the British luxury liner *Lusitania* in May 1915 further exacerbated tensions.

One social gospel leader who was an early advocate of intervention was Lyman Abbott. Abbott had a long and prolific career as an author and a respected Congregational minister, who succeeded his friend Henry Ward Beecher as pastor of the Plymouth Congregational Church, Brooklyn. An enthusiastic supporter of religious modernity, Abbott endorsed Darwinism, social reform, and the role of religion—specifically Protestantism—in making America a righteous nation. For decades, Abbott served as the editor of the *Outlook*, a journal that became associated with a wide range of progressive causes, and that vigorously supported American intervention in the war. A diverse cross section of America's religious leaders shared the attitude toward the war expressed in Abbott's 1918 book *The Twentieth Century Crusade*, especially the connection he drew between the war's outcome and the survival of two interconnected institutions, Christianity and democracy:

> Democracy is not a mere form of government. It is a religious faith. . . . We are fighting to maintain the right of eager peoples to organize their institutions in harmony with this spirit of brotherhood. We have joined with all the free peoples of the world in a stern resolve, not that all Nations shall be Christian, but that all Nations shall be at liberty to be Christian if they wish.[19]

Abbott saw the war as a postmillennial struggle between good and evil, viewing Germany's defeat as holding out the possibility for a new epoch in human history. With echoes of Wilson's declaration of war, Abbott asserted, "We are going to make the whole world safe for the Brotherhood of Man—Germany no less than the countries which the German autocracy has attacked. And we are going to do it whatever it costs us and whatever it costs those who we are fighting."[20]

While less jingoistic than Abbott, numerous social gospel leaders gave their support to the war. Stephen Wise wrote to Wilson that "the time has come for the American people to understand that it may become our destiny to have part in the struggle which would avert the enthronement of the law of might over the nations."[21] Washington Gladden, who had initially opposed American intervention, ultimately came to support the war, as did Vida Scudder. America's war aims, Gladden asserted, were not for the nation's own gain, but "for the supreme good of freedom, which shall be shared with all the nations, the least and the greatest."[22]

The growing international antagonism toward Germany also played into emerging theological differences in American Protestantism. Some religious leaders who became associated with the fundamentalist movement claimed that part of Germany's diabolical heritage rested with its support of biblical higher criticism and liberal modernist theology. By 1917, the association of Germany with all things anti-Christian would become a common sentiment among many American Protestant leaders. Democracy for many religious leaders was not just a political system; it was a sacred religious ideal that needed to be defended at all costs—including by war.

The consequences of this view of Germany as tantamount to the anti-Christ had dire consequences for millions of American citizens of German descent. After America's declaration of war, Congress passed the Espionage Act, a law that targeted not only German Americans but also anyone who resisted the war. Although some religious leaders spoke out in defense of American civil liberties, the vast majority of social gospel leaders quickly embraced Wilson's view that the war was a battle pitting Western democracies against militaristic forces out to destroy democracy. Harry Emerson Fosdick, one of hundreds of American ministers who served as volunteer chaplains on the Western Front in 1918, initially expressed the view that America had a moral obligation "to be champions of humanity" when he wrote in a prayer,

> We have grown weary, to the sickness of our souls, sitting comfortably here, while others pour their blood like water forth for those things which can make this earth a decent place for men to live upon. . . . And now we lay our hand upon the sword. Since we must now draw it, . . . help us to play the man and to do our part in teaching ruthlessness once for all what it means to wake the sleeping lion of humanity's conscience.[23]

In the years following the war, Fosdick and hundreds of other American clergymen would openly repent of their support of this sort of sentiment.

Social Gospel Internationalism

At the same time that the Federal Council of Churches was maturing in the 1910s, a wide range of Protestant mission organizations was helping to craft a vision of the social gospel that supported both the ecumenical movement and the war. Many of these organizations had come out of the revivalist crusades of Dwight Moody in the late nineteenth century and were forged out of a desire to recruit young people into missionary service. While devoted to international mission, these groups, including the Young Men's Christian Association and the Young Women's Christian Association, became important conduits for the spread of social gospel ideals just prior to and following World War I.

The YMCA and YWCA were founded in England in the mid-nineteenth century and established American chapters in 1851 and 1866, respectively. Initially, both the YMCA and YWCA emphasized urban evangelism, with their missions largely defined through Y centers that opened in major American cities. By the end of the Civil War, the Y movement increasingly promoted in its centers the importance of exercise and physical fitness as a way of building Christian character. Toward the end of the nineteenth century, however, the YMCA and YWCA were at the epicenter of a growing international movement geared toward recruiting young people for foreign mission service. The person most responsible for the growing success of youth mission service in American Protestantism was a Methodist layman, John R. Mott.

Mott was brought up in rural Iowa, the son of a Methodist minister, and ultimately studied at Cornell University. After college, he went to work for the YMCA and became one of the principal organizers of the Student Volunteer Movement. Like Dwight Moody, Mott strove to place mission over matters of theology, and his associates represented a wide network of leaders with varying theological commitments. Mott became one of the most significant American leaders of the international ecumenical movement, and in 1910 he was an important catalyst behind the World Missionary Conference in Edinburgh, Scotland, which helped to spawn the international Protestant ecumenical movement in the twentieth century. Mott's vision was firmly rooted in the belief that evangelism of university-age students was essential to the winning of the world to Christ. In 1895 he helped to found the World Student Christian Federation, an umbrella organization that was designed to coordinate the activities of Protestant youth organizations like the SVM, YMCA, and YWCA. The WSCF reflected a vision that appealed to late nineteenth-century Protestant ideals of mission, embodied by the Student Volunteer Movement motto, "The evangelization of the world in this generation."[24]

In the early years of the twentieth century, the Protestant student movement sponsored thousands of youth as foreign missionaries, many of whom came out of collegiate chapters of the YMCA and YWCA. Of the approximately 4,500 SVM missionaries who came from the United States and Canada between 1899 and 1914, more than 3,400 were from the YMCA or YWCA.[25] Although both organizations at this time were still primarily motivated by a desire to promote individual salvation, the Y movement's zeal for mission was also interconnected with a growing desire to use the platform of mission to create international understanding and to teach America's youth about the social problems brought on by modern industrialization.

Initially, the YMCA and YWCA held closely to predominant evangelical themes, stressing the role of personal conversion and the cultivation of personal morality. For example, the YWCA often expressed a goal of cultivating women's "femininity," whereby "in every setting the YWCA sought to protect young and vulnerable girls, to inculcate Christian teachings so as to guard their virtue."[26] Like their women counterparts in Protestant home missions, however, many YWCA leaders increasingly took interest in a wide range of social gospel themes. At a series of international YWCA gatherings prior to World War I, women were called to examine Christianity's response to the challenges of industrialization. A 1910 conference in Berlin noted that "present social and industrial conditions . . . militate against the highest development of Christian womanhood." YWCA members were told that it was "a definite duty to study the social and industrial problems of the day."[27] As this quote illustrates, many missionaries sponsored by the student Christian movement were being exposed to predominant social gospel themes, especially surrounding economic justice. This vision was readily embraced by one of John Mott's most influential protégés in the student movement, Sherwood Eddy.

Born in Leavenworth, Kansas, in 1871, Eddy, like Mott, headed east to college, graduating from Yale University in 1891. That same year, Eddy attended one of Dwight Moody's summer youth conferences at Northfield, Massachusetts, and came to a "conviction" of his own sinful nature. While attending Union Theological Seminary in New York, Eddy became involved in a local branch of the YMCA, beginning an association with that organization that would last until he retired in 1948.

Soon after graduating from Union Seminary, Eddy became a traveling secretary for the American YMCA, and for several decades he oversaw mission work in China and India. Eddy's extensive international travels made him question some of the dominant missionary suppositions of Western churches. In particular, he was troubled by how aspects of Western colonialism carried over into the mission field. Was the task of the missionary to share the Gospel of Jesus or was it to impose the values of American society? Eddy's vacillations were part of a wider debate among Protestant leaders about the role of foreign missions in the early twentieth century. Increasingly, he believed that the goal of missions was to raise up indigenous leaders, and that World War I exacerbated larger issues of economic inequality that plagued the so-called Christian nations of the West. As Eddy wrote,

> The conviction formed in my mind that the Christian gospel is more than good news for individuals in their interpersonal relationships; it is also a message about the Kingdom of God and the way of life for men in their group and corporate affairs—in economics, politics, international relations, and all other interrelationships.[28]

Eddy's questions about the nature of evangelism reflected a larger transformation taking place in the YMCA and other youth mission organizations during the 1910s. Through its American publishing arm, the Association Press, the YMCA published numerous books, focusing on a college-aged audience, that strongly advanced social gospel themes. Two of the best-selling YMCA books in that decade were Walter Rauschenbusch's *Social Principles of Jesus*, published in 1916, and *Manhood of the Master*, published in 1918 by another prominent Baptist minister, Harry Emerson Fosdick.

The impact of the social gospel on Protestant youth organizations like the YMCA and YWCA was substantial. First, the Y movement's work brought many American church leaders into contact with a range of international issues, as well as with religious leaders outside the West. Increasingly, these American social gospelers critiqued many aspects of earlier Western suppositions about the goals of foreign mission and the cultural superiority of the West. When World War I ended, Eddy still shared the dominant Protestant view that America and its allies had succeeded in advancing the cause of democracy and Christianity globally. However, he soon evidenced a growing disillusionment toward the war that would impact the direction that the social gospel would develop during the 1920s:

> Our task, then, was not only to win or change individuals, all-important as that was, but to build a new social order and to Christianize the whole of life and all its relations, industrial, social, racial, and international. . . . We had not only to relieve poverty and misery but to remove their causes.[29]

Second, by the end of World War I, the YMCA/YWCA solidified a presence on college campuses throughout the country. These intercollegiate Y chapters not only were centers to recruit youth for mission, but increasingly became key institutions that exposed young people to a range of themes associated with the development of the social gospel after World War I. The Y movement's presence on American college campuses helped to sow the seeds for a developing social radicalism that played a major role in shaping the worldview of many young activists who came of age in the decades following the war.[30]

Although Eddy's social gospel convictions were firmly in place by 1917, he shared a common vision that the war was a great crusade that required the support of American Protestant churches. After America entered the war, the YMCA sponsored a number of Protestant ministers who served in England and France as chaplains. Yet even as most Americans supported the war effort, doubts soon emerged about the war's role in creating a righteous society.

World War I and the Birth of the "Religious Left"

In the spring of 1917 Walter Rauschenbusch gave the prestigious Lyman Beecher Lectures at Yale Divinity School. Despite his disillusionment over the escalating conflict and the fact that America had declared war less than a week before he gave his lectures, Rauschenbusch increasingly turned his attention to Christianity's role in the postwar world.

In November 1917 these Yale lectures were published as his last book, *A Theology for the Social Gospel.*

For Rauschenbusch, the war years had been difficult. When the conflict began in 1914, he strongly advocated for American neutrality and hoped that the United States might serve as an international mediator. However, Rauschenbusch quickly found himself attacked publicly as pro-German, and suspicions about his patriotism grew more heated by the time America declared war in 1917. Much to Vida Scudder's disappointment, Rauschenbusch never joined the Socialist Party. At the same time, he made his support for the Socialist Party more vocal as the 1910s progressed. At a Socialist-sponsored antiwar rally just prior to America's entry into the war, Rauschenbusch noted that the war largely reflected the interconnection between militarism and economic greed. If America entered the war, those who would pay the greatest price would be the poor. "It is dishonor for the richest country in the world to let mobs of poor women cry for bread for their children" and "to let the price of living be pushed up till all wage earners and salary earners are being jammed against the wall."[31]

A Theology for the Social Gospel became an influential book in the subsequent development of American theological liberalism as it sought to provide a clear theological template for interpreting what was now widely called the "social gospel." Even as Rauschenbusch fleshed out many points of his earlier theological idealism, compared with many of his earlier writings, this book reflected a chastened tone. The book contains no references to "Christianizing" America, and while Rauschenbusch articulates a desire for theology to adapt itself to the conditions of the modern world, there was a discernible pessimism about the future. He noted that "super personal" forces of evil were present in the world, not through traditional Christian understanding of the Devil, but manifested in the systemic economic structures of capitalism that victimized the poor. For Rauschenbusch, the war was not about making the world safe for democracy; it was part of larger capitalist forces—including the major combatants in the war—running amok on an international scale.

As he reflected back on his career, he recalled with fondness Dwight Moody's late nineteenth-century revivals and noted that this sort of personal faith had a kind of nostalgic appeal for him. However, this brand of piety was not fully formed. "The social gospel furnishes new tests for religious experience," he argued. "Some who have been saved and perhaps reconsecrated a number of times are worth no more to the kingdom of God than they were before. Some become worse through their revival experiences, more self-righteous, more opinionated" and "more devoted to emotions and unresponsive to real duties."[32] Rauschenbusch chastised an emerging generation of biblical scholars in the 1910s who began to question the social gospel's reliance on the historical Jesus. Rauschenbusch steadfastly held to the belief that any apocalyptic interpretation of Jesus robbed Christianity of its revolutionary power. These scholars "who belong by kinship and sympathy to the bourgeois classes and are constitutionally incapacitated for understanding any revolutionary ideas, past or present, have overemphasized the ascetic and eschatological elements in the teachings of Jesus. They have classed as ascetic or apocalyptic [Jesus's] radical sayings about property and non-resistance which seem to them unpractical or visionary."[33]

At one point in the book, Rauschenbusch makes reference to a concept used by the Harvard University philosopher Josiah Royce, "the beloved community." Analogous in many ways to social gospel conceptions of the kingdom of God, the term was used by Royce to summarize the social idealism of Christianity. While Royce used the term as a symbol of the church, Rauschenbusch asserted that the beloved community was impossible to achieve unless the realities of Jesus's radical spirit changed individuals and social structures. Rauschenbusch did not abandon his hope that the church would be a vital conduit for social change. However, the church's "revolutionary force" to change systemic injustices in America came through the power of Christ:

> The saving qualities of the Church depend on the question whether it has translated the personal life of Jesus Christ into the social life of its group and thus brings it to bear on the individual. . . . The saving power of the Church does not rest on its institutional character, . . . or its doctrine. It rests on the presence of the Kingdom of God within her.[34]

Forty years after Rauschenbusch published this work, Martin Luther King Jr. would use the term "beloved community" to speak of the ideal of America as an interracial society.

Rauschenbusch would not get the chance to play a role in shaping the postwar social gospel. When *A Theology for the Social Gospel* was published he was already showing the first symptoms of the cancer that took his life in July 1918. A few weeks before Rauschenbusch's death, Washington Gladden also died. The passing of perhaps the two most important social gospel figures came to be interpreted by later scholars as a symbolic ending of the social gospel era in American Protestantism. However, the culmination of World War I provided many American Protestants with the grounds for new optimism, and in many ways a desire to move forward with Rauschenbusch's vision of postwar America.

Walter Rauschenbusch's death was mourned by many religious and secular leaders. An executive for the YMCA summed up the feelings of many social gospel figures by noting that Rauschenbusch "was our admiration and our despair. We looked up to him, but none of us could climb to his height."[35] The figure who perhaps was most motivated to try to live up to Rauschenbusch's legacy was Harry Ward. In many ways, it fell upon Ward to galvanize what a later era would call the "religious left."

Harry Ward was preparing to take up full-time teaching as a professor of social ethics at Union Theological Seminary in New York when he received word of Walter Rauschenbusch's death. Writing to Rauschenbusch's widow, Pauline, Ward noted his desire to continue her late husband's work: "The banner he so gallantly lifted will not fall. It will be carried forward by many of those whom he has taught by word and pen."[36] Several months after her husband's death, Pauline Rauschenbusch wrote Ward that he now wore her husband's mantle: "Walter has gone on, and is out of this phase of the strife and so I'm doubly glad you are still here."[37]

In 1918 Ward seemed well positioned to carry forward Walter Rauschenbusch's legacy. In many ways, his credentials as an organizer and activist were better than Rauschenbusch's and his position at Union Theological Seminary gave him an ideal platform for his future work. Founded in 1836, by the end of the nineteenth century Union had assembled a faculty that included some of the most prominent figures in the study of scripture, theology, and church history. In the 1890s Charles Briggs, an Old Testament scholar, was put on trial for heresy by the Presbyterian Church for his teaching of biblical higher criticism, an event that ultimately made Union sever its formal denominational connections with the Presbyterians. By the early twentieth century, Union faculty vigorously supported the social gospel, and its graduates would become important leaders in propagating the movement within American Protestantism.[38]

When Union opened its academic year in September 1918, Ward gave the inaugural address at the seminary and stated his vision for postwar America. His speech exemplified the zealous and uncompromising perspective that characterized his activism for the rest of his career: "In a desperate military situation, oftentimes the only possible defense is a vigorous offensive. This is now the case with the ethical teaching and practice of Christianity."[39] Ward asserted that the ethical imperatives of Christian theology needed to find their way into concrete programs of reform:

> The situation is critical, because the organized form of human life for the future is necessarily the industrial state and human destiny hinges upon the question of whether the industrial world-community . . . shall be organized for material ends around the ethics of self-interest or around the ethics of cooperative service with the common spiritual development as the goal.[40]

He often spoke in dualistic terms about a tension between the forces of self-interest and the forces of collective service to society, at the same time that his understanding of a cooperative "Christianized" commonwealth grew more radical.

Ward had an important ally in his Methodist colleague Francis McConnell. McConnell was born in 1871, and his father was a Methodist pastor who served numerous churches in the Midwest. Like Rauschenbusch, McConnell maintained a degree of affection for aspects of his evangelical piety, while also adopting a more liberal theology. As a student at Boston University, McConnell primarily focused on the study of theology and philosophy, as opposed to social reform. While a student, he came under the influence of Borden Parker Bowne, who by then was well established as professor of philosophy at the university and a spokesperson for the philosophical idealism of personalism.

After a pastorate in Brooklyn, McConnell became president of DePauw University in Greencastle, Indiana. In 1912 he was elected a bishop of the Methodist Episcopal Church and was also appointed president of the Methodist Federation for Social Service, serving alongside that body's executive director, Harry Ward. The pairing of McConnell and Ward seemed an odd combination. While Ward would develop a reputation as an uncompromising idealist whose interests would move him further from institutional Christianity, McConnell became the consummate spokesman for the ecumenical mainline. Introducing him to a political gathering in the 1920s, Stephen Wise referred to McConnell as "the Protestant pope," implying that McConnell had come to embody the public face of American Protestantism after World War I.[41] In addition to becoming a prolific author whose publications included biographies of both John Wesley and his mentor, Bowne, he became a driving force in the Federal Council of Churches, eventually serving as its president. In the 1920s a young Detroit minister, Reinhold Niebuhr, cited McConnell as his model of a modern-day prophet.[42]

McConnell and Ward soon became involved in a wide spectrum of social activism. In 1916 workers in the Methodist Episcopal Church's publishing house went on strike, ironically because the publisher denied workers the right to unionize. Ward and McConnell took a strong stance in support of the strikers, noting that the Methodist Book Concern was in violation of the denomination's social principles affirming the right of workers to unionize. That same year, McConnell heavily criticized President Wilson for sending American troops into Mexico in pursuit of the Mexican revolutionary Pancho Villa. McConnell contended that American policy in Mexico was dictated more by economic self-interest than by a desire to preserve American security.[43]

Like the majority of Protestant leaders, McConnell and Ward came to support American involvement in the war. However, their worldview had little in common with Lyman Abbott's sense of American manifest destiny. McConnell and Ward increasingly argued that Allied victory would be fully realized only to the extent that America and other Western democratic nations could redefine the meaning of democracy in the postwar world. Although they enthusiastically backed President Wilson's call for a League of Nations, they wanted to make sure that this vision of internationalism was connected to an expanded view of democratic freedom. Both leaders objected to the government crackdown on civil liberties, criticizing various methods of government surveillance for violating individual rights to privacy.

McConnell brought a particular sensitivity to his understanding of social issues. In the final months of the war, he toured British and American army camps on the front lines of France, seeing firsthand the physical and psychological consequences of the war. While McConnell decried the ideology of German militarism that in his mind caused the war, the postwar world needed to provide political and economic alternatives to the predominant policies of the West. This meant that the nation's Protestant church leaders had a unique calling to be social prophets in their promotion of a just society. "The duty of the Church toward forward social movements ought to be . . . to hold on high the human ideals so that all men can see them," McConnell wrote toward the end of the war.[44] For McConnell and Ward, the great task of the church in the postwar world was to be open to the ways that prophetic Christianity called on Americans to embrace alternative social-political models.

While Ward and McConnell called for Protestant churches to take up the cause of creating a just postwar America, another church leader advanced his own vision of religiously based reform. For John Ryan, the war years brought a level of personal vindication for his outlook. While *A Living Wage* attracted serious attention among a range of religious progressives, he was still seen by many within the Catholic Church hierarchy as a socialist maverick. Ryan's 1916 book *Distributive Justice* added to his reputation as a radical voice within Catholicism. However, Ryan's perspective gradually found institutional acceptance in the Catholic Church. In 1917 American Catholic bishops formed the National Catholic War Council to promote a range of service initiatives geared toward the needs of American Catholics in the armed forces. Increasingly, this group evolved into a policy-making body that focused on social-economic conditions in the postwar world. In 1919 Ryan authored a "Bishop's Program Report" under the sponsorship of the National Catholic War Council (soon to be renamed the National Catholic Welfare Council) that helped to inaugurate a wider twentieth-century tradition of U.S. Catholic bishops taking progressive, if not radical, stands on social-economic issues.

The National Catholic Welfare Council's administrative committee was chaired by Bishop Edward Hanna, a childhood friend of Walter Rauschenbusch's and noted throughout his career as a conservative church leader. While the council's report distanced itself from socialism as a violation of individual rights, it issued a strong plea that businesses had a moral obligation not to cut worker wages in the war's aftermath: "The wage-earners would lose more in remuneration than they would gain from whatever fall in prices occurred as a direct result of the fall in wages. On grounds both of justice and sound economics, we should give hearty support to all legitimate efforts made by labor to resist general wage reductions." When it came down to a choice between capital and labor, Ryan's report solidly backed the labor movement. Yet the bishops' report reaffirmed that the Catholic Church's goal was to reform the capitalist system, not abolish it: "It is to be noted that this particular modification of the existing order, though far-reaching and involving to a great extent the abolition of the wage system, would not mean the abolition of private ownership. The instruments of production would still be owned by individuals, not by the State."[45]

For all their differing outlooks, both Protestant and Catholic social gospel leaders embraced a growing conviction that social reform required more than fidelity to social ideals; it required picking up Walter Rauschenbusch's urgent tone about the need to make major changes in American political and economic structures. In a college student study guide published in 1917, Harry Ward and Richard Henry Edwards, a YMCA secretary, noted that "the social program of Jesus calls not simply for deeds of service, but for social reconstruction."[46] As opposed to his assertions earlier in the decade that the church's primary goal was to be a shaper of ideals, Ward's anticapitalist rhetoric became more strident: "The most powerful enemy of community life is predatory business—business that seeks to make profit out of the whole community, regardless of the results to the community life." Ward cast a wary eye on religious institutions that had accepted large financial contributions from wealthy patrons without critically examining the ways these donors may have abused their wealth:

> For the sake of profit men have locked the doors of their factories and their workers have burned to a crisp; they have adulterated the food that children eat and the medicines that babies take; . . . they have double-crossed child-labor and safety-first legislation; they have broken down the health, the strength, and the morals of the community in their factories and mines.[47]

Although he conceded that there were some Americans who used wealth responsibly, Ward was increasingly clear that the spirit of capitalism and the spirit of Christianity were incompatible. The sense that capitalism was under assault from a wide range of church leaders was exacerbated by unsettling political developments occurring in Russia.

The Red Scare and the Interchurch World Movement

What the varied social outlooks of Ward, McConnell, and Ryan had in common is that they were increasingly viewed with suspicion by many Americans, as part of a "Bolshevik" conspiracy represented by the Russian Revolution. In the spring of 1917 the overthrow of the tsarist regime, led by a democratic socialist, Alexander Kerensky, and Kerensky's subsequent overthrow at the hands of Vladimir Lenin's Bolshevik Party that autumn, caught Americans off guard. As Russia was engulfed in a bloody civil war between 1918 and 1922, Lenin presented himself to the West as a leader who espoused an internationalist vision of a workers' proletariat, hostile to Western democracies and in particular to its religious institutions.

As the twentieth century progressed, many segments of American society would draw a false correlation between Soviet communism and progressive movements of religious social reform. In some ways, that perception was created in the aftermath of World War I. For the most part, social gospel leaders up to the time of the Russian Revolution had little sympathy for the ideals of Marxism. Despite his strong socialist tendencies, figures like Walter Rauschenbusch were appalled by the antireligious sentiments of Karl Marx. While Marx believed that religion was the "opiate of the people," social gospelers asserted that true democracy and freedom were inseparable from the truths of religion. For the social gospelers, Jesus modeled the ideals and teachings that would help create the conditions of modern social equality.

The growing concern among a range of religious leaders about the creation of a just postwar world led to a critical moment for the social gospel. Many Protestant leaders had hoped that the war signaled a new golden age for their churches. In July 1919 Congress passed the Volstead Act, which prohibited the sale and consumption of alcoholic beverages in the United States. The enactment in January 1920 of the Eighteenth

Amendment to the U.S. Constitution appeared to mark a decisive victory for American Protestants. Many social gospel liberals united with conservatives in the belief that Prohibition would make society more righteous and assist them in the goal of creating a Christianized social order.

However, many social gospel leaders worried that jingoism over Allied victory would obscure the wider social-economic objectives that they believed justified the war. They looked with expectation to a future that they hoped would present the nation's churches with an opportunity to remake American political and economic institutions in a way that would create greater social equality.

In December 1918, one month after the armistice ending World War I was signed, 135 prominent Protestant leaders organized the Interchurch World Movement (IWM). Heavily financed by wealthy patrons like John D. Rockefeller Jr. and with John R. Mott serving as chairman of the executive committee, the IWM sought to expand on the efforts of the Federal Council of Churches through an unprecedented range of proposed programs of evangelicalism and social outreach. IWM leaders dreamed that their efforts could fund a wide range of mission-oriented projects that would unite churches in their mission objectives, both in the United States and abroad.

The IWM laid out ambitious financial goals, with plans to raise over $335 million by the spring of 1920.[48] One of the guiding forces behind the IWM was the Presbyterian mission executive Robert Speer, who had a providential sense that Allied victory in the war, the Prohibition Amendment, and the IWM went hand in hand. He felt that Americans were at the dawn of an era when "institutions of lust and evil and sin" would be "extirpated" from America. "But what we are being told today is just what Christians have known from the very beginning, that any generation might have the Kingdom of God if it would open itself to the full inpouring of the will and power of God."[49] While not identified with the social gospel, Speer had a deep passion for Protestant mission and church unity, seeing the IWM as the culmination of earlier Protestant (and social gospel) desires to Christianize the nation. As one scholar noted, IWM leaders were flushed with a sense of possibility that the war literally put the world in the position to be "saved."[50]

However, Protestant leaders had little time to celebrate the founding of the IWM or the enactment of the Prohibition amendment in early

1920. By mid-1919, many American corporations were beset by labor disputes. Numerous industries drastically cut production in the aftermath of the war, leading to layoffs and slashed wages. By late 1919, a series of strikes broke out throughout the country, the largest being in the U.S. Steel Corporation, where approximately 300,000 workers walked off their jobs.

Social gospel leaders faced a dilemma at war's end. On one hand, several figures believed that victory in the war and the passing of the Prohibition amendment had ushered in a new era of optimism in America. On the other hand, many conceded that events like the U.S. Steel strike reflected the dangers of economic exploitation that the war only seemed to bring to the surface. As Fred Fisher, chairperson of the IWM's Industrial Relations Department, asserted, the social teachings of Jesus needed to be "the dominating force in the adjustment of industrial relations."[51] The acid test for Fisher's assertion came when a special IWM task force was formed to investigate the conditions of the steel industry. Chaired by Francis McConnell, the commission included a cross section of social gospel leaders, including George Coleman, the Baptist layperson responsible for organizing Boston's Ford Hall Forum, and Charles Williams, a prominent bishop in the Episcopal Church.

The extensive report produced by the McConnell Commission was a severe indictment of the steel industry, taking particular aim at the president of U.S. Steel, the Methodist layperson Judge Elbert Gary. The *Report on the Steel Strike*, released to the public in the spring of 1920, had as its goal "to find peaceable ways out of the present industrial tension" by fostering "enlightened public opinion."[52] The main report and its numerous sub-reports explored a range of issues pertaining to U.S. Steel corporate practices, including wage cutting, strike breaking—noting the use of corporate spies to undercut union organizing—and most especially the harsh working conditions endured by U.S. Steel's predominantly immigrant labor force. It examined the company's use of a twelve-hour day that the report labeled "the most iniquitous of the by-products of the Corporation's labor policy; which is to get cheap labor and keep it cheap."[53] The report also went to great lengths to disassociate the strikers from affiliation with "Bolshevism," noting that reports of workers' devotion to communism had been fabricated by U.S. Steel leadership and did not reflect the actual sentiments of steel company employees.[54]

Although the report did make reference to the IWM leadership's desire to discern the facts "from the Christian viewpoint," the report's tone sought a level of objectivity as it presented a range of statistics on workers' wages and living conditions, as well as the reasonableness of the steel union's demands for job safety and a reduction of working hours. Repeatedly the IWM report criticized the steel owners, especially Judge Gary, for their unwillingness to negotiate with the workers and their use of a "spy system" to undermine and ultimately break the strike.

The IWM's *Report on the Steel Strike* gave the American Protestant social gospel one of its chief institutional triumphs and, in many ways, served as a model for a range of ecumenical documents on social issues that would emerge later in the twentieth century. The report helped galvanize public opinion, leading to the passing of legislation abolishing the twelve-hour workday in the steel industry in 1923.[55] However, the IWM's goals to assert its institutional muscle and to endorse specific policies of social amelioration proved not to be compatible. Financial donations to the IWM plummeted, and by 1922 the IWM had dissolved. Stephen Wise, a firm supporter of the strikers and harsh critic of Judge Gary, observed that the death of the IWM reflected the resiliency of belief in the idea that religious leaders should only discuss so-called spiritual matters, and "when a minister interfered with current politics he was exceeding his ecclesiastical authority."[56] The IWM's demise related to the fact that the U.S. Steel strike report directly challenged the prerogative of business leaders to determine the fate of their companies. Although the report sought to distance itself from labor radicalism, it was perceived by many wealthy business leaders as an assault against the free enterprise system and an individual's right to earn wealth.

The report signaled a growing tension that would develop throughout the twentieth century between religious leaders committed to radical iterations of the social gospel and conservatives, who viewed the efforts of leaders like Ward and McConnell as communism masked as religion. For many religious leaders who wanted to build on the legacy of Walter Rauschenbusch, a question that had been debated by social gospel leaders since the late nineteenth century was still unresolved: Was the ultimate goal of religious-based social reform to promote broadly defined social ideals that would lead to societal change, or was it to advocate for specific social-economic remedies?

Conclusion

In early 1928 Stephen Wise wrote to Walter Rauschenbusch's widow, Pauline, to pay tribute to Rauschenbusch as "one of the great spirits of our day" while lamenting his absence from the contemporary religious landscape. "I have always felt, and I dare say you know I have said it from time to time, that he was one of the real prophets of the religious social awakening of our time. He was a beautiful spirit and I wish I might have seen very much more of him in recent years." Wise's letter also noted that Rauschenbusch's 1910 *Prayers of the Social Awakening* reflected the essence of Rauschenbusch's personality: "The spirit of the man is in these prayers. It is that which makes them so precious."[57]

Wise reveals how the social gospel in the early twentieth century strove to be an irenic movement, balancing a concern for the care of souls with the care of society. Several of the chief representatives of what Wise called the "social awakening"—Rauschenbusch, Washington Gladden, Emil Hirsch, and Wise himself—identified themselves as clergy who struggled to find a balance between being prophetic and serving the demands of their congregations. This tension between the pastoral and the prophetic would continue to be part of the American social gospel tradition in decades ahead, embodied by important figures such as Harry Emerson Fosdick. By the early 1920s, many religious leaders were raising questions about how, and whether, the social gospel would survive in the churches. One person who was raising this question was Harry F. Ward. Through his growing activism outside the church, and through his influence on many of his students at Union Theological Seminary, Ward helped to convince a post–World War I generation of Union Seminary graduates that the radicalism of Jesus needed to move beyond the "pious platitudes and undiscriminating generalities" of church pronouncements into concrete actions to change society.[58] In the early 1920s Ward continued to insist that Christianity's goal was to promote a "cooperative commonwealth" based on the social teachings of Jesus.[59] Yet in the aftermath of the war, he expressed growing disillusionment about the ability to reform American capitalism. Just prior to the steel strike of 1919, the Methodist Federation for Social Service had published a series of pamphlets in which Ward gave an assessment of the recent Bolshevik Revolution. Although he castigated the Bolsheviks for their hostility toward religion and their sanction of violence, Ward expressed a degree of hopefulness about events in Russia and called on Americans to keep an open mind toward this workers' revolution. Events in Russia convinced him that the "aim of the Bolsheviks is clearly the creation of a state composed entirely of producers and controlled by producers. This is manifestly a Scriptural aim."[60]

Ward's controversial assessment of the Soviet Union in the early 1920s was accompanied by the sense among some social gospel adherents that the movement, if not dead, was seriously crippled. In 1926 the liberal Protestant magazine the *Christian Century* published an editorial on the legacy of Walter Rauschenbusch. The editorial writer seemed pessimistic about the future of the social gospel, lamenting that "nothing in the social thought of American protestantism has occurred which deserves to be dignified by the term 'a new reformation.' . . . We are living under a highly competitive economic system which remains unchallenged by the cooperative ideal of the gospel."[61] Taking stock of the social context of the mid-1920s, the *Century's* editors believed that the nation's churches had become apathetic in the face of postwar prosperity: "There are hardly more than a score of men in the entire church in America who are really feared by the forces which are intent upon maintaining the status quo inviolate." Reflecting on the administration of President Calvin Coolidge, the magazine asserted that "we are living under an administration which more frankly espouses the cause of a secularized and impersonal capitalism than any administration since [William] McKinley and that this administration is subject to practically no criticism from the churches or their leaders."[62] While the *Century* was not willing to concede the demise of the social gospel, it wondered how the tradition could be rejuvenated:

> It may be that underneath the surface of religious life the emphasis in Christian ethics is gradually and imperceptibly shifting until some day we will awaken to discover that we have a church with the ambition of conquering the whole of life in the name of Christ. But we must confess that we see waves without evidences of a tide at the present time.[63]

At the same time that Harry Ward and the *Christian Century* wondered whether Americans could move beyond "pious platitudes," Euro-

pean Protestantism was experiencing the first aftershocks of the work of
the Swiss theologian Karl Barth. Studying at the University of Marburg,
Barth had been steeped in German liberalism. However, at war's end he
shared with many continental theologians a growing disillusionment toward liberal theology. Barth's *Epistle to the Romans*, originally published
in 1918, was called by many a "theological bombshell" against liberalism.
With his emphasis on God's transcendence and the unique revelation
of Jesus Christ as the only means by which believers could encounter
God in history, Barth set the stage for a spate of theologians who questioned social gospel suppositions about the kingdom of God and human
progress. As the 1920s progressed, theologians such as Rudolf Bultmann
and Paul Tillich made their own theological syntheses that summoned
Christian communities to both reclaim a sense of divine transcendence
and embrace the power of scripture to transform churches.

Although the neo-orthodox tradition would not take full root in
America until the 1930s, the tradition anticipated a broader backlash
against the social gospel. Part of that critique emerged in 1928, when
W. A. Visser't Hooft, a Dutch theologian who would later become one
of the principal founders of the World Council of Churches, wrote one
of the first theological critiques of the social gospel in the United States.
Visser't Hooft was critical of the social gospel and found it lacking a great
deal of theological substance. Yet he acknowledged that it manifested
beliefs and practices that were distinctive from Europe, noting that it
would be foolish to consider this theological movement dead. "Humanly
speaking there is no single nation in the world which is more important to the future of Christianity than America. One cannot therefore
be indifferent to the question in which direction American Christians
are moving." Visser't Hooft believed that the social gospel represented
an effort of American churches to define their theological identity outside Europe, but he also saw it as the emergence of something radically
new in theology, even as he questioned where this tradition would lead
Americans: "The social gospel is therefore in a sense the first expression
of American religious life which is truly born in America itself. May it
therefore not be that America is yet at the beginning of the process of
finding itself?"[64]

Visser't Hooft's analysis largely focused on formal theological developments in American Protestant denominations, failing to see that by

the mid-1920s an important new chapter of the social gospel was being forged outside these institutions. Although the progressive optimism that undergirded much of the social gospel in its development in the late nineteenth and early twentieth centuries had crested, the movement was far from dead. In the early 1920s, social gospel thinking was still very much ensconced within religious institutions, and it had a solid base within what would be an expanding network of collegiate organizations, epitomized by the YMCA and YWCA. Over the next several decades, these groups would be connected by an expanding network of organizations, both within and outside church denominations, that characterized the subsequent development of the social gospel movement through the middle part of the twentieth century. Not only had the social gospel established deep roots within American religious institutions, but it was forging new understandings of social justice, setting the stage for a new phase in the evolution of the social gospel movement in American religion.

5

"Since Rauschenbusch—What?"

The Social Gospel between the World Wars

In 1923 Bishop Francis McConnell observed that there was a new spirit of radicalism emerging in the nation's churches. In the aftermath of the Interchurch World Movement's collapse, McConnell conceded that the postwar era was creating a complicated social context that required established religious leaders to make room for more radical perspectives coming from a younger generation of activists. "So the first duty toward the social radical is to let him talk," McConnell asserted. "The next duty is to listen to him, and the next is to try to put into effect whatever of his teaching seems sound." Although noting that for many church leaders political radicalism was hard to embrace, McConnell believed that these youth articulated an important message: "It is necessary to remember that among the cranks and wild fellows there are some true prophets of the Most High—men who stand in the direct line of succession from the prophets of old. Let them speak forth."[1]

McConnell's comments are instructive for understanding the development of the social gospel movement after World War I. Many historians have argued that the social gospel declined sharply after the war. By the 1930s, American proponents of the neo-orthodox theological tradition, associated with Reinhold Niebuhr, called for Christians to rearticulate a historical Protestant theology that underscored humanity's sinfulness and the naïveté of social gospel liberals in the face of societal evils.[2] While Niebuhr's critique of theological liberalism is important to the story of the social gospel's history after World War I, his influence often overshadows the fact that the social gospel did not disappear in the 1920s and 1930s. Rather, a "revival" of the social gospel in the 1930s built on a growing movement of what one scholar termed "social gospel radicalism."[3] In the 1920s and 1930s, these radicals took the earlier idealism of the social gospel, epitomized by figures like Wal-

ter Rauschenbusch, and rechanneled it to engage a range of social issues in the war's aftermath.

While some Protestant leaders worried that nobody appeared ready
to pick up the prophetic mantle from Walter Rauschenbusch, during
the 1920s and 1930s the earlier idealism of the social gospel impacted
a number of older religious institutions as well as newer groups. Organizations such as the YMCA, the YWCA, the Fellowship of Reconciliation, the Socialist Party, and religiously oriented youth movements were
infused with a greater urgency to experiment with more radical models of social-political change. As the historian William McGuire King
noted, in juxtaposition to the gradualist measure of earlier reformers,
"the social gospel radicals were now ready to use the tactics of direct
social and political confrontation. In place of progressive optimism, they
were now convinced that America was headed in the wrong direction
and that only a drastic cultural reorientation could stave off disaster."[4]
Post–World War I social gospel leaders not only looked to more radical means of economic reform, they also insisted that questions of economic justice were inseparable from issues such as racism, the defense
of civil liberties, international cooperation, and a growing commitment
to various models of religiously based pacifism.

Although many aspects of this radicalism were rejected by mainstream religious leaders and institutions, the radical activism spoken
of by Francis McConnell would contribute to the creation of a broad
coalition of religious and secular organizations on the political left, a
coalition that helped to spawn the civil rights movement of the 1950s
and 1960s.

The Social Gospel Confronts the 1920s

One cannot overstate the impact that World War I had on many American religious leaders. The mass scale of wartime casualties, in which
over 11 million were either killed or wounded, created a growing sense of
revulsion against the prospect of any future wars. This was true among
hundreds of American clergy who had witnessed the war firsthand in
Western Europe while serving as YMCA chaplains. As one of these former chaplains reflected in the immediate postwar period, "We thought,
at least many of us did, that we were fighting for great ideals, and that

the winning of the war would give us a better world. Well, we know differently now."[5] This sentiment not only underscores a disillusionment about the war's outcome, but highlights how many social gospel Protestants and their religious allies were committed to mobilizing around a range of social issues. These included a heightened anticapitalist stance, a growing international consciousness, and a commitment to various models of religiously based pacifism.

One of the groups that epitomized these themes in the interwar period was the Fellowship of Reconciliation (FOR). Founded in Great Britain in 1914 by British pacifists, the American FOR was established in November 1915 by a coterie of Protestant activists with the goal of keeping the United States out of World War I, embracing a vision that was "no less than a quest after an order of society in accordance with the mind of Christ."[6] It was "a political organization committed to using 'the method of Jesus' to resolve vexing industrial, racial, and international problems."[7] Although the FOR lacked a high level of public visibility during the war, membership rose steadily in the war's aftermath, attracting a range of individuals who shared a commitment not only to pacifism but also to democratic socialism. Among the early leaders and supporters of the FOR were Jane Addams, Vida Scudder, John Haynes Holmes, and a Presbyterian minister who would become the standard bearer for the American Socialist Party in the 1920s and 1930s, Norman Thomas.

Thomas was committed to following Walter Rauschenbusch's desire to create a democratic socialist political alternative in the United States. Growing up in a traditional Presbyterian household, he embraced the social gospel while a student at Union Theological Seminary in the early 1910s. Thomas credited Rauschenbusch with leading him to democratic socialism and, like Rauschenbusch, began his career as minister of a small church in a poor immigrant neighborhood in New York.[8] By 1920, Thomas had left the ministry, and for the next several decades would serve as the party's primary spokesperson.

Under Eugene Debs's leadership, the Socialist Party reached its height of popular appeal when Debs received approximately 6 percent of the popular vote in the 1912 presidential election. However, World War I and the Russian Revolution created dissension among many American socialists, ultimately causing ruptures in the party in the 1920s and 1930s.

While some socialists embraced the newly formed American Communist Party, Thomas was committed to a vision of social change that attempted to draw together Americans disillusioned with the capitalist
policies of the Democratic and Republican Parties. This socialist vision
for change was inspired in part by earlier social gospel beliefs that democratic socialism represented the pure ethical motives of Jesus. Although
many religious leaders supported and joined the Socialist Party during
the 1920s, several of these leaders expressed a disillusionment with institutional forms of religion. Thomas noted in 1919 that "it is the church
that needs our concern—the church which is committing suicide by the
neglect of things which pertain to her salvation."[9] Dan McKanan observes that as the Socialist Party moved into the 1920s it increasingly
viewed socialism as a "universal religion," whereby socialist reforms
were seen as the embodiment of God's love for humanity.[10]

The strong support for the Socialist Party by many Protestant clergy
in the war's aftermath demonstrated that earlier themes of late nine-
teenth- and early twentieth-century Christian socialism continued to
exert a powerful appeal on a wide range of social gospel Protestants. In
1921 Sherwood Eddy and his younger colleague Reinhold Niebuhr were
instrumental in founding the Fellowship for a Christian Social Order
(FCSO). The FCSO included a spectrum of members who broadly interpreted the concept of a "Christian social order." With a membership that
included Eddy and Niebuhr, as well as Francis McConnell, G. Bromley
Oxnam, and the prominent liberal theologian William Adams Brown,
the group linked together liberal and more radical perspectives. Most
significantly, the FCSO included a core of leaders who were involved
in the Socialist Party, the FOR, and the YMCA/YWCA.[11] Although the
Fellowship for a Christian Social Order was short-lived, merging with
the FOR in 1928, it reflected the dedication of numerous Protestant
leaders to continue the prewar social gospel quest to flesh out political
and economic alternatives to capitalism. The development of organizations like the FOR, as well as the strong appeal of socialist political
alternatives among many social gospelers, demonstrates their growing
uneasiness about the political character of postwar America. Increasingly, these leaders became pacifists as a means to live out Jesus's ethical
teachings while creating a more just society.

Some social gospel figures who embraced pacifism in the 1920s became international isolationists. However, several leaders such as Sherwood Eddy connected pacifism to a robust commitment to internationalism—especially critiquing long-standing assumptions that equated American imperialism with missionary success. The YMCA/YWCA, which had been moving in this direction before the war, played an even greater role in the interwar period in inspiring many social gospel leaders to recalibrate their thought. Eddy emphasized that the way to create world peace was through a thoroughgoing assessment of the social-economic practices of the West—practices that many social gospel leaders believed had helped to cause the war. For many social gospelers, part of the war's impact was to increase their sense of urgency concerning the implicit evils of the capitalist economic system, reflected in what many of them saw as the symbiotic connection between capitalism, militarism, and imperialism.[12] In 1920, at a time when his own disillusionment toward the war was becoming more pronounced, Eddy offered his resignation as a Y secretary, telling the YMCA leader John R. Mott that he felt uneasy asking for financial donations from the rich people that he criticized. "[I] knew that many of the men I had solicited would never tolerate the social gospel I felt impelled to proclaim."[13] After being reassured by Mott that the YMCA "needed a social gospel," Eddy began a new phase of his work.

Between 1920 and 1939 Eddy conducted a series of travel seminars, sponsored by the YMCA, to war-ravaged regions of Europe. These YMCA-sponsored trips included some of the most significant heirs of the post–World War I social gospel, such as G. Bromley Oxnam, Harry F. Ward, and Reinhold Niebuhr. Eddy's work not only decried the war's devastating consequences for European nations, but also promoted a broader awareness of post–World War I independence movements in developing nations in Asia and Africa, and increasingly focused attention on issues of racial justice in America.

A source of critical assistance to Sherwood Eddy's work in the YMCA was Kirby Page. Born in Texas in 1890, Page had an early association with the YMCA. After his ordination as a Disciples of Christ minister and serving a church in Chicago, he became Eddy's personal secretary in 1916. In the aftermath of the war, Page was instrumental in organizing and leading Eddy's travel seminars, as well as an important figure in linking together the work of the YMCA and the FOR.[14]

Page's theological and social commitments picked up where Walter Rauschenbusch left off, in analyzing the range of issues exacerbated by capitalism and the war. Reflecting many of the social gospel themes in Rauschenbusch's later writings, Page not only stressed the nonviolent character of Jesus's social teaching, but also called on American Christians to engage questions of internationalism, particularly examining the interconnection between capitalism and militarism. In 1927 he praised independence movements in younger nations that attempted to break out of long-standing cycles of Western colonialism. As a nation, Americans "are inordinately proud and are slow to recognize our own faults and excesses. Indeed, we are exceedingly self-righteous and honestly believe that we are ethically superior to other peoples."[15] At a time when several religious leaders supported what was referred to as the "outlawry of war" movement—epitomized by the Kellogg-Briand Pact of 1928—Page noted that these efforts, while to a degree laudable, failed to engage the economic and imperialist motivations that often lay behind the causes of modern warfare. On the eve of the Great Depression in 1929, Page noted how Western militarism accentuated runaway economic and political forces that made future international conflicts inevitable. "The growth of industrialism makes it impossible for nations to live apart, each being dependent upon other regions for raw materials and food, markets and fields of investment. Rivalry for control of the economic resources of the earth has grown keener and keener."[16] Along with Sherwood Eddy, Page noted that economic justice required Christians to engage a multitude of issues related to internationalism, nonviolence, and, increasingly, American racism.

Page was well aware of the changing American demographics after World War I that saw increasing African American migration from the South to major industrial cities in the North. In the late 1910s and early 1920s, race riots broke out in several northern cities, including Chicago in 1919, resulting in the deaths of thirty-eight people. For Page, a great deal of the culpability for racism rested with white Christian churches: "First, many white Christians hold the extreme attitude toward the inferiority of Negroes and support discriminatory measures; and second, by silence, evasion, and neglect they permit unjust measures to be perpetuated."[17] By the late 1920s, the YMCA and its sister organization, the YWCA, partnered with the FOR in sponsoring conferences and gatherings that brought together black and white college-age youth. These gatherings were designed to create the conditions for transformative interracial encounters between young people representing diverse racial-ethnic backgrounds, building the basis for more long-term movements of social change in America.

Despite the fact that they remained administratively segregated until the late 1940s, the collegiate branches of the YMCA and YWCA played a critical role in the development of the social gospel in the interwar period. Led by figures like Sherwood Eddy and Kirby Page, the YMCA/YWCA not only promoted social gospel teachings related to economic justice and pacifism, but along with the FOR worked to create cross-cultural and cross-racial gatherings, internationally and domestically. Despite the perceived radicalism of these movements, their work drew support from influential leaders and networks in many long-standing Protestant institutions. By the early 1930s, the one place that came to embody the institutional stature of the social gospel heritage in American Protestantism was Riverside Church, New York, led by its popular minister, Harry Emerson Fosdick.

Harry Emerson Fosdick and the *Christian Century*'s Social Gospel Liberalism

Although many segments of American Protestantism yearned to embrace the economic prosperity and "return to normalcy" ethos associated with the 1920s, perhaps no figure embodied the vibrancy of the social gospel legacy after World War I more than Harry Emerson Fosdick. When Fosdick went to France in 1918 to serve as a YMCA chaplain, he accepted the predominant view that the war was a struggle between the forces of democratic freedom and militaristic tyranny. Like many other YMCA chaplains, when Fosdick returned from the war, he soon became a pacifist. Describing this decision in his autobiography, he noted his disillusionment at the war's outcome, "confronting with increasing agony the anti-Christian nature of war's causes, processes and results. I could not dodge my conscience: I must never again put my Christian ministry at the nation's disposal for the sanction and backing of war."[18]

Fosdick's early ministry drew mostly from social gospel figures like the liberal Baptist theologian William Newton Clarke as well as Walter Rauschenbusch.[19] Yet even before his pacifist turn, Fosdick imbibed a religious mysticism from a person who had influenced many social gospel leaders during the interwar period: Rufus Jones. In the early twentieth century, Jones played a critical role in integrating aspects of a Quaker tradition of nonviolence into the theological framework of social gospel liberalism. A professor at Haverford College, Pennsylvania, Jones was a founder of the American Friends Service Committee during World War I, an organization that offered food and refugee assistance to civilian populations displaced by the war.[20]

While Jones was committed to the reform initiatives of the social gospel, ministers like Fosdick were also drawn to the therapeutic implications of Jones's theology, a template that Fosdick would later develop in many of his own writings in the 1920s and 1930s. Echoing themes explored in William James's seminal 1902 book *The Varieties of Religious Experience*, Jones's work combined a stress on religious experience with an emphasis on the dignity and worth of the individual that paralleled many strands of social gospel thinking. As Jones asserted in his enormously influential 1904 book *Social Law in the Spiritual World*, God's nature postulated a continuous ground for hope in a better future: "The entire progress of the race toward goodness, the coercive power of our own ideals which shape our lives, proclaim the truth that goodness belongs to the eternal nature of things. . . . Our own life, if it is to have meaning and significance and value at all, compels such faith."[21] Jones's combination of piety, mysticism, and social action would be fleshed out by a wide range of social gospel leaders like Fosdick in the interwar period.

Fosdick's stature in American Protestantism increased during the climactic battles between fundamentalists and modernists in the early and mid-1920s. In addition to teaching responsibilities at Union Theological Seminary, he was the preaching minister at the affluent First Presbyterian Church in New York. Fosdick's 1922 sermon "Shall the Fundamentalists Win?" was paradigmatic of the growing theological rift that ultimately led to the departure of numerous conservatives from many northern-based Protestant denominations in the 1920s and 1930s.[22] Fosdick's symbolic place in American Protestantism was secured in 1930 with the founding of the institution that became a symbol of the social gospel's institutional legacy in America: the Riverside Church. Built across the street from Union, and heavily financed by John Rockefeller Jr., Riverside modeled the long-standing social gospel tension between liberal-progressive proclamations of reform and the realities of institutional wealth. Fosdick's career paralleled those of numerous other social gospel preachers during the interwar period who built national reputations as ministers of upper-middle-class churches. Among these well-known clergymen were the New York City ministers Ralph Sockman, George Buttrick, and Henry Sloane Coffin, who in 1926 became president of Union Theological Seminary, as well as Ernest Fremont Tittle in suburban Chicago and Henry Hitt Crane in Detroit. Significantly, several of these "pulpiteers," including Fosdick, Coffin, and Tittle, also were major leaders of the mid-twentieth-century Protestant ecumenical movement.

Like famous nineteenth-century ministers such as Henry Ward Beecher, Fosdick used his various pulpits, culminating with Riverside Church, to draw large crowds to hear his sermons, many of which received a wide circulation in published form as articles or in books. Fosdick's popularity had as much to do with his pastoral and therapeutic demeanor as it did his outspokenness on issues related to economic justice, pacifism, and racism. The therapeutic themes in his sermons resonated with many Americans, while members of Fosdick's congregations often looked to him for pastoral care, relying on Fosdick to baptize their children, officiate at weddings, preside over funerals, and comfort those who mourned. Although his parishioners may not have shared Fosdick's politics, they were drawn to the ways he connected his theology to a deep care for the individuals in his church.

In many ways, Fosdick epitomized a broader movement toward exploring the psychological implications of religious faith, a movement that helped to spawn the wider development of therapeutic religious models in the aftermath of World War II. Not only did Fosdick find a popular market, but his example illustrates the growing popularity of religious book clubs in the 1920s, 1930s, and 1940s that included a number of Protestant, Catholic, and Jewish authors. The historian Matthew Hedstrom observes that these book clubs illustrate the rise of a "religious middlebrow culture" that exposed Americans to emerging theories of psychology and religious mysticism.[23] A great deal of Fosdick's public success revolved around his ability to balance his social gospel theological commitments with a deep-seated pastoral-therapeutic sensitivity. His example would pave the way for a wide range of mid-twentieth-century Protestant, Jewish, and Catholic leaders who increasingly appropriated popular therapeutic models of religious liberalism in their ministries. While Fosdick often expressed his support for pacifism and socialism, he also cultivated the friendships of some of the most powerful leaders in the realms of business, politics, and academia.

Harry Emerson Fosdick's status as the most prominent social gospel liberal in the interwar years paralleled the rise in the 1920s of the *Christian Century* as the primary periodical of liberal Protestantism and the social gospel. While its circulation in the interwar period was modest, hovering between 30,000 and 40,000 subscribers, the magazine enjoyed wide cultural appeal as the major voice of liberal Protestant political and cultural aspirations.[24] The *Century's* origins date to 1884, when it was founded as the *Christian Oracle*, a journal of the Disciples of Christ, a denomination formed in the aftermath of the Second Great Awakening. In 1908 the magazine was purchased by a Disciples minister, Charles Clayton Morrison, who refashioned it as an ecumenical periodical. Morrison's theological commitments were firmly rooted in the progressive tradition of the social gospel, and he was determined to advance the broader movement of theological modernism in America. A staunch supporter of Prohibition, Morrison reflected an early twentieth-century progressivism that backed both the social gospel and the Republican Party. His conservatism was evident during the 1928 presidential election, when the *Century* not only endorsed Republican candidate Herbert Hoover but also echoed long-standing Protestant fears of Catholicism in its attacks on the Democratic Party nominee, the Roman Catholic Alfred E. Smith, who campaigned on the promise to repeal Prohibition.

Morrison embodied many of the aspirations of the early twentieth-century social gospel. At the same time, he cultivated a talented network of young clergy and social gospel activists to write editorials and articles in the *Christian Century*. One of his biggest stars was Reinhold Niebuhr. Like Walter Rauschenbusch, Niebuhr was the son of German immigrants, with his father serving as a minister in the predominantly German immigrant Evangelical and Reformed Church. After Niebuhr

graduated from Yale Divinity School, he served an urban parish in Detroit. Embracing pacifism after the war, Niebuhr developed a reputation
as a social activist during his Detroit ministry, standing up for the rights
of workers in the automotive industry. More important, however, was
Niebuhr's growing number of organizational commitments, including
the Fellowship for a Christian Social Order, the Fellowship of Reconciliation, and the Socialist Party. These circles introduced Niebuhr to
a broad sphere of influence and a widening audience to hone his ideas.
Throughout the 1920s, Niebuhr was a tireless speaker in numerous local
churches and college campuses throughout the country, in events sponsored by organizations such as the Student Volunteer Movement, the
YMCA, and the FOR.[25]

Niebuhr's post–World War I theology echoed important themes associated with social gospel liberalism. Writing in the *Christian Century*
in 1924, he called on readers to work for the formation of a Christian socialist political alternative that would galvanize Americans toward more
radical social action. Such a political party

> must have the courage and the imagination to conceive an ideal social
> order in which the human spirit can triumph over every social custom
> and economic relationship which now depreciates human personality
> and debases human life. At the same time it must believe that such a
> world can be built without violence and without hatred; it must have suf-
> ficient confidence in people to believe that most of them can be brought
> to detect the social ills from which they and their fellows suffer and to
> desire their abolition.[26]

While he conceded that the post–World War I church was reluctant to
take up the cause of radical reform, Christians needed to stay focused
on this goal. Niebuhr concluded, "One wonders what kind of a Christian
political party could be created if the church really took the social implications of its gospel seriously and became the trusted champion of every
cause which seeks to free men from the forces which enslave his life and
debase his worth."[27]

The *Christian Century* had enormous influence in tying together a
wide spectrum of American Protestant social gospel figures who encompassed both liberal and radical perspectives. Not only did it publish

articles by leading social gospel figures, but the magazine served as a bridge between Protestant institutions and the wider culture. Although the *Century* remained extremely popular in the 1930s, its articles increasingly demonstrated how social gospel leaders were divided on how America should be reformed—and the role that religion should play in that process.

The Great Depression and the Social Gospel

Despite the immense popularity of ministers like Harry Emerson Fosdick, other social gospel leaders believed that these individuals were held captive by capitalist wealth. On the eve of the Great Depression in 1929, Reinhold Niebuhr highlighted a growing belief that the Western world was on the precipice of disaster. While he remained hopeful that the ideals of a just society were obtainable, and although he was still committed to the principles of pacifism, Niebuhr's doubts about the future grew more pronounced: "I saw the modern nation as a great economic unit without a moral will strong enough to restrain or check the almost automatic processes which brought it in conflict with other nations." Niebuhr still affirmed the power of Christian love to create a just society. However, he asserted that "there is tragedy in all the beauty which life reveals." He summarized that "it is not impossible for society to overcome conflict and develop into a brotherhood, but there is something divinely foolish about the hope of such a consummation."[28] Four years later, Niebuhr would conclude one of his most famous books, *Moral Man and Immoral Society*, with a variation of this assertion. His growing disillusionment with earlier social gospel arguments related to the power of love to create a just society revealed the ways that his thought by the early 1930s was increasingly embracing Marxist analysis of class conflict.

 The willingness of a once-committed pacifist like Niebuhr to examine Marxist models of social change, including the possibility that violence was an acceptable means to achieve justice, reflected a broader skepticism on the part of social gospel radicals toward American democratic processes of gradualist reform. This tension was exacerbated by the onset of the Great Depression. When Franklin Roosevelt was elected president in 1932, he signaled a dramatic change in direction for the government in its regulation of the nation's economic life. Roosevelt's New Deal policies of the 1930s demonstrate how earlier reform initiatives supported by the social gospel were becoming part of American national policy. Roosevelt's cabinet included individuals who endorsed many aspects of social gospel thinking, in particular his secretary of the interior, Frances Perkins, as well as Harry Hopkins, head of the New Deal's Works Progress Administration and one of Roosevelt's most important advisors. Perkins and Hopkins had deep roots in the social gospel, and both had spent their young adulthood working in the settlement house movement, with Perkins spending her formative years with Jane Addams at Hull House. Another New Deal advisor was Father John Ryan.

Ryan's association with Roosevelt, through which he earned the nickname the "Right Reverend New Dealer," illustrated how aspects of the social gospel dovetailed with emerging theories of economic reform. Much of New Deal economic policy owed a great deal to economists such as John Maynard Keynes, who emphasized the role of government in regulating the private sector. However, many New Deal priorities, including unemployment compensation, work-hour regulation, labor rights to collective bargaining, and the establishment of social security, have roots in the worldview of the social gospel.

Although the religious idealism of the social gospel was making inroads in mainstream American politics, a range of religious radicals increasingly debated specific social-political models of reform. While many clergy continued to embrace the Socialist Party, by the early 1930s support for the party was dwindling, polling just over 2 percent of the population in the 1932 presidential election.[29] The Great Depression prompted many socialists to reassess both ideas and tactics; some social gospelers concluded that leaders like Norman Thomas did not go far enough in offering economic alternatives to capitalism. With approximately 15 million unemployed Americans by the time Franklin Roosevelt was inaugurated president in 1933, some social gospel leaders saw radicalism as the only hope for the nation—including the possibility of turning to the politics of the American Communist Party. Two individuals who exemplified this radicalism were Methodist Federation for Social Service colleagues Harry Ward and Winifred Chappell.

In 1916 Chappell, a Methodist deaconess, noted the expanding arenas for women in church and society. Reflecting upon Walter Rauschenbusch's calls for social evangelism, Chappell affirmed the central role that women would play in creating God's kingdom: "A fairer day has dawned for women. They are no longer hidden away within the enclosures of their four home walls. They are out in the strong wind of world affairs. And as if with a sense of the responsibility which their new position brings, they are seeking for opportunity to serve."[30] By the end of World War I, however, the Protestant deaconess movement was in decline. The campaign in the 1910s for a suffrage amendment was led by a younger generation of feminist activists who often challenged the Victorian feminism that had been central to an earlier generation of women like Lucy Rider Meyer and Frances Willard. By the mid-1930s, however, Winifred Chappell had developed a reputation as one of the staunchest radicals in America, and her embrace of radicalism reflects the distance that she traveled in her life's journey. As one person commented about Chappell, "everyone on the left knew her."[31] Born in 1879, Chappell had enjoyed an extensive career as a Methodist deaconess, including service in the 1910s as assistant principal of the Chicago Training School. Chappell had been a longtime member of the Methodist Federation for Social Service, and in 1922 she left her position in Chicago to become assistant secretary of the federation and, with Harry Ward, the editor of the organization's periodical, the *Social Service Bulletin*.

However, a great deal of her work moved beyond the MFSS, leading Chappell into various forms of labor organizing. Numerous American industries were beset with continuous labor unrest in the 1920s and 1930s, including debates over wages, worker safety, and the right to unionize. In 1926 Chappell reported on a major textile strike in Passaic, New Jersey, and raised a question in a report in the *Christian Century* about the church's ability "to repair the breaches which this strike has certainly driven between them and the laboring portion of this industrial community."[32] By the start of the Great Depression, Chappell had traveled extensively through coal mining communities in Pennsylvania and West Virginia, reporting back to her readers about worker conditions in these mining towns.

During the 1930s, Chappell increasingly traveled in the South, seeking to build coalitions between poor whites and African Americans, and arguing that the capitalist system was at the center of the nation's economic woes. As the decade progressed, she helped to create numerous academies of "applied religion" in the rural South. In 1937 she became one of the principal organizers of what was called the People's Institute of Applied Religion (PIAR). The PIAR was largely the vision of a Presbyterian minister, Claude Williams, who during the 1920s had become a labor activist and union organizer, using his church in Paris, Arkansas, as a base. After his presbytery forced him out of his parish, Williams set off on a peripatetic path as a full-time social activist who during the Great Depression worked with a coalition of leftist activists like Chappell. The PIAR partnered with a network of religious radicals to conduct a series of institutes in the South and in the North, offering seminars on labor organizing, and it stressed "a positive message of active brotherhood, democracy and justice."[33] Although a short-lived experiment, it illuminated a wider legacy of interracial cooperation in the rural South and highlighted a growing network of youth activism that was centered on numerous Protestant denominations.

Chappell's effort to create a broad-based coalition of poor whites and African Americans in the South highlights the political radicalism of the Methodist Federation for Social Service and its controversial leader, Harry Ward. As a professor at Union Theological Seminary, Ward had a major impact on a number of his students who pursued ministries devoted to social change. In the 1930s, two of Ward's former Union students, Myles Horton and James Dombrowski, were the principal founders of the Highlander Folk School in rural Tennessee. Highlander became a prototype for many experimental communities that developed in the American South during the height of the Great Depression. These "folk schools" attracted interracial communities, offering instruction and fellowship surrounding a range of issues associated with the mid-twentieth-century political left.

While Union students like Horton and Dombrowski were committed pacifists, Ward's rhetoric in the 1930s grew more strident in his attacks against capitalism and his advocacy of a global workers' revolution. Ironically, Ward often professed to be nonpartisan in his political affiliations, and his biographers suggest that he showed little interest in participating in electoral politics.[34] Yet Ward grew increasingly explicit in his faith in the Soviet Union as an earthly embodiment of the kingdom of God. By the early 1930s, Ward's anticapitalist stance became more pronounced. He noted in a 1932 *Christian Century* article that capitalism was beyond reform, and the task of religion was to espouse new models of economic justice based upon collectivism. "If organized Christianity is so tied in with the capitalist order that it can offer no regenerative power but only consolation in the day of its decline, then it cannot avoid repeating the story of those religions of the past which have gone down with the civilizations in which they grew."[35]

Ward's admiration of the Soviet model was strengthened after he spent a sabbatical year in Russia in 1931–1932. His 1933 book *In Place of Profit* reflected the distance he had traveled since his days early in the twentieth century as a pastor in the Chicago stockyards. Ward's analysis of the Soviet Union was highly paternalistic. As one historian noted, Ward viewed Russia as an example of how a backward, nondemocratic society was taking a bold leap into the future. While appalled by aspects of what he saw in his travels in the Soviet Union, he embraced a utilitarian view of Soviet communism, believing that whatever violence was committed by Joseph Stalin might be justified if it led to the future realization of a just social order.[36] This faith in Soviet-style communism was evident in *In Place of Profit*, especially the contrast Ward drew between the Western world's fixations on profit over the ethical necessity to embrace a collectivist society. "The powerful profit motive that still dominates the capitalist world, driving it toward war against its own judgment and to the repression of liberties against its own professed principles, is [in the Soviet Union] but a pale ghost flitting about in dark places with a lessening company of cringing speculators and bewildered peasants."[37] Ward viewed the Soviet Union as a society that was striving to place collectivist ideals ahead of the selfish motives of profit. He believed that the ends for which the Soviet Union was striving illustrated the idealistic precepts of social change for which he had spent much of his life fighting. "The Communists are doing what the idealists have long desired, they are turning the battle spirit of man into constructive channels. . . . Eastward as well as Westward it is opening up the last great reservoirs of undeveloped human energy at the bottom of society."[38]

Ward's positive assessment of the Soviet Union demonstrates a larger rupture that occurred among many social gospel adherents throughout the 1930s. By the mid-1930s, both Ward and Reinhold Niebuhr had resigned from the Fellowship of Reconciliation, and Ward applied much of his energies to an organization called the American League Against

War and Fascism. Founded in part as a response to the rise of Adolf Hitler in Germany, the league became very controversial among religious leaders because it was seen as a popular front group whose real agenda was to support the Communist Party. Ward's leadership in this organization drew criticism from many former allies who increasingly called into question both Ward's radicalism and his judgment for aligning himself so directly with the aims of communism.

By the mid-1930s, Ward became a lightning rod figure in a renewed battle between liberals and conservatives in American Protestantism. One of the most prominent critics of Ward and other religious leftists was Elizabeth Dilling. A leader in the Daughters of the American Revolution, Dilling was a vehement critic of many politicians associated with the New Deal, claiming that several figures in Franklin Roosevelt's administration had connections to the Communist Party. Her vitriol frequently targeted many American religious leaders, as she identified high-profile figures such as Harry Emerson Fosdick and Stephen Wise as being communist "fellow travelers." She published a spate of works including *The Red Network* and *The Plot against Christianity* that brought out both her anticommunism and anti-Semitism.

Dilling's accusations and the national publicity she received illustrate a growing conservative resistance to social gospel–oriented leaders during the 1930s. In 1936 the media mogul William Randolph Hearst funded a national network of "laymen's caucuses" that concentrated their efforts on rooting out various leaders and organizations from American Methodism. In the 1930s, Methodism was the largest Protestant church in the nation, and its leaders played a disproportionately large role in ecumenical organizations like the Federal Council of Churches. Additionally, Methodism's involvement in supporting international organizations like the YMCA and the Student Volunteer Movement made it easily susceptible to charges of political radicalism. One of the common themes of the various campaigns waged against religious organizations was not simply that they advocated communism, but that social gospel radicals opposed the true teachings of Jesus that supported individual freedom, including an individual's right to earn money. "Christianity is the father of the individual," one layman wrote. "The supreme achievement of Christianity is to open and expand the souls of men into noble characters through which it influences and molds the social system; Socialism subordinates the happiness, the liberties, and the characters of men to the economic welfare of the mass."[39]

During the 1930s Americans were deeply divided over matters of economic and political justice, and religious groups were often seen as some of the principal proponents of radicalism. On one extreme were those like Dilling, who expressed a staunch anticommunism and a commitment to the American free enterprise system. On the other extreme were people like Ward, who appeared to embrace the state-controlled economy of the Soviet Union. Yet the Depression years also brought together a wide spectrum of religious leaders, especially within Protestantism, whose vision of religious radicalism still kept them firmly connected to religious institutions. While they often espoused views that allied them closely with churches, their radicalism linked them to movements like the YMCA and YWCA that increasingly looked beyond Western institutions for inspiration.

Mediated Idealism: The Example of Georgia Harkness

In 1936 the program services committee of the YMCA drew up a list of principles designed to give guidance to that organization's young adult work. Although this list of principles stressed the Y movement's historical commitment to physical fitness and Christian morality, it emphasized the interconnection between "developing Christian personality and building a Christian society." Part of this goal was centered in the role of the YMCA to "challenge men to explore the meaning of Christian principles and of the gospel and bring them to feel and understand the tension between life as it is and as it would be if the Christian ideals operated more fully in our economic, political, business, interracial and national affairs."[40] While radicals like Niebuhr, Chappell, and Ward offered distinctive variations of religious activism, many Protestant social gospel leaders continued to uphold older notions of working for a Christian social order, even as they critiqued many aspects of that goal. One of the best representatives of this tension was the Methodist theologian Georgia Harkness.

Later in her career, Georgia Harkness referred to herself as a "hardy perennial"—an apt term, given her extensive work as a theologian, church leader, writer, and activist whose public career stretched from the end of World War I to the end of the Vietnam War. The term also highlights her perseverance as a woman who fought to be heard within the male citadels of Protestant power. Harkness was the embodiment of post–World War I social gospel radicalism, who embraced a number of causes of the political left. Nevertheless, she devoted much of her career to upholding long-standing Protestant institutions.[41] Growing up in rural upstate New York and attending Cornell University, Harkness had initially planned to pursue a career in the Student Volunteer Movement. After a stint as a schoolteacher, she attended Boston University, where she received a master's degree in religious education and then a Ph.D. in theology and philosophy from Edgar Brightman, a disciple of Borden Parker Bowne, the principal architect of the philosophical tradition of personalism. After graduating from Boston University, Harkness had a distinguished academic career, culminating in 1939 with her faculty appointment at Methodist-related Garrett Biblical Institute and later, in 1950, as a professor at the Pacific School of Religion. Harkness's writings became especially popular among Christian laity during the 1940s and 1950s, when much of her work sought to bridge the gap between her academic training and a popular audience. Her book *Dark Night of the Soul* echoed many aspects of religious mysticism associated with the work of Vida Dutton Scudder, reflecting her efforts to integrate her liberalism into more classical sources of Christian theology.[42]

Harkness also fully engaged Reinhold Niebuhr's increasingly critical stance against liberal theology. As the 1930s progressed, Niebuhr's books, including *Moral Man and Immoral Society* (1932) and *An Interpretation of Christian Ethics* (1935), illustrate his break from liberalism and his identification with an American tradition of neo-orthodoxy, or Christian realism. Niebuhr always insisted that he embraced the broader social gospel aim of using religion to create a just society. At the same time, he came to castigate liberals for their naïve beliefs in an ethics based on love to create social change. "The sum total of the liberal Church's effort to apply the law of love to politics without qualification is really a curious medley of hopes and regrets," Niebuhr asserted in 1935. "If the liberal Church had had less moral idealism and more religious realism its approach to the political problem would have been less inept and fatuous."[43] This statement exemplifies the caustic tone that Niebuhr often took with his former allies in the social gospel, especially pointing to what he saw as liberalism's inadequate doctrine of sin and myopic views of Christian love and social progress.

Like many social gospel liberals of her generation, Harkness embraced aspects of Reinhold Niebuhr's Christian realism, often referring to herself as a "chastened liberal." However, she and other liberals criticized Niebuhr's tendency to caricature their tradition as hopelessly naïve.[44] She continued to stress the potential power of religious idealism to build a "Christian democracy" centered on the radical implications of Jesus's teachings.[45] As she wrote in 1937,

> If the church is to have a prophetic function, Christian leaders must be willing to challenge comfortable, traditional modes of thought, and do it in terms not glossed over with vague generalities. Such challenge is imperative in the areas of economics, of militaristic nationalism and of race, and because in these areas we are now least Christian, it is in these most dangerous to be prophetic.[46]

One principle that Harkness embraced consistently for much of her adult life was pacifism. In 1924 she had participated in one of Sherwood Eddy's YMCA travel seminars in Western Europe, and remained committed to pacifism after the United States entered World War II. During the war, Harkness commented on her continued commitment to nonviolence, reflecting that pacifism "grows best in the soil of social-gospel liberalism."[47] Harkness criticized Reinhold Niebuhr's opposition to pacifism, noting that he often resorted to caricatures and oversimplifications. Harkness did not believe that Christian pacifists were naïve, and she thought that nonviolent engagement was far more effective than resorting to armed aggression as a means to cast out evil:

> If one believed that Jesus regarded persons—all persons—as of supreme worth, this is bedrock for the pacifist position. Add to it the fact that Jesus himself chose the way of the cross instead of military force in a situation tense with nationalism, and one finds more potent testimony in this fact than in any specific word about non-resistance.[48]

Harkness's legacy was significant not only for her role as a theologian and denominational and ecumenical leader, but also for the key part she played in helping to bridge Protestant institutions with a range of more radical voices coming from the Protestant student movement. In 1941 Harkness served as one of the principal advisors for a new publication coming out of the Methodist student movement: *motive* magazine. *motive* (intentionally spelled with a lowercase *m*) was a publication of the Youth Division of the Methodist Church. While the journal was recognized as an official denominational publication, *motive*'s editorial board and staff consisted of individuals like Harkness who were steeped in the social gospel. The magazine offered its readers articles on contemporary social issues, commentary, poetry, and original artwork. From the perspective of many of its readers, *motive* was "the virtual national magazine of the entire American student Christian movement."[49] *motive*'s articles in its early years strongly advocated ideals associated with the social gospel, supporting civil liberties, international understanding, and the rights of conscientious objectors. Over the next three decades, *motive*'s editorial staff and contributing writers consisted of prominent religious leaders, public intellectuals, contemporary authors, and social activists, including Howard Thurman, Pearl Buck, Albert Einstein, Howard Zinn, and William Stringfellow. The magazine bridged institutional Protestantism with radical idealism that called for dramatic changes in American social-political life.

motive's editorials and articles not only examined changes in American society, but also underscored the growing commitment to religious internationalism that many organizations like the YMCA and YWCA had long supported. An example of this internationalism emerged in the 1930s through the impact of three individuals—two from Asia and one from the United States—who enabled many Americans to merge earlier traditions of social gospel liberalism with a developing faith in the power of nonviolent direct action to transform society.

Nonviolent Internationalism: Toyohiko Kagawa, Mohandas Gandhi, and A. J. Muste

The heightened critique of the imperialist assumptions of Protestant foreign missions led to fresh questions about the nature and purpose of global mission. If the kingdom of God was not dependent on the outreach of Western churches, then how should mission be defined? In the late nineteenth and early twentieth centuries, the majority of Protestant social gospel leaders took for granted the singular role of Western churches in the wider work of global mission and evangelicalism. Josiah Strong's views about the cultural superiority of the Anglo-Saxon race remained a strong sentiment even among the most progressive church leaders before World War I. However, the social gospel's view of social salvation animated a range of mission leaders to rethink their purpose. Consistent with Sherwood Eddy's own faith pilgrimage, a range of mission executives in major Protestant denominations increasingly raised questions related to the ultimate goals of missions. As mission leaders debated whether foreign missions should be primarily focused on personal conversion or social outreach, they also wrestled with the question of whether the very presence of Western missionaries created a barrier to raising up indigenous leadership.

This debate was central to a Laymen's Foreign Missions Inquiry and a 1932 summary report entitled *Rethinking Mission*, written by a Harvard University philosophy professor, William Ernest Hocking. The report reveals the wider tensions in the 1920s between fundamentalists and modernists in American Protestantism, concluding that modern mission needed to move beyond efforts to convert "heathens" and instead should focus on the social-economic conditions in indigenous communities. Hocking and other influential Protestants felt increasingly uneasy about traditional missiology, and determined that Americans needed to learn from the religious leaders in the so-called mission field. By the mid-1930s two very different Asian religious leaders—Mohandas Gandhi and Toyohiko Kagawa—were raising these questions in new ways for American social gospel leaders.

Gandhi's nonviolent campaign for Indian independence from Great Britain increasingly drew the attention of numerous mission leaders in the West. In the 1920s E. Stanley Jones, a prominent Methodist missionary, helped introduce Gandhi to many Americans with written accounts of his friendship with the Indian leader. Though Gandhi was a Hindu, his public addresses and writings contained strong echoes of liberal Protestantism, especially his emphasis on the historical example of Jesus. For example, Gandhi was extremely fond of the hymn "When I Survey the Wondrous Cross" for its emphasis on Jesus's earthly suffering. As we saw earlier, this emphasis on Jesus's humanity played into a long-standing social gospel theme that the true disciple of Jesus needed to be prepared to suffer, and perhaps even die, for his or her beliefs.

While Gandhi's affinity for liberal interpretations of Jesus appealed to many social gospel figures, he also accentuated an emerging worldview among many liberal Protestants that America needed to embrace and learn from the wisdom of the East. Sherwood Eddy noted succinctly that Gandhi was "the greatest personality I ever met and the greatest saint on earth during our generation."[50] Although Gandhi became a frequent point of reference among a wide range of religious leaders during the 1920s and 1930s, Toyohiko Kagawa represented for many social gospel Protestants the hope of an emerging global Christianity.

Born in Japan in 1888, Kagawa was disowned by his family as a teenager after his conversion to Christianity. Becoming a Presbyterian, he received the opportunity to attend Princeton Theological Seminary, and upon returning to Japan, engaged in a well-publicized ministry in the industrial slums of Kobe, Japan. Kagawa's theology reflected a mix of influences. Unlike Gandhi, who affirmed religious diversity, Kagawa tended to promote more traditional evangelical Protestant notions of the exclusive truth of Christianity. Yet Kagawa strongly embraced many aspects of the social gospel. Influenced by Walter Rauschenbusch, Kagawa frequently wrote and preached about Jesus's life and death as a model for creating a transformed society. "Jesus' understanding of the Gospel included economic emancipation (preaching to the poor), psychological emancipation (healing the broken-hearted), social emancipation (recovery of sight to the blind), and political emancipation (setting at liberty them that are bruised)."[51] While not an absolute pacifist like Gandhi, Kagawa was seen as an antimilitarist who challenged the growing culture of Japanese militarism during the 1930s. When Kagawa toured the United States in 1936, he stressed economic models of "cooperative Christianity." Like earlier social gospel leaders such as Washington Gladden, Kagawa believed that the creation of small groups of producers and workers could allow for shared ownership and accountability over goods produced. Although Kagawa disavowed communism and was critical of socialism, he also espoused the classic social gospel position that the spirit of capitalism was antithetical to the spirit of Christianity. "The poverty of to-day is not the poverty of want but the poverty of plenty," he wrote in 1936. Stressing what he called "Brotherhood Economics," Kagawa castigated capitalism as "a system of exploitation; the accumulation of capital in the hands of the few."[52] In its place, he argued for indigenous communities of worker collectives that would control their own fates.

Public reaction to Kagawa's 1936 American "crusade" was mixed. Although he drew large crowds at many of his appearances, including at Fosdick's Riverside Church, he was denounced by many conservatives as a religious modernist and a communist. One Methodist conservative reacted to Kagawa's desire to "teach the world's Christians the co-operative way" as "a Mongolian trick for bringing in coercive communism, to replace American constitutional capitalism."[53] Even many of his supporters conceded that his economic ideas were naïve.[54] However, Kagawa and Gandhi had a huge influence on many Protestant leaders, exposing Americans to religious and cultural ideas coming from parts of Asia and reinforcing the social gospel appeal to nonviolence. This legacy would become especially vital to the Fellowship of Reconciliation and its most important leader by the end of the 1930s, A. J. Muste.

Muste's early life provided little hint that he would emerge as one of the most prominent leaders of the religious and political left during the first half of the twentieth century. Born in Michigan in 1885, he came out of a background in the Dutch Reformed Church, a denomination with strong historical ties to conservative Calvinism. Muste became pastor of a Dutch Reformed church in New York City, where he studied at Union Theological Seminary. Heavily influenced by Walter Rauschenbusch and Rufus Jones, Muste became a pacifist in 1916 and left parish ministry to become a full-time social activist. In 1921 he helped establish the Brookwood Labor College in Westchester County, New York, with a faculty that included a range of social activists and labor leaders. Brookwood was a prototype of various labor "colleges" that were established in different parts of the country in the 1920s and 1930s. Its mission was to foster community among its students while training labor leaders in various aspects of political activism, particularly labor union organizing. Although he remained active in the FOR, he found himself increasingly gravitating toward an analysis of social inequalities that embraced aspects of Marxist views of class conflict, including the possibility that violence might be justified in the overthrow of oppressive social structures.

However, by the mid-1930s Muste experienced a "reconversion" to pacifism, and much of his subsequent professional life, until his death in 1967, was devoted to his work for the FOR. Perhaps more than any other figure of the interwar period, he helped to translate Gandhian views of nonviolence into a working strategy for social change. In the 1920s and 1930s, most social gospel pacifists tended to see pacifism as an act of individual conscience. Nonviolence was based on a desire not to participate in any way in any coercive actions that could be interpreted as promoting violence or harm to another person. In other words, it wasn't envisioned as a method of political action. However, Gandhi's philosophy promoted the idea that nonviolence could be used as a form of action with the potential to change society—a means to confront the violent acts of oppressors with the "weapon" of nonviolent protest. Muste's adaptation of Gandhian nonviolence in some way served as a middle ground in various theological debates that had been ongoing in the FOR throughout the 1930s. On one hand, he questioned the views of older social gospel pacifists who often equated pacifism with one's individual choice to do no harm in one's personal behavior. On the other hand, he also rejected the Christian realist perspective of Reinhold Niebuhr that pacifism represented the failure of liberals to understand the collective nature of social sin. The historian Leilah Danielson notes that Muste's embrace of a variant of Gandhian nonviolence was heavily derived from Muste's interpretation of the social gospel. While he embraced traditional social gospel views of the inherent sacredness of the individual, he "believed that Christianity was not an unrealizable ideal, as Niebuhr suggested, but rather a blueprint for how to bring 'peace and the Kingdom of [God].' For Muste, in other words, suffering love as exemplified by Jesus Christ was a 'social concept' as opposed to an individual ethic."[55] While experiments in nonviolent direct action were not employed on a large scale initially, when Muste became executive director of the FOR in 1941, he helped to turn that organization into a major conduit for training a wide range of religious radicals in the methods of nonviolent direct action.

The impact of Kagawa and Gandhi on American religious leaders like A. J. Muste was significant in the development of the social gospel in America. For many church leaders influenced by the idealism of the social gospel, Gandhi and Kagawa demonstrated how religious leaders of the East were challenging Western colonialism, imperialism, and militarism. They also helped many social gospel leaders in the 1930s envision new possibilities for societal change that did not succumb to the pessimism of leaders like Reinhold Niebuhr, who by the end of the 1930s dismissed pacifism as a myopic philosophy. Although World War II appeared to cull the ranks of those willing to embrace nonviolent direct action, this emerging vision of social change did not die out with the war.

Conclusion

In the inaugural issue of *motive* magazine, published in February 1941, Ernest Fremont Tittle, prominent minister of the First Methodist Church of Evanston, Illinois, wrote the lead article on the topic "Can Democracy Be Made to Work?" Writing less than a year before American entry into World War II, Tittle summarized the view of many social gospel leaders on the social-political state of America in the interwar period:

> The only way to preserve democracy . . . would mean to make govern-
> ment of the people, by the people, and for the people a reality. It would
> mean to maintain civil liberties and freedom of expression for minority
> groups. It would mean to secure just and fair treatment of all political,
> racial, and religious minorities. It would mean honest and persisting at-
> tempts to create economic conditions that would offer to all men [sic]
> equal and adequate opportunity to earn a livelihood, to educate their
> children, and to develop the best in themselves. That, of course, would
> mean the end of "extreme contrasts of poverty and riches, of misery and
> luxury, of material degradation and ostentatious living." It would mean
> the beginning of economic justice and of the association of patriotism
> with a lively and loyal dedication to the welfare of all the people.[56]

Tittle could hardly be labeled a radical. Like Harry Emerson Fosdick, he enjoyed the prestige of pastoring one of the most prominent churches in the country, with a membership drawn from a cross section of social-economic elites. In his defense of racial justice and of various religious and political minorities, along with his castigation of American capital-ism, Tittle was typical of many religious leaders on the left who were deepening their commitment to radical political activism, even as many of them spoke from the perspective of "religious insiders" within the institutional structures of American Protestantism. Between the end of World War I and the beginning of World War II, many religious leaders were pulled by numerous political-economic currents to examine what they saw as a range of economic and political alternatives to capitalism. At the same time, the idealism propagated by many religious leaders like Tittle had ramifications that extended beyond the parameters of Protestant-based institutions.

By the end of the 1930s, social gospel idealism had made numerous inroads—both on the margins and at the center of American life. The New Deal, under the influence of one of its key architects, Harry Hopkins, and one of its advisors, John Ryan, had achieved many of the goals aspired to by original adherents of the social gospel, including provisions for unemployment insurance and a social security system. In 1938 the Fair Labor Standards Act "set parameters for an eight-hour workday, prevented the use of children as laborers, provided some security for workers in retirement . . . and established the right of workers to organize."[57] This piece of legislation encompassed many of the critical demands made by early twentieth-century social gospel leaders like Rauschenbusch.

However, iterations of social gospel radicalism that in different ways flourished in the 1920s and 1930s were submerged amid the overwhelming patriotism unleashed by World War II. With the coming of the war, many religious leaders renounced their pacifism and fully supported the American war effort. During World War II and the postwar aftermath, Protestantism apparently found a new public voice akin to the earlier social gospel. Protestant goals during the war and postwar era were centered on the creation of a just world, premised on the social gospel assumption that American democratic institutions had the power to save the world.

Despite the fact that the vast majority of American religious leaders vigorously supported the country's entry into World War II, the religious radicalism epitomized by a commitment to pacifism that had been fermenting in the 1920s and 1930s did not die out. In 1943 Bayard Rustin, a staff member for the Fellowship of Reconciliation, went to prison for refusing to be inducted into the U.S. military. Rustin grew up outside

Philadelphia in a small African American community. Raised in his grandparents' Quaker faith, Rustin fully embraced this tradition in his twenties as he read individuals like Rufus Jones, and later as he began his work at the FOR, with A. J. Muste as his mentor. While often work-ing in obscurity, Rustin became one of the central figures in promoting the teachings of nonviolent direct action. In the mid-1950s he became one of Martin Luther King Jr.'s principal advisors. In 1963 Rustin was the chief architect of the March on Washington, one of the most prominent moments of the civil rights movement and an event that was supported by a wide range of the nation's religious leaders.[58]

In microcosm, Bayard Rustin's work reflects Francis McConnell's words at the opening of this chapter on the consequences of religious radicalism—and highlights the ways that the social idealism of the early twentieth-century social gospel evolved by the mid-twentieth century. In 1920 many Protestant social gospel leaders still believed that their churches had a unique role to play in Christianizing the nation in the af-termath of World War I. Stressing the power of moral suasion, they un-dertook a range of measures to promote the social witness of the church. By World War II, this tradition was still evident in the activism of ecu-menical assemblies like the Federal Council of Churches. At the same time, the interwar period saw the formation of numerous religiously motivated groups that believed that these mainline churches were not going far enough in their advocacy. Scorning social prestige, these radi-cals waged a range of campaigns against militarism while promoting economic reform and racial justice, helping to lay the groundwork for the rise of the civil rights movement in the 1950s and 1960s.

The sociologists Luther Gerlach and Virginia Hine noted that suc-cessful social movements seldom emerge out of large-scale organiza-tions that claim to speak for the masses. Rather, they develop out of a network of small, "reticulate" groups that often share a cadre of leaders and a common vision for change.[59] The civil rights movement owed a great deal to organizations like the FOR, the Protestant student move-ment, and a spate of smaller radical groups in the North and South that were inspired in some way by the legacy of the social gospel.

Although American entry in World War II brought about an unprec-edented mood of national unity, the social gospel did not disappear. Even as many religious bodies, especially within American Protestantism, felt they were ascending to a new level of institutional prestige, an earlier legacy of religious radicalism was being rechanneled through a range of institutions. After the war, this radicalism would become highly visible in many black churches in the South. In this context, a new American revolution of social change would occur that represented the crowning achievement of the social gospel movement in American history. The figure who served as the embodiment of that legacy was Martin Luther King Jr.

6

Achieving the "Beloved Community"

Civil Rights, Vietnam, and the Twilight of the Social Gospel

In 1949 Howard Thurman, an African American minister of the Church for the Fellowship of All Peoples in San Francisco, published one of the most important, and in some ways overlooked, theological works of the mid-twentieth century, *Jesus and the Disinherited*. Like an earlier generation of social gospel liberals, Thurman asserted that Jesus's teachings needed to be primarily understood in terms of how he reached out to the poor. However, Thurman drew close parallels in the book between Jesus's mission to serve the marginalized and the historical plight of African Americans. For Thurman, racial justice not only depended on how individuals understood the prophetic teachings of Jesus, but also required a deeply felt personal sense that Jesus's message empowered people of faith to confront the social sins of racism in order to create a just world: "[Jesus] knew that the goals of religion as he understood them could never be worked out within the then-established order. Deep from within that order he projected a dream, the logic of which would give to all the needful security." In this new society "there would be room for all, and no man would be a threat to his brother. 'The kingdom of God is within.'"[1]

Thurman's faith pilgrimage carried him far from his early years growing up in a segregated community in Daytona Beach, Florida. His theological development exemplified how different aspects of the social gospel heritage were converging into a broader national movement for social change in the decades following World War II. As an undergraduate in the early 1920s Thurman studied at Morehouse College, Atlanta, a historically African American college where an emerging generation of young faculty exposed him to many aspects of the social gospel. This immersion in the social gospel became more pronounced when Thurman traveled north to receive his theological education at

Walter Rauschenbusch's Rochester Theological Seminary, followed by studies with the Quaker theologian and mystic Rufus Jones. During the 1930s Thurman's ministry intersected with a wide range of Protestant social gospel networks. He was especially active in the YMCA and the Fellowship of Reconciliation, where, like other social gospel liberals of the interwar period, he encountered Gandhi and his teachings on non-violence. Thurman's professional and personal odyssey came to a climax in 1953, when he became dean of the chapel at Boston University, where he mentored a young graduate student in philosophy, Martin Luther King Jr. Years later, after King emerged as a national civil rights leader, he often carried a copy of Thurman's *Jesus and the Disinherited* in his travels.[2]

Thurman's influence on Martin Luther King was matched by that of Benjamin Mays, an often overlooked African American theologian and educator. As the longtime president of Morehouse College, Mays helped to shape the religious and social worldview of many African American leaders in the mid-twentieth century, including King. It would be Mays who first exposed King to the legacy of religious reform associated with figures like Walter Rauschenbusch.

Howard Thurman and Benjamin Mays shared many similarities as religious leaders. While their work was rooted in the struggle of African Americans to fight racism, each viewed the fight for racial justice as part of the larger need to build an integrated society in America—a vision of what Martin Luther King called the "beloved community." King's leadership of the civil rights movement represented one of the great triumphs of the social gospel's legacy in America. However, King's legacy would not have been possible without the contributions of Mays and Thurman.

African American Christianity and the Social Gospels of Howard Thurman and Benjamin Mays

In 1924 Reverdy Ransom, at the culmination of a long career as a minister, activist, and writer, was elected a bishop in the African Methodist Episcopal Church. Ransom continued to express aspects of the idealism that he had preached since the 1890s, praising the social advancements of American society and the growth of Christendom, particularly the rise of the Protestant ecumenical movement. Yet he frequently challenged African Americans to remember their history of slavery and the oppression they endured in the face of racism: "The question before us is not what kind of Negroes the white people want us to be, but what kind of Americans and men do we ourselves intend to be." For Ransom, this required African American churches to confront America's legacy of racial injustice and the American legal system that too often denied African Americans their rights. "We must ceaselessly agitate and work for the repeal of every law . . . that in any way discriminates against American citizens on the grounds of race, color, or religion; any public convenience, recreation, amusement, or necessity that is labeled 'for Negroes,' we should reject as an insult to our American citizenship and manhood."[3] African American churches in the early twentieth century were prophetically creating a strong foundation to engage racism, while producing a range of religious leaders in the tradition of the Black Social Gospel. Benjamin Mays and Howard Thurman were two of the most important leaders to emerge out of this tradition.

Born in Daytona Beach, Florida, in 1899, Thurman, like other African Americans of his time, lived in a segregated society in which the "white and black worlds were separated by a wall of quiet hostility and overt suspicion."[4] Inspired by the mentoring of the prominent African American reformer and Daytona Beach resident Mary Bethune, Thurman saw education as a means to raise himself out of poverty. Although most of the public schools in Florida excluded African Americans, Thurman won a scholarship to attend one of the few private high schools in the state for African Americans in nearby Jacksonville. Upon graduation, he received a scholarship to Morehouse College.[5]

Morehouse College's early history reflected the social reform zeal that characterized many evangelical Protestant campaigns for abolitionism prior to the Civil War. Founded in 1867 as an African American Baptist seminary, by the early twentieth century the school had transformed itself into one of the leading liberal arts colleges for African American men in the country. At a time when the dominant educational model for black education propagated Booker T. Washington's understanding of industrial schools, designed to teach African Americans skills to pursue a trade, Morehouse emphasized W. E. B. Du Bois's ideal that the future of African Americans rested on an educated elite. Educated in a liberal arts curriculum as well as professional training, many "Morehouse men" became prominent ministers and major spokespersons in African American denominations such as the National Baptist Convention, founded in 1895. During Thurman's years at Morehouse, between 1919 and 1923, he studied with faculty such as the sociologist E. Franklin Frazier, whose work pioneered the study of the Black Church experience in America. Thurman also established a lifelong friendship with his philosophy teacher Benjamin Mays, who also served as Thurman's coach on the college's debating team. After graduating from Morehouse in 1923, Thurman headed north to attend Rochester Theological Seminary.

Although Walter Rauschenbusch had died five years earlier, Rochester Seminary still carried the torch of the social gospel. Three of Thurman's professors, Henry Burke Robins, George Cross, and Conrad Moehlman, were prominent social gospel liberals, and had been close colleagues of Rauschenbusch. Thurman noted how his education at Rochester not only taught him "the essential religion of Jesus," but also exposed him for the first time to living and working with white people.[6] As Thurman reflected years later in his autobiography,

> Until I went to Rochester I had accepted the fact that I was a Christian, a practicing Christian. I believed sincerely in the necessity for loving my fellow man. It was a serious commitment; however, it had not ever occurred to me that my magnetic field of ethical awareness applied to other than my own people.[7]

Thurman's emerging sense of integrating a commitment to fight racism, while working toward a multiracial vision of reform, was also important to his Morehouse colleague Benjamin Mays.

While Thurman was a Morehouse undergraduate, Mays was at the beginning of a career that would make him one of the most influential African American educators and ministerial leaders in the country. Like Thurman, Mays grew up poor in the South and saw education as a means to achieve a better life. After graduating from high school, Mays went north to attend Bates College in Maine, where he was drawn to the writings of Walter Rauschenbusch and the social gospel.[8] Although Mays recognized Rauschenbusch's failure to engage with racial justice in a sustained way, he remained committed to Rauschenbusch's basic premise of creating a just society. In 1950 Mays edited an anthology of Rauschenbusch's work that helped to create renewed interest in this pioneer social gospel theologian.[9] After his tenure at Morehouse, Mays served as a national secretary for the YMCA. Ultimately, he received a Ph.D. at the University of Chicago and served for many years as dean of the faculty of Howard University in Washington, D.C., before returning to Morehouse in 1940 as president. In 1944 Mays became the first African American to serve as vice president of the Federal Council of Churches.[10]

One of Mays's biographers referred to him as the "schoolmaster" of the civil rights movement.[11] Mays played a vital role as a mentor to many generations of his students at Howard University and Morehouse College, including Martin Luther King; he also had a major impact on African American churches in promoting the progressive theological and social reform agenda of the social gospel. Like many predominantly white denominations in the early twentieth century, African American churches engaged in numerous debates over whether the purpose of Christianity was chiefly to promote individual or social salvation. These debates divided many constituencies in Mays's tradition, the National Baptist Convention, with one prominent NBC minister noting in 1934, "I am sick and tired of this Social Gospel bunk; you need to be born again."[12] Along with another Rochester Theological Seminary graduate, Mordecai Wyatt Johnson, the longtime president of Howard University, Mays argued for the centrality of a religious progressive vision that engaged the historical legacy of the black church experience. At the same time, Mays frequently attacked the racism of white churches: "The basic differences between the black and white churches is that the black church has never had a policy of racial exclusiveness. The white church has."[13]

Benjamin Mays and Howard Thurman developed similar vocational trajectories, despite the differences in their career paths. Mays's theological orientation demonstrates an affinity with the public church liberalism associated with the mid-twentieth-century American Protestant ecumenical movement. Thurman's liberalism owed a debt to the classic social gospel of Rauschenbusch and the Quaker mysticism that he learned when he studied with Rufus Jones in the late 1920s. Mays and Thurman also had a shared foundation in the social gospel internationalism of the YMCA. During the 1930s, both men traveled to Asia in YMCA-sponsored travels and had the chance to meet Mohandas Gandhi; their encounters with Gandhi were transformational and had a major impact on their attitudes on issues of race, religious interna-tionalism, and interracial fellowship. After serving for several years as dean of the chapel at Howard University, in 1944 Thurman moved to San Francisco to become pastor of the interdenominational Church for the Fellowship of All Peoples. This fledgling church had been the brain-child of A. J. Muste and was initially supported by the Fellowship of Reconciliation. The church was rooted in the premise that it was open to all persons, Christian or non-Christian, as well as stressing no racial barriers to membership.

Thurman and Mays both believed fervently in the idea that reli-gious faith was central to a society predicated on social equality for all Americans, while acknowledging that the persistence of racism made achieving that vision difficult. Although deeply ecumenical, Thurman's mysticism made him wary of aspects of institutional religion. On the other hand, much of Benjamin Mays's public career was shaped by his longtime involvement in the ecumenical movement. His leadership in organizations like the Federal Council of Churches came at a time when Protestant ecumenism was achieving a new public stature.

Ecumenical Aspirations and a Just and Durable Peace

Those involved in the classic social gospel movement emerging out of early twentieth-century American Protestantism believed in the power of churches to disseminate their teachings on social questions to the larger culture. Many social gospel leaders hoped that their policies would carry over into the nation's political institutions, whereby Prot-estant social-ethical teachings might be responsible for "perfecting" American social-political institutions. In many ways, a minister-turned-politician like Norman Thomas was indicative of how some advocates of the social gospel sought to move their vision of social reform outside the nation's churches.[14] At the same time, for those in the classic social gospel movement, American democracy depended on strong prophetic churches to safeguard the nation. While these social gospel leaders vigorously embraced the separation of church and state, they saw organizations like the Federal Council of Churches as essential bodies that could act prophetically to challenge injustices, while linking influential church leaders to important figures in government. In many ways, World War II represented a revival of this earlier social gospel ideal.

At the culmination of the war in 1944–1945, the Federal Council of Churches had entered a new era of public visibility and prestige. During the interwar period, its principal leaders included some of the most prominent figures of the post–World War I social gospel movement. Several of them, including Shailer Mathews, played important leadership roles in the first international Life and Work Conference held at Stockholm, Sweden, in 1925.[15] The ecumenical Life and Work movement, rooted in many of the theological foundations that had been critical to the establishment of the Federal Council of Churches in 1908, emphasized the role of applied ethics among member churches, as opposed to matters of religious doctrine.

Although the Federal Council strongly echoed social gospel teachings after World War I, its ability to shape social action mostly relied on appeals to moral suasion, as opposed to binding resolutions upon its member churches.[16] Federal Council pronouncements on economic justice issues veered to the left during the Great Depression, as the council increasingly sided with Franklin Roosevelt's New Deal initiatives, supporting greater government regulation of the private sector. In fact, Roosevelt cited the Federal Council's support of his policies when he addressed the FCC assembly on the occasion of its twenty-fifth anniversary in 1933. Having noted that he wished he was "as radical as the Federal Council," Roosevelt proudly "equated the ideals of the church and the government" in the building of an equitable society.[17] Roosevelt's comment underscores the continuation of a tradition that began with Woodrow Wilson and would continue in the years after World War II, in which the Federal Council and its successor organization, the National Council of Churches, enjoyed the symbolic support of many American presidents and other important political leaders, who regularly addressed these assemblies and met with influential ecumenical leaders.[18]

As the Federal Council moved into the late 1930s and early 1940s, the attitudes of its principal leaders reflected Reinhold Niebuhr's growing influence on American theology and ethics. The Federal Council stressed that Christianity needed to transcend matters of political partisanship in order to create a prophetic international witness. The second international Life and Work Conference, held at Oxford, England, in 1937, was noted for its assertion, "Let the Church be the Church!" Amid the rise of totalitarian regimes in Japan, Italy, and Germany, the Oxford conference emphasized that the only way Christianity could be prophetic was if it transcended specific social-political ideologies. Even as Oxford proclaimed a view of justice that its leaders hoped would speak to the international tensions brought about by the rise of fascism, its pronouncements steered clear of endorsing specific international solutions. Oxford was strongly motivated by a desire to create an international religious witness against fascism. However, it stressed a duality that saw the church's social witness as indispensable to preserving democratic freedoms and staving off totalitarianism. Before and during World War II, the American ecumenical movement primarily saw the greatest threat to world peace as fascism. In the war's aftermath, it identified communism as the greatest deterrent to world peace.

Oxford's stance on the relationship of the church to international affairs had a major impact on the wider development of America's international ecumenical witness throughout the mid-twentieth century. Although that witness demonstrated the impact of Reinhold Niebuhr's Christian realism, Niebuhr's theological orientation also affirmed the church's role in uniting disparate theological and social movements behind a common goal of creating a just world. Even as Niebuhr castigated the earlier idealism of the social gospel, he was not averse to speaking of Christianity's ultimate purpose in a way that harkened back to earlier social gospel aspirations of a Christianized society. As he noted during World War II, "we must seek to fashion our common life to conform more nearly to the brotherhood of the Kingdom of God."[19]

The idea that the Christian church needed to be a transcendent body, free of political partisanship, reflected the emerging geopolitical realities of the time. However, church leaders also manifested a long-standing social gospel hope that American Protestant churches could serve as the moral force leading the nation and the world to the realization of a just world order. This ecumenical ethos shaped the Federal Council, and later the National Council of Churches, as well as the efforts of western European church leaders in founding the World Council of Churches, which held its first general assembly in Amsterdam, Netherlands, in 1948.

Amid these successes the mid-twentieth-century ecumenical movement found itself wrestling with a question that had plagued early twentieth-century social gospel leaders: If the church was to create an international witness that stood above political partisanship, then to what extent should churches embrace specific models of social reform? For many ecumenical leaders, the answer was a rarefied social gospel vision that tied together Christian teaching with the precepts of American democracy. In 1940 the Federal Council established a Commission for a Just and Durable Peace. During the war this commission would play a critical role in articulating a reform vision that reflected wider Protestant aspirations nationally and internationally. Two symbols of this new religious and social vision were G. Bromley Oxnam and a Presbyterian layperson, John Foster Dulles.

The Ecumenical Movement and Global Unity

By 1944, G. Bromley Oxnam had traveled a great distance from his early vision of religious activism, which he had learned from Harry Ward as a student at Boston University. After a number of years as a pastor in Los Angeles, as well as serving as Sherwood Eddy's secretary in the YMCA, Oxnam eventually became president of DePauw University in Greencastle, Indiana, before being elected a bishop of the Methodist Church in 1936. During and following World War II, Oxnam continued to embrace many aspects of the social gospel. While he oversaw Protestant military chaplains during the war, he also defended the right of Americans to conscientious objector status based on religious grounds. In the postwar era, Oxnam vigorously denounced political and religious groups who created a new "Red Scare" anticommunist hysteria. In 1953 he made a highly publicized appearance before the House Un-American Activities Committee, where he denounced the committee for using questionable evidence and resorting to scare tactics in accusing many high-profile Americans of Communist Party membership.[20]

However, Oxnam increasingly followed Reinhold Niebuhr's political drift. In addition to vigorously supporting American participation in

World War II, Oxnam and Niebuhr were committed to the goal of creating a new international political order that would be undergirded by ecumenical Protestant pronouncements. In 1942 Oxnam spearheaded within Methodism what was called a "Crusade for a New World Order." The crusade, whose motto was "We must save the world,"[21] was an effort to raise money and win public support for American participation in an international peacekeeping organization—what would eventually become the United Nations. Oxnam tirelessly stumped the country, urging Methodists to lobby their congressional leaders for support of an international peace organization. Earlier themes of social gospel triumphalism can be found in his rhetoric, as Oxnam demonstrated the confidence expressed by many contemporary American church leaders that they were building an international community of brotherhood based on the democratic precepts of the United States. "In discovering the techniques whereby the ethical ideals of our faith may be translated into the realities of the common life, Jesus Christ will become the ruler of the earth." As he further noted, "we must take the next step up in the evolution of government and do for the world what our forefathers did for us. . . . We must build the United States of the world."[22] No one in the ecumenical Protestant establishment expressed this vision more fully than Oxnam's colleague in the Federal Council of Churches, a Presbyterian layman, John Foster Dulles.

By the end of World War II, Dulles had emerged as one of the most important figures in the American ecumenical community. A prominent attorney before the war, Dulles served as a critical link between important ecumenical leaders like Oxnam and Niebuhr and the nation's political elites. In 1953 he became President Dwight Eisenhower's secretary of state. In his role as chairperson of the Just and Durable Peace Committee, Dulles championed an internationalist ideal for global cooperation in the postwar era. Invoking the committee's "six pillars of peace," Dulles called for the formation of an international organization that would create fraternal bonds among the nations of the world, overseen by a vision that affirmed "that the right of spiritual and intellectual liberty must be both recognized and made a matter of international concern."[23] The Dulles Commission on a Just and Durable Peace included some of the most prominent Protestant leaders in the country, including Oxnam, Henry Pitney Van Dusen (Reinhold Niebuhr's faculty colleague at Union Seminary), and Harry Emerson Fosdick. Many scholars have noted that the commission helped to garner widespread support for the formation of the United Nations, and its policies served as a template for the UN's Declaration of Human Rights.[24]

However, Dulles's vision of ecumenical Protestantism also accentuated a staunch belief that religion, specifically Protestant Christianity, was essential to stave off the growing menace of communism. One critic of Dulles noted that "as the years passed, and especially following his categorical commitment to anti-Communism, this quality seemed to fuse with his thin but firm religious tenets in an awesome self-righteousness, as though . . . he were acting as the agent of a Higher Power."[25] Throughout the 1940s, Dulles was the embodiment of mainline Protestant cultural aspirations, in part because he helped to project a high level of public visibility for organizations like the FCC and its leaders.

The ecumenical movement was a critical context in which the objectives of Christian realists like Niebuhr merged with those of liberal Protestant ecumenical leaders like Oxnam. While less jingoistic than ecumenical groups after World War I, these mid-twentieth-century leaders still believed that their mission was to preach a salvific message to Americans and to the world. However, the post–World War II ecumenical outlook also owed a great deal to developments within American Catholicism, as the earlier social-ethical tradition of John Ryan was being developed by an emerging generation of thinkers.

During the 1940s, ecumenical leaders endorsed long-standing Protestant beliefs that their particular religious traditions should dominate American society. However, the years prior to and following World War II increasingly saw Protestant leaders emphasizing the idea that the nation's religious heritage was the product of the major movements of Protestantism, Catholicism, and Judaism—what popularly became known as the "Judeo-Christian" heritage. This term was used to signify not only a perceived cultural unity, but also the ways these three traditions appeared to be advocating a shared moral and civic faith that could unite the nation. Since the late nineteenth century, social gospel Protestants and numerous leaders in Judaism had shared similar theological ideas on how their religious traditions might reform the country. By the mid-twentieth century, many ecumenical Protestants, while still suspicious of Catholic religious and political motives, were increasingly drawn to the social thought of numerous Catholic theologians, public intellectuals, and grassroots activists.

On the radical end was the work of Dorothy Day and the Catholic Worker Movement. Day's pilgrimage to radicalism was highlighted in her autobiography *The Long Loneliness*, which explores how by the early 1930s she had converted to Catholicism and embraced a ministry dedicated to hospitality to the poor, a commitment to pacifism, resistance to militarism, and radical economic reform. Day's activism, particularly her strong pacifist advocacy, attracted a loyal group of followers on the left, including the American socialist Michael Harrington and the prominent 1960s Catholic radicals Daniel and Philip Berrigan.[26] Also, in the post–World War II era, the work of the Jesuit theologian John Courtney Murray anticipated the groundbreaking reforms of the Second Vatican Council, held from 1962 to 1965, that opened the Roman Catholic Church to ecumenical dialogue with Protestants and Jews. An especially important public intellectual in the postwar era who has often been overlooked was a French intellectual, Jacques Maritain.

In his extensive writings Maritain sought to reconcile a synthesis of late medieval scholasticism with the emerging social and philosophical developments of the modern Western world. He looked to medieval Catholic tradition as a means to unify society around a shared religious and moral vision. Prior to and following World War II, Maritain's work resonated with ecumenical Protestants who sought to create a culture that would, in some fashion, be dominated by a Christian worldview. As the historian Eugene McCarraher notes, Catholics and Protestants increasingly found common ground in their pleas to create a Christian society. These leaders "insisted that theology occupy the center of social criticism and sought to bestow on the churches a primary agency in social and cultural politics."[27]

Ecumenical Protestants, along with many Catholic intellectuals like Maritain and activists like Day, endorsed various versions of natural law theology, connecting pre-Reformation interpretations of Christianity with the public role of religion. However, ecumenical leaders, like early twentieth-century social gospelers, often struggled with the issue of how to assess the effectiveness of the church's social witness, especially when religious leaders were seeking to build alliances with political leaders like John Foster Dulles, whom they were supposedly critiquing. At the onset of the Cold War between the United States and the Soviet Union, ecumenical Protestants wrestled with the age-old question of how the church's social witness should be defined: should the church proclaim general assertions about its role in promoting a democratic society, or did it need to engage in a more sustained analysis of social institutions to propose specific remedies on issues such as economic justice, racism, and international justice? As ecumenical leaders struggled to decide how far they could push their ideals of social reform, one of Benjamin Mays's former students was emerging with a radical new vision of how religious faith might unite Americans.

The Civil Rights Movement and the Idealism of Martin Luther King

In August 1954 Benjamin Mays delivered an address to the Second General Assembly of the World Council of Churches in Evanston, Illinois. Mays's WCC address framed the issue of race internationally, and evoked the philosophical and theological themes of nonviolence that in a few years would characterize the career of Martin Luther King. Mays noted the impact of racism not only on the oppressed, but also on the oppressors:

> It scars not only the soul of the segregated but the soul of the segregator as well. When we build fences to keep others out, erect barriers to keep others down, deny to them the freedom which we ourselves enjoy and cherish most, we keep ourselves in, hold ourselves down, and the barriers we erect against others become prison bars to our own souls.[28]

His address not only shows how ecumenical leaders were beginning to see issues of racism in an international context, but also illustrates the full-orbed development of the social gospel ethos of theological personalism that became a major characteristic in the social thought of Martin Luther King.

King was thoroughly immersed in a tradition of African American evangelicalism, represented by his father, Martin Luther King Sr., the longtime pastor of Ebenezer Baptist Church in Atlanta. At a young age King resolved to follow his father into the ministry. However, King shared Benjamin Mays's opposition to much of the theological conservatism of many southern black churches and, against his father's wishes, made the decision after graduating from Morehouse to pursue his theological studies in the North. Although King was influenced by a wide range of intellectual currents, he was always clear that the foundation of his thought was the theological liberalism that he learned at Morehouse and later as a student at Crozer Theological Seminary in suburban Philadelphia, culminating with his Ph.D. studies at Boston University.

Crozer was a small northern Baptist seminary that had a distinct place in the wider history of American liberal theology. Established in 1867, by the early twentieth century Crozer had a distinguished faculty of liberal scholars, including Henry Vedder, who like Walter Rauschenbusch saw Christianity as an idealistic faith that made possible the transformation of societies as well as individuals. King also studied with Kenneth "Snuffy" Smith, a theologian who helped to introduce him to figures like Reinhold Niebuhr. The culmination of King's academic journey would take him to one of the major academic centers that promoted the social gospel's legacy: Boston University.

When King entered Boston University in the fall of 1951, he did so primarily to study with the personalist theologian Edgar Brightman. After Brightman's death in 1953, L. Harold DeWolfe, who had been a student of Brightman's, became King's principal academic adviser. As King noted in his first book, *Stride toward Freedom*, Brightman, DeWolfe, and Walter G. Muelder, the dean of Boston University School of Theology, inculcated in him a religious idealism that became the basis of his social thought: "It was mainly under these teachers that I studied personalistic philosophy—the theory that the clue to the meaning of ultimate reality is found in personality. This personal idealism remains today my basic philosophical position." King added that personalism provided him with a firm philosophical basis to believe in "the dignity and worth of all human personality."[29]

King owed a tremendous debt to the personalist tradition that he was introduced to at Boston University. Because of the value he placed on "personality," he was able to understand the individual in the context of an increasingly pluralistic society. King used the term "beloved community," a concept originally used by the early twentieth-century Harvard University philosopher Josiah Royce, as a way to understand the importance of creating a society that allowed individuals to embody Jesus's love ethic to the fullest. For King, this meant a deep-seated belief that all people, oppressors and oppressed alike, were connected to an interrelated purpose. "All men are caught in an inescapable network of mutuality, tied in a single garment of destiny," King noted in one of his sermons. "I can never be what I ought to be until you are what you ought to be, and you can never be what you ought to be until I am what I ought to be."[30] While the conclusion of this sermon reflects the personalist idealism that he learned in Boston, it also reveals the spirituality of Howard Thurman: "Our hope for creative living lies in our ability to reestablish the spiritual ends of our lives in personal character and social justice. Without this spiritual and moral reawakening we shall destroy ourselves in the misuse of our own instruments."[31]

Belac l
Communzy ,,

As he approached his graduation from Boston University, King struggled over the question of his vocation. Benjamin Mays had offered him a teaching position at Morehouse College, but King decided that pastoral ministry experience would help him to balance his competing vocational interests in ministry and teaching.[32] When King graduated from Boston University with his Ph.D. in 1955, he was already serving as pastor of the Dexter Avenue Baptist Church in Montgomery, Alabama. Ironically, King was called to Dexter Avenue out of the belief that his ministry would be devoted primarily to the pastoral needs of his congregation. King had succeeded the Reverend Vernon Johns, a minister who strongly promoted a social activist vision for the church.[33] When the Montgomery Bus Boycott began in December 1955, King was seen by many African American leaders in Montgomery as a relatively unknown and untested leader. Yet beginning with his leadership in Montgomery, King would emerge as the primary catalyst for the national civil rights movement that would transform the social-political dynamics of the country.

Discussions of King often focus on his adoption of the tactics of nonviolent direct action associated with Mohandas Gandhi. Certainly Gandhi was a central influence on King, but social gospel teachings also played an important role in King's commitment to nonviolence and his vision of reform. Rooted in the African American churches in the American South, numerous associates and allies of King had important connections to a range of social gospel organizations, including the Fellowship of Reconciliation and the Highlander Folk School, as well as the support of ecumenical organizations like the National Council of Churches and an interfaith network of religious leaders.

One of King's most important allies in the civil rights movement was Rabbi Abraham Joshua Heschel. Born in Poland, Heschel was raised in the teachings and culture of Orthodox Judaism. At the same time, he was educated in a Jewish tradition of religious modernism, and his subsequent writings often demonstrated that Jewish tradition and modern liberalism could coexist. In the 1930s he received a doctorate from the University of Berlin and began teaching at a school for Jewish studies in Frankfurt that had been established by the famous Jewish mystic Martin Buber. In 1938 Heschel was expelled from Germany by the Nazis; a year later, just prior to the German invasion of Poland, he received a visa to travel to the United States. Initially teaching at the Reform Hebrew Union College in Cincinnati, in 1951 he joined the faculty at the Jewish Theological Seminary in New York, where he taught Hebrew Bible until his death in 1972.

Part of Heschel's popularity during the 1950s and 1960s, like that of Martin Buber, was the result of his ability to make aspects of Jewish tradition relevant in the broader cultural context of post–World War II America. Many of Heschel's books, such as *Man Is Not Alone* and *God in Search of Man*, helped to introduce Jewish mysticism to a broad audience of Jews and non-Jews. Heschel became especially interested in Jewish-Christian dialogue, and in the mid-1960s he served as a visiting professor at Union Theological Seminary.[34]

Heschel's reputation as a public figure and religious activist was cemented in the 1960s, first through his role in the civil rights movement and later in his activism against the Vietnam War. An early supporter of Martin Luther King, he participated with King in the 1965 voting rights march from Selma to Montgomery, Alabama. Later Heschel reflected on the significance of this event: "I felt a sense of the Holy in what I was doing. . . . Even without words our march was worship. I felt my legs were praying."[35]

Heschel's support of the civil rights movement was indicative of the creative tension that existed between institutional religion and more radical social movements that converged around King. A part of this emerging coalition came from Jewish leaders like Heschel, as well as a wide range of Roman Catholic activists and numerous Protestant groups associated with the National Council of Churches. While often critical of these religious institutions, King believed that these bodies needed to play a vital role in redeeming America from the sins of racism.

Martin Luther King, the Beloved Community, and a Christian America

King's theological worldview differed from the earlier social gospel in several ways. Like Mays and Thurman, King understood social reform as directly tied to the struggle of African Americans for freedom and justice. African American critics of the social gospel tradition have drawn attention to the fact that social gospelers like Rauschenbusch were relatively silent on issues of racial justice.[36] While laudatory toward Rauschenbusch, King also criticized him for falling victim to what King referred to as the nineteenth-century "cult of inevitable progress." In other words, King believed that Rauschenbusch embraced a gradualist ethic of reform, a concept that King strongly rejected in his "Letter from Birmingham Jail." Citing Reinhold Niebuhr, King asserted that "history is the long and tragic story of the fact that privileged groups seldom give up their privileges voluntarily."[37] Yet King's theology also demonstrates the influence of Rauschenbusch, in particular, Rauschenbusch's view of history. Both Rauschenbusch and King shared the idealistic notion of the "zeitgeist," a belief that God was active at distinctive moments of history to create the conditions of social change. William McGuire King refutes the assertion commonly made by Reinhold Niebuhr that social gospelers had a superficial optimism about historical progress: "Progress took place, but it was episodic. Moments of victory emerged only out of a web of suffering and tragedy."[38] In addition, Martin Luther King shared with social gospelers a belief in redemptive suffering—that is, the idea that persons committed to changing society needed to be prepared to suffer the consequences of their convictions, just as Jesus had suffered.

King's belief that God partnered with humans in the process of changing society strongly reflected the legacy of the social gospel. He saw the zeitgeist at work in the twentieth century driving persons of color toward the realization of freedom and justice. "Oppressed people cannot remain oppressed forever," King asserted. "This is what happened to the American Negro. Something within has reminded him of his birthright of freedom; something without has reminded him that he can gain it."[39] King's major sermons, speeches, and writings and his social witness not only embody the personalist grounding that he learned at Boston University, but echoed Catholic social teaching associated with figures like John Ryan. Citing Thomas Aquinas in his "Letter from Birmingham Jail," King noted, "An unjust law is a human law that is not rooted in eternal and natural law. Any law that uplifts human personality is just. Any law that degrades human personality is unjust."[40]

Another aspect of King's thought related to the social gospel was the high premium he placed on the moral authority of the Christian church to bring about justice in America. A great deal of King's larger appeal, especially among leaders in predominantly white mainline churches, was that he tied a vision of American uniqueness to the prophetic role of the church in shaping a just society. His "I Have a Dream" speech reflects a blending of religious and secular imagery. Like the abolitionist leaders before the Civil War and the postmillennial optimism of the original social gospelers, King offered a vision of a transformed America, predicated on racial harmony. King's dream was "deeply rooted in the American dream that one day this nation will rise up and live out the true meaning of its creed—we hold these truths to be self-evident, that all men are created equal."[41] Throughout his public career, King spoke of his disappointment with religious institutions, and insisted that the church had a mandate to lead American society "as a thermostat" with the power to transform "the mores of society."[42]

King's understanding of the church as the "moral compass" of the nation drew not only on the social gospel, but also on a deeply entrenched cultural worldview of American Protestantism. The historian James Washington notes the affinity of King's moral vision with the Puritan ethos of the first governor of Massachusetts, John Winthrop, who saw the church as a "city upon a hill" that would serve as the moral beacon for society. However, King's vision of American uniqueness did not translate into a priestly faith. "He certainly was an Americanist, but not a nationalist ideologue."[43] While he was very clear that religion was a matter of personal choice, his understanding of social reform was rooted in his view of a personal God working out

God's purposes in history—and the best means for people of faith to discern these divine purposes was through nonviolence. Using arguments made by many social gospel pacifists like Georgia Harkness and A. J. Muste, King asserted that "returning hate for hate multiples hate, adding deeper darkness to a night already devoid of stars." Echoing words from the Apostle Paul, he frequently noted that "darkness cannot drive out darkness; only light can do that. Hate cannot drive out hate; only love can do that."[44] In many ways, King's theology revived and reinterpreted an earlier social gospel hope that American churches would serve as the nation's moral conscience, guiding Americans to prophetic action.

King's campaigns of nonviolent direct action succeeded in large part because of his ability to mobilize a disparate range of social activists, while also garnering significant media attention. Toward the end of his life, however, King's leadership was challenged by an emerging network of African American activists. At the same time, King's own moral discernment surrounding American escalation of the Vietnam War caused him to rethink aspects of his earlier vision of justice. Vietnam became a symbol of the collapse of both King's vision of a "beloved community" and a wider tradition of progressive activism associated with the history of the social gospel in America.

The End of Common Dreams: The Churches Confront Vietnam

If the social gospel achieved its greatest public prominence in American history through Martin Luther King, the Vietnam War represented its twilight. The war revealed broader tensions that lay beneath the surface of mainline Protestantism's mid-twentieth-century social witness. Specifically, it revealed the gap between ecumenical Protestant policies of reform and grassroots constituencies.

After John Foster Dulles became Dwight Eisenhower's secretary of state in 1953, his relationship with the National Council of Churches became more strained. Although many social gospel leaders in the ecumenical Protestant establishment agreed with Dulles on the centrality of American democracy, they did not concur with Dulles's view that America was a nation beyond reproach. In particular, influential Protestant leaders increasingly criticized Dulles's insistence that the ends of a just society required the eradication of global communism. Even Reinhold Niebuhr, Dulles's longtime collaborator in the ecumenical Protestant establishment, conceded that Dulles's "moral universe makes everything quite clear, too clear. . . . self-righteousness is the inevitable fruit of simple moral judgments."[45] In the early twentieth century, social gospel leaders like Walter Rauschenbusch often defined religious reform as an expansion of American democracy. Yet their view of democracy was predicated on a democratic socialist future that they hoped could unite persons of different social classes, races, and religious affiliations. In contrast, figures like Dulles saw American democracy as a system that strongly supported individualism through a free enterprise economic system. For Dulles, this meant that Americans had to commit themselves to the singular goal of eradicating communism.

Ultimately, National Council of Churches leaders distanced themselves from Dulles's sentiments, rekindling some of the NCC's more radical reform visions from the 1930s. By the early 1960s, the NCC's critique of American democratic shortcomings emerged through its engagement with the civil rights movement. For several years, the Federal Council of Churches' Department of Race Relations, under the direction of George Haynes, had engaged in important but often neglected studies of religion and race in the United States. Like Benjamin Mays, Haynes was part of a cadre of early twentieth-century African American ecumenical leaders who publicly asserted that the best means for churches to overcome racial prejudice was the creation of networks of interracial cooperation.[46] By the 1950s and especially during the early 1960s, however, the National Council began a vigorous effort to connect its policy statements with direct support of King and other civil rights leaders. During the early and mid-1960s, National Council representatives took an active role in civil rights demonstrations, including the March on Washington and the Selma voting rights campaign. Although the National Council of Churches was not in the forefront of civil rights protests, it increasingly extended financial support to King's primary organization, the Southern Christian Leadership Conference, as well as to other civil rights groups allied with King. Crucially, the National Council's various educational initiatives generated public support, particularly in northern churches, for the civil rights movement.

When President Lyndon Johnson began his military escalation in Vietnam in 1965, the National Council of Churches attempted to engage in several "fact finding" efforts that were designed, much like the Interchurch World Movement's steel strike report in 1920, to educate the American public on issues surrounding the conflict. As the historian Jill K. Gill observes, National Council leaders believed that they could employ the same strategy of laity education that had united many Americans behind the civil rights movement. "They extended their sense of accomplishment in moving laity and government on civil rights into similar high expectations for the churches on Vietnam. Their desire for a direct action program on the war stemmed from their belief that this had worked on civil rights."[47] The leadership of the National Council of Churches by the mid-1960s included many individuals who came of age during the 1940s and were shaped by the ecumenical views of Christian realism and the social gospel. These leaders also shared the social gospel belief that churches had an obligation to educate Americans on wider social-political issues from a religious point of view. By 1966 the National Council of Churches began to issue statements calling for a ceasefire in Vietnam and a negotiated settlement. That same year, Clergy and Laymen Concerned about Vietnam (CALCAV) was founded as an effort among a cross section of religious leaders to stop American escalation of the war and work for a negotiated settlement. With a membership that included Abraham Heschel, the theologian Robert McAfee Brown, and the Yale chaplain and later Riverside Church senior minister William Sloane Coffin, CALCAV represented one of the first concerted efforts of antiwar mobilization by a religious group in the country.

Between 1966 and 1969, the National Council of Churches expressed increasing condemnation of American participation in Vietnam, repeatedly calling on the United States to pursue a negotiated settlement between North and South Vietnam. However, while the civil rights movement had garnered significant public support through the mid-1960s, American public opinion on Vietnam strongly supported U.S. intervention—a reality that would begin to change only after the North Vietnamese Tet offensive in January 1968. A wide range of religious leaders, including those in the National Council of Churches, frequently heard public accusations that they were far too radical, misinformed, and elitist in their antiwar advocacy.

The ecumenical movement became further separated from grassroots constituencies in 1966, when the World Council of Churches Life and Work Conference in Geneva, Switzerland, strongly condemned U.S. involvement in Vietnam. The Geneva conference revealed the growing participation of churches from the developing nations of the Southern Hemisphere, who challenged the theological and political suppositions of church leaders from North America and Western Europe. These leaders from emergent, "third world" nations castigated Western churches for their culpability in policies of colonialism and imperialism that kept these younger nations in a serf-like posture.

The response of many American religious leaders to these various developments was mixed. Many in the National Council of Churches attempted to respond favorably to these international ecumenical critiques of the war. However, a cross section of American church leaders saw Geneva as another sign that groups like the NCC were out of touch with "ordinary" church people, underscoring that the Geneva report did not speak for American Christians on a grassroots level.[48] By the late 1960s, ecumenical Protestant leaders began to experience something that had not occurred since the foundation of the Federal Council of Churches in 1908—they were increasingly denied access to political leaders in the executive branch of the government.

Although public opinion began to swing decisively against the war in 1968, many progressive bodies like the National Council of Churches found public witness difficult. Not only was the NCC attacked by conservatives who noted the organization's lack of grassroots appeal, it was accused by religious radicals of being too tied to the interests of its member churches. One consequence of this agitation is that the NCC lost the support of younger activists, who became part of an increasing pattern of desertion from mainline churches that would only escalate in the 1970s.[49]

As groups like the NCC mounted a social witness against Vietnam, Martin Luther King grew more strident in his critiques of American social-economic life.[50] On April 4, 1967, exactly one year before his assassination, King gave his first major public address against American involvement in Vietnam, delivered at Riverside Church in New York. King noted that America as a nation was charged to look beyond its own self-interests, in an effort to understand that the circumstances of the war were antithetical to a moral outlook: "We are called to speak for the weak, for the voiceless, for victims of our nation and for those it called enemy, for no document from human hands can make these humans any less our brothers."[51] King laid out steps that he hoped the U.S. government would follow for a ceasefire and troop withdrawal from Vietnam. He concluded his address with an observation that illustrated his liberal view of history, echoing Walter Rauschenbusch's assertion prior to World War I that historical opportunities for social change don't last for long. "In this unfolding conundrum of life and history there is such a thing as being too late," King asserted. "Procrastination is still the thief of time. Life often leaves us standing bare, naked and dejected with a lost opportunity. . . . There is an invisible book of life that faithfully records our vigilance or our neglect."[52]

King's sense of urgency was seen in the frenetic pace of his final year, not only opposing the Vietnam War but also drawing connections between the war and America's economic and political malaise. His assassination came on the eve of his efforts to organize a Poor People's Campaign in Washington, D.C., in order to engage in massive nonviolent protests aimed at changing the conditions facing poor people in the United States. On the Sunday before he died, King preached at the National Cathedral in Washington, expressing his concerns about America's moral plight, but also his hope that the nation was on the cusp of a great opportunity to transform itself:

> This can happen to America, the richest nation in the world—and nothing's wrong with that—this is America's opportunity to help bridge the gulf between the haves and the have-nots. The question is whether America will do it. There is nothing new about poverty. What is new is that we now have the techniques and the resources to get rid of poverty. The real question is whether we have the will.[53]

While King's social thought evolved in various ways after the Montgomery Bus Boycott in 1955–1956, his theology remained rooted in the suppositions of social gospel idealism. Like Howard Thurman and Benjamin Mays, King sought to show Americans how the African American experience was central to a larger vision of American culture that these thinkers believed was essential if America was to be, in King's words, "a society at peace with itself."[54] However, by the end of the 1960s, an emerging generation of African American leaders articulated goals that were very different from the interracial beloved community envisioned by Benjamin Mays, Howard Thurman, and Martin Luther King.

The Beloved Community Challenged: The Rise of Liberation Theology

On April 9, 1968, Benjamin Mays delivered the eulogy for Martin Luther King at Morehouse College. Now president emeritus of Morehouse, Mays noted in his sermon that he had hoped and expected that King would deliver Mays's own eulogy. While noting the tragedy of King's assassination and death at a young age, Mays asserted that King's life revealed the power of the prophets of scripture. "If Jesus was called to preach the Gospel to the poor, Martin Luther King, Jr. fits that designation. If a prophet is one who does not seek popular causes to espouse, but rather the causes he thinks are right Martin Luther qualified on that score."[55] Mays concluded his eulogy by emphasizing a theme that King had used in many of his major orations—that unearned suffering was redemptive:

> Let black and white alike search their hearts; and if there be prejudice in our hearts against any racial or ethnic group, let us exterminate it and let us pray, as Martin Luther King, Jr. would pray if he could: *Father, forgive them for they know not what they do.* If we do this, Martin Luther King, Jr. will have died a redemptive death from which all mankind will benefit.[56]

However, even before King's death, his idealistic vision of an integrated society was being challenged by a new generation of African American leaders and scholars. By the end of the 1960s, an earlier vision of social gospel liberalism was under assault not just from conservatives but also from increasingly radical voices in church and society. Critiques of racism by Malcolm X and Stokely Carmichael drew attention to issues of power and identity that reflected wider tensions that broke apart King's vision of beloved community. In the spring of 1969 James Foreman, a longtime civil rights activist in the Student Nonviolent Coordinating Committee (SNCC), staged a series of well-publicized demonstrations, including at Riverside Church and the headquarters of the National Council of Churches, demanding that millions of dollars in reparations be paid to African Americans for the ways that they had been victimized by slavery. Also in 1969, James Cone, a professor at Adrian College in Michigan, published his first major book, *Black Theology and Black Power*. This book was followed by *A Black Theology of Liberation*, which galvanized a wider movement of black liberation theology. Cone, who became a professor of theology at Union Seminary in 1970, asserted that the only way to understand scripture and Christian theology was through the category of God's "blackness." "Black Theology is survival theology because it seeks to provide the theological dimensions of the struggle for black identity. It seeks to reorder religious language, to show that all forces supporting white oppression are anti-Christian in their essence."[57] Cone directly challenged earlier social gospel liberal views that saw integration as the ultimate goal of racial justice. "The role of Black Theology is to tell black people to focus on their own self determination as a community by preparing to do anything which the community believed to be necessary for its existence."[58]

Cone's castigation of American Christianity exemplified how a wide range of American religious leaders reassessed their mission in the 1970s. The rise of black liberation theology underscored the belief of many African American leaders that King's moral vision of social reform had exhausted itself. Liberation theologians believed that their critiques of race "confronted more realistically the stubbornness of white racism, recognized an implicit whiteness in the ideal of integration, and demanded the hard currency of power over the bad credit of love."[59] By the end of the 1970s, several theologians followed James Cone's example by stressing the central importance of racial, ethnic, and gender identity among oppressed and marginalized groups, as opposed to earlier faith in creating an integrated society. Liberation theologians frequently shared a belief that more traditional forms of Christian theology did not take seriously the sufferings of oppressed people, whether African Americans, women, Latinos, or, by the end of the twentieth century, movements of lesbian, gay, bisexual, and transgender liberation, or what has often been referred to as queer theology.

Liberation theology dramatically transformed the study of American theology in the late twentieth century, epitomized by the attention received by this movement in the nation's leading theological seminaries. However, liberation theology, like many brands of social gospel liberalism that preceded it, was often judged by critics as elitist, and not necessarily translatable to the real-life conditions of grassroots communities. In many ways, the end of the 1960s represented a collapse of the broadly based Protestant social gospel hope to unify the nation around concerted ecumenical activism. On one hand, historians have noted that the statements coming from the National Council of Churches and other religious bodies played an important role in helping to foster a wider public discussion on Vietnam that led to a shift in public opinion toward the war by 1968. By the same token, the NCC found itself, much like the Interchurch World Movement in the early 1920s, struggling to secure grassroots support. By the early 1970s, the NCC was struggling financially and was forced to dramatically cut its staffing.

In the 1970s and 1980s, public disillusionment over many aspects of leftist-based religious activism would feed into the growth of conservative evangelical political activism. In many ways, these religious conservatives became the heirs of the social gospel movement in American religion, as they often carried on earlier social gospel visions of using religious faith to unite the nation—even as they rejected the progressive political and theological orientations of the classic social gospel.

Conclusion

In 1943 Howard Thurman delivered the commencement address at Garrett Biblical Institute in Evanston, Illinois. At a moment when World War II was at its height, he asserted his faith in a peaceful world that would unite the world's peoples in a common social fabric of brotherhood: "We must proclaim the truth that all life is one and that we are all of us tied together. Therefore it is mandatory that we work for a society in which the least person can find refuge and refreshment." Thurman issued a plea to the graduates who were about to enter the Christian ministry that they needed to be prophets in the face of international uncertainty, concluding, "You must live and proclaim a faith that will make men affirm themselves and their fellowmen as children of God. You must lay your lives on the altar of social change so that whatever you are there the Kingdom of God is at hand!"[60] The causes Thurman advocated—nonviolence, internationalism, and the hope of a vision of social/cultural unity—were foundational social gospel themes of the mid-twentieth century that also influenced Martin Luther King and the nonviolent phase of the civil rights movement from 1955 to 1965.

Seen in the broader context of the twentieth century, the civil rights era represented the culmination of the social gospel's influence on the religious and cultural landscape of America. Highlighted by the work of Martin Luther King, earlier themes associated with the classic social gospel tradition of Walter Rauschenbusch were reformulated into one of the most influential social movements in American history. The legislative successes of the civil rights movement, particularly the passing of the Civil Rights Act of 1964, the Voting Rights Act of 1965, and the Fair Housing Act of 1968, were partly achieved by the religious activism inspired by King. Like earlier social gospel leaders, King appealed to the power of moral suasion to change the hearts and minds of Americans.

After King's assassination in 1968, however, the liberalism of the social gospel was critiqued and challenged by religious and secular voices on the left, as seen in public disillusionment with the Vietnam War and the movement toward liberation theology. Further, the activism of organizations like the NCC illustrates wider ruptures that were taking place in American religious institutions that signified waning public support of more radical political solutions to the nation's social problems. As the historian James Findley Jr. observes, while ecumenical Protestants elevated the social gospel's legacy during the 1960s, "in retrospect one can view the involvement of the churches in the civil rights movement of the sixties as a last hurrah of sorts of the [Protestant] establishment."[61]

By the early 1970s, numerous commentators began to discuss the decline of churches that supported the historical social gospel, including the Episcopalians, Presbyterians, Congregationalists, and the largest mainline tradition, the Methodists. These studies often took note that the social gospel commitments of church leaders did not match the attitudes of those who sat in the pews. In 1972 Dean Hoge, a sociologist working for the National Council of Churches, published a study finding that conservative churches—those that stressed a strict theology and an otherworldly orientation—were growing. Hoge's study would be debated by scholars for decades. However, during the late twentieth century conservative religious groups experienced a significant upturn in growth, and some scholars asserted that it was these churches, rather than the more liberal ones, that now represented the true American mainline.[62] As the mainline Protestant denominations struggled during the 1970s to reassess their mission, conservative religious movements found themselves embracing the cultural mantle of the social gospel mission to save America, even as they rejected its theology and its political agendas.

Not only does Martin Luther King's life embody numerous aspects of the social gospel's legacy in America, but his career symbolizes the institutional peak and the decline of the social gospel as a progressive institutional movement in American religion. The years following King's assassination in 1968 were marked by increasing contention and division over strategies of social change that reflected how many religious communities, especially in mainline Protestantism, were struggling to articulate their message amid declining public stature. From the 1970s on, institutional forms of religious activism that have sought to propagate the legacy of figures like Rauschenbusch and King have often struggled to define their message, their objectives, and the means to change society. The idea that religion could shape national identity and public policies was no longer championed by the heirs of the social gospel on the left; in fact, by the end of the 1970s, that idea would be embraced by what became known as the Christian Right.

7

An Evangelical Social Gospel?

The Christian Right and Progressive Evangelicalism

In 2008 the popular evangelist and author Rick Warren referred to the social gospel as "Marxism in Christian clothing."[1] Warren's assertion could have been uttered by any number of conservative critics of the social gospel movement since the early twentieth century. Yet, at the same time that he castigated the social gospel as incompatible with the Bible, Warren reflected a late twentieth-century shift among many evangelicals toward a vigorous engagement with social issues. In the early 1980s an eclectic coalition of evangelicals and conservative Catholics helped to forge what became known as the Christian Right. Ronald Reagan's election in 1980 signaled a major sea change not only in American politics, but also in American religion.

For much of the twentieth century, religious movements allied with the social gospel played the dominant role in public advocacy, endorsing a range of progressive political causes. However, in the final decades of the twentieth century, the most prominent calls for political change in American religion came from leaders who allied themselves with conservative movements. These groups built on a template used by religious conservatives earlier in the twentieth century in their support of pro-capitalist and anticommunist policies. Yet what distinguished the late twentieth-century conservative Christian activists was their advocacy of a variety of "family values" issues rooted in support of school prayer, anti-abortion, and anti–gay rights campaigns. These issues placed religious conservatives at the center of what became known in the late twentieth century as the "culture wars." A variety of liberal political and religious groups castigated the Christian Right for what they saw as the movement's exclusionary and homogeneous vision of America. However, many progressives failed to notice how this conservative resurgence resembled aspects of the classic social gospel movement of the early twentieth century. While an increasing number of leaders who came out of churches with historical connections to the earlier social gospel distanced themselves from earlier rhetoric of making America a Protestant nation, numerous evangelicals picked up the older social gospel quest to "Christianize" America, even as most of them rejected the progressive political and theological visions espoused by social gospel leaders like Walter Rauschenbusch.

By the late twentieth century, churches and religious activists who identified with liberal mainline churches increasingly embraced leftist political causes and advocated for religious and cultural pluralism—stances that often put them at odds with the religious right. The historian David Hollinger observes that as more social gospel and ecumenically oriented Protestants lost their public influence after the 1960s, conservative evangelicals thrived in part by affirming a traditional vision of American homogeneity. "Politically and theologically conservative evangelicals flourished while continuing to espouse popular ideas about the nation and the world that were criticized and abandoned by liberalizing, diversity-accepting ecumenists."[2] Despite the fact that many conservatives would not identify themselves openly with the tradition of the social gospel, their mission, at points, coincided with one of the primary goals of the early social gospel: to use religion as a means to unify the nation.

Early twentieth-century social gospelers were unequivocal in their belief that part of the purpose of "social salvation" was to create a "Christian America," in which religion, specifically Protestantism, would play a dominant role in shaping the political values of the nation. Even as various proponents of the social gospel differed on matters of theology and specific policies, they appealed to a broader vision of national unity that came about through religious faith. Yet the fallout from the 1960s—which increasingly moved liberal churches to engage issues such as feminism and African American liberation—created uncertainty among many mainline Protestant heirs of the social gospel regarding whether such visions of national unity forged by religious faith were still possible, or even desirable. During the 1970s and 1980s, the growth of liberation theologies and the decline in mainline Protestant membership led many individuals associated with the religious left to acknowledge institutional complacency in the face of patriarchy, racism, nationalism, and homophobia, and a taken-for-granted sense of cultural privilege. For many conservative evangelicals, however, these positions of liberal churches reflected not only a concession to secular norms of cultural pluralism, but an abandonment of the long-standing Protestant goal to Christianize America in terms of personal morality and public policy. Increasingly conservatives argued that their traditions could save America from godlessness by bringing religion back to shape the public values of the nation.

Francis Schaeffer and the Anti-Abortion Movement

During the first half of his life, Francis Schaeffer was a little-known fundamentalist preacher who largely accepted the view that there was little value in modern America outside the saving message of Christianity. Ordained into a conservative Presbyterian denomination, he was a follower early in his ministry of the firebrand fundamentalist Carl McIntire. Not only did McIntire support biblical inerrancy—rejecting liberal interpretations of biblical higher criticism—but from the late 1930s until his death in 2002, he repeatedly attacked liberal religious groups for their apostate doctrines and their liberal politics of social reform. In the 1950s and 1960s he was a critic of Billy Graham, believing that Graham compromised his theology to attract a popular audience. McIntire espoused a dispensationalist theology of the end times, while also stressing the dangers to America posed by the Soviet Union and communism.

By the 1950s, however, Schaeffer's commitment to a hardcore fundamentalism began to soften. After spending years living in Europe, in 1955 Schaeffer and his wife, Edith, established L'Abri (the Shelter) in a chalet in the rural Swiss Alps. In the years ahead, L'Abri became a place of refuge for a number of restless youth who found themselves disillusioned with their lives and in search of personal direction. By the 1960s, L'Abri became associated with an evangelical Protestant model of the 1960s counterculture—and Schaeffer looked the part of a middle-aged hippie. He grew his hair long, sported a goatee, and often wore Swiss knickers, becoming a popular lecturer at evangelical colleges in the United States throughout the 1960s and 1970s. Schaeffer identified himself as a Christian philosopher, who could reference in his lectures and sermons a disparate range of figures from Jean-Paul Sartre to the Beatles.[3]

However, the core of his theology was a rarefied conservative evangelicalism. As many scholars have noted, Schaeffer's theology was at times hard to place. In the 1960s he was drawn for a time to a position known as Christian Reconstructionism, a movement whose members believed that secular society needs to be ordered and maintained according to the precepts of biblical (specifically Old Testament) law. Although Schaeffer rejected extreme interpretations of this worldview, he increasingly became convinced that the foundations of American democracy rested on Protestant Christianity, since America was originally established as a Christian nation. Schaeffer's refurbished version of an argument used by many Protestants since the time of the Civil War became the basis for his rising popularity in the 1960s. During the 1970s and 1980s he exerted a major influence on the rise of the Christian Right.

In the late 1970s Schaeffer and his son, Frank, produced two highly successful films among evangelicals: *How Shall We Then Live?* and *Whatever Happened to the Human Race?* These films underscored a common message in Schaeffer's theology—namely, that the Western world had abandoned a philosophical worldview rooted in Christianity and instead embraced an ideology grounded in "secular humanism." Schaeffer was not always precise about his use of this term; basically, he believed that Western society was abandoning God and putting its trust in false notions of human superiority. As he saw it, "either anarchy, tyranny, or the imposition of the will of the majority—no matter how corrupt—would prevail, and minorities and the defenseless would have no protection from a society that no longer acknowledged the absolute value of human life."[4] Schaeffer blamed the Enlightenment not only for leading Westerners to abandon God, but also for a wide range of contemporary moral and ethical abominations, the most striking of which, for Schaeffer, was legalized abortion.

By the early 1980s, conservative Christians became strongly associated with the leadership of the anti-abortion movement—a cause that had been largely ignored by evangelicals during the 1970s. The 1973 Supreme Court *Roe v. Wade* decision legalizing abortion created little initial stir among most evangelical Protestants, the vast majority of whom saw abortion as a Roman Catholic issue. Scholars have pointed out that the rise of the Christian Right had more to do with efforts of evangelicals to preserve the tax-exempt status of fundamentalist-related colleges than it did fighting abortion.[5] In the aftermath of the *Roe* decision, some evangelical churches, including the Southern Baptist Convention, even passed resolutions praising the *Roe* decision, seeing abortion primarily as a woman's choice. By the late 1970s, however, evangelicals like Schaeffer were beginning to frame abortion as a critical issue to mobilize conservative activism.

For Schaeffer, and increasingly other evangelical activists like Jerry Falwell, abortion came to symbolize the triumph of a humanistic "liberal" worldview over the biblical values of Christianity. These evangelicals argued that abortion was nothing short of genocide; Falwell himself noted that "abortion is a weapon that has annihilated more children than Pharaoh murdered in Egypt, than Herod murdered when seeking the Christ child, than the Nazis slaughtered of the Jews in World War II."[6] The foundation of the Moral Majority in 1979 was a milestone in the emergence of the late twentieth-century Christian Right. Although the Moral Majority seized upon the abortion issue, the organization also embraced a staunch anticommunist platform and firmly supported conservative free market economic policies, positions that aligned perfectly with the politics of Ronald Reagan.

At the same time, leaders like Francis Schaeffer and Jerry Falwell reinterpreted a long-standing tradition related to evangelism's role in shaping a Christian culture in America. Schaeffer insisted that all of the most permanent social institutions in America, including democracy, were the products of the Protestant Reformation. As his biographer, Barry Hankins, noted, "Only with a Christian worldview . . . could freedom be kept from degenerating into chaos. Thus the replacement of the Christian base of American government with the humanist worldview would lead either to chaos—the lack of form—or to authoritarian government—the lack of freedom."[7] For Schaeffer and many of his allies on the Christian Right, proclaiming the truths of Christianity was necessary in order to return America to a lost state of grace.

Schaeffer's theological commitments were firmly rooted in the traditions of American fundamentalism and a more moderate neo-evangelicalism often associated with the rise of Billy Graham in the 1940s and 1950s. However, he helped to forge a template of conservative social activism echoing the early twentieth-century social gospel. Schaeffer believed that religion had the power to transform the social

mores of American culture. At times his rhetoric came across as politically radical in his attacks on American affluence and, in certain moments, his defense of the environment from industrial pollution. By the
end of the 1970s, however, Schaeffer's anti-abortion message increasingly found a hearing among conservative evangelicals, not only to
lobby against abortion, but to advance a broader conservative political
agenda against "secular humanism."

Francis Schaeffer's message would increasingly be used by religious
conservatives in the 1980s and 1990s to rewrite the story of Christianity's
role in American history. Like Walter Rauschenbusch and other figures
of the classic social gospel era, these conservatives believed that American society needed models of faith-based activism to redeem the nation.
Yet while the tradition of the progressive-based social gospel saw religious faith as a means to create systemic structural changes in American society, conservatives like Schaeffer wanted to return America to
the perceived purity of an earlier era in the nation's history, an America
dominated by evangelical Protestant presuppositions.[8]

The Christian Right and the Legacy of Martin Luther King

In the 1980s and 1990s, influential leaders of the Christian Right attacked
a range of liberal-progressive groups that they associated with the wider
problems of secular humanism. At the same time, many prominent
conservatives appropriated selective parts of the social gospel's heritage.
Many evangelical activists used the legacy of Martin Luther King in
particular, connecting King's nonviolent direct action campaigns of the
1950s and 1960s to the anti-abortion movement. One prominent evangelical activist who regularly appealed to King was Randall Terry, head
of the anti-abortion group Operation Rescue. Terry was a minister in
the Elim Gospel Church, a small pentecostal-leaning movement. Operation Rescue was founded in November 1987, and within a few years the
group had staged a range of nonviolent demonstrations at abortion clin-
ics throughout the country, attracting the support of an eclectic array
of conservative Protestant and Catholic activists. Terry viewed Martin
Luther King as his personal hero, and increasingly conservative evangelical groups employed nonviolent tactics in a range of protests, including

anti-abortion rallies and, by the early twenty-first century, anti–gay rights demonstrations.

Terry's rise to prominence in the late 1980s reflected a change of tactics among many conservatives in their broader strategy to "Christianize" America. Like early twentieth-century social gospel leaders, conservative Christian groups in the early 1980s such as the Moral Majority made it their mission to lobby influential political leaders. In the early years of Ronald Reagan's presidency, Moral Majority leaders like Jerry Falwell were flush with the sense of a rising political status, as they were regularly invited to meet with Reagan and his key advisors. Just as previous American presidents had courted influential figures associated with the Federal and National Council of Churches, in many ways Reagan's presidency seemed to brand evangelicals as the country's new "mainline" religious body. Throughout Reagan's administration, these conservatives had direct access to the president and other key political leaders in numerous high-profile gatherings, similar to the public access enjoyed by liberal Protestant ecumenical leaders prior to the Vietnam War. However, the stature of prominent conservative evangelical ministers like Falwell, Charles Colson, and James Dobson didn't last. Efforts to get Reagan to push federal anti-abortion legislation were unsuccessful, and the election of George H. W. Bush in 1988 signaled that perhaps the impact of religious conservatism had crested. By the end of the 1980s, however, a new conservative Christian group emerged that dramatically succeeded in building a grassroots movement of political activism: the Christian Coalition.

While Francis Schaeffer played a major role in galvanizing evangelical Protestants to public activism in the 1970s, and Jerry Falwell became an embodiment of that activism for much of the 1980s through the Moral Majority, no figure did more to ground the Christian Right in both an ideological and political strategy in the 1990s than Ralph Reed. Raised a Methodist, Reed gained his early experience as an organizer for the Republican Party in college. After a conversion experience while attending an evangelical nondenominational church and graduate school at Emory University, where he received a Ph.D. in history, Reed emerged by the late 1980s as one of the most effective Republican political strategists. Along with Pat Robertson, in 1989 Reed launched the Christian

Coalition out of a desire to reinvigorate an evangelical grassroots base in American politics.

Like Jerry Falwell, Reed wanted to pass legislation that reflected what he saw as an evangelical "pro-family" agenda. Yet the Christian Coalition proved much more effective as a political organization. In contrast to the Moral Majority, which primarily sought to pass legislation on a federal government level, Reed concentrated his energies on grassroots organizing. In its early years the Christian Coalition succeeded in mobilizing conservative political candidates on a state and local level. With its election guides that steered potential voters to its slate of "Christian" candidates—those who took strong positions against abortion and embraced other politically conservative causes—Reed believed that evangelical Christians were using their faith to restore America to its greatness. "For today, religious conservatives are poised to enter an era of American life in which moral issues, and the pro-family agenda, will predominate."[9]

In his 1996 book *Active Faith*, Reed appealed to the wider history of evangelical social action in American history, extending from the First Great Awakening to the social witnesses of Charles Finney and Frances Willard in the nineteenth century, and the civil rights movement in the twentieth century. Notably, his historical assessment of evangelical social action positively highlights the model of the classic social gospel, particularly the thought of Walter Rauschenbusch. Reed conceded that aspects of the social gospel legacy were problematic for him, especially its anticapitalist tendencies and the desire to promote government solutions, rather than seeing churches as the natural place to engage in grassroots social change. Yet Reed saw the social gospel as a historical movement that demonstrated how Christian values might influence national politics in ways that could inspire contemporary evangelical social action. Like religious conservatives in the 1980s, Reed strongly identified with the legacy of Martin Luther King, seeing in King the basis by which evangelicals could challenge what Reed perceived as anti-Christian laws related to abortion and gay rights.

Reed accurately noted the affinities between social gospel leaders like Walter Rauschenbusch and Martin Luther King and earlier traditions of historical American evangelicalism, especially in its pre–Civil War postmillennial varieties. Yet Reed's lack of historical nuance is evident when he notes that most social gospelers "retained many traditional Christian tenets, such as belief in a sovereign, all-powerful God; the imminent millennial return of Christ; and the power of prayer."[10] While theological liberals like Rauschenbusch and King certainly stressed prayer and spirituality, none of the major social gospel figures embraced premillennialism, and they stressed a liberal Protestant doctrine of divine immanence as opposed to divine sovereignty.

However, in many ways the Christian Coalition accomplished what Walter Rauschenbusch and other social gospelers never fully could in the early twentieth century: a religious movement that empowered grassroots constituencies to engage in concerted political action. The high-water mark for the Christian Coalition occurred during the 1994 elections, when conservative Republicans took control of both the House and Senate by substantial majorities. Emboldened by Representative Newt Gingrich's "Contract with America," the new Congress promised to deliver on an agenda shaped by Christian conservatives like Reed. But while the Christian Coalition remained active in the early twenty-first century, it found itself losing its political muscle in the face of scandal, marked by the eventual resignation of Ralph Reed, and its splintering into other conservative movements.

The rise of the Christian Right in the 1980s and 1990s demonstrates how the cultural mantle of American Protestantism was passing from liberal mainline denominations to conservative evangelical churches. These movements have often been criticized as being theocratic, or part of a wider movement of Christian Reconstructionism. At the same time, the rhetoric of several twenty-first-century political leaders such as former congresswoman Michele Bachmann and former Texas governor Rick Perry reflects long-standing conservative religious claims that American democracy is rooted in the suppositions of evangelical Christianity.[11]

Ironically, both the progressive social gospel tradition and the late twentieth-century Christian Right share a rhetoric that often equates Christianity with the "sacred" precepts of American democracy. While the social gospel strongly identified democracy with the social-political initiatives emerging from a range of liberal and radical political movements, figures like Falwell and Reed embraced the broader conservative economic agenda, supporting limited government and a pro-business agenda. Further, religious conservatives attacked liberals associated with the nation's mainline Protestant churches for abandoning Christian teaching in favor of secular norms and ideals. These accusations were coming not only from predominantly conservative churches, but increasingly from evangelicals within the historical mainline churches that gave birth to the social gospel.

Mainline Religion and Conservative Resurgence

Despite the association of the Christian Right with churches and leaders that were independent from liberal churches, several religious conservatives in the late twentieth century had developed a strong base within more liberal, mainline Protestant churches. Throughout the rise of the social gospel in the twentieth century, these leaders struggled with the challenge of gaining grassroots support. Although the movement interpenetrated networks of clergy and influential laity—especially among college-age young adults—the 1960s witnessed a renewed effort within several Protestant denominations of religious conservatives to stave off the influence of liberals.

Throughout the twentieth century, conservative resistance to various iterations of the social gospel had been strong within mainline Protestantism. In the aftermath of the social and cultural upheavals of the 1960s, a new generation of activists emerged in these churches, representing a coalition of more traditional Protestant evangelicals and individuals often dubbed "neoconservatives" for their embrace of anticommunism and support of free enterprise economic theory. This synergy can be seen in the founding in 1981 of the Institute for Religion and Democracy (IRD). The IRD was established by a number of leading American neoconservatives, the most prominent being Richard Neuhaus. In the 1960s Neuhaus had been a leading voice in the ecumenical movement and a staunch critic of the Vietnam War. By the end of the 1970s, however, like many former activists in the 1960s, he shifted toward the political right.[12] Neuhaus served as the principal author of the IRD's founding manifesto in 1981, noting that its mission was to extend "an invitation to Christian leadership in this country to consider the Christian stake and the Christian warrant for democratic government."[13] Neuhaus's manifesto echoed social gospel themes from earlier in the twentieth century by calling on the church to stand above political partisanship and by affirming the need for the church to become "a zone of truth-telling in a world of mendacity."[14]

On the other hand, Neuhaus, like John Foster Dulles in the 1940s and 1950s, made clear assertions in his IRD manifesto that Christianity could exist only in societies made up of free economic markets. Echoing strong anticommunist themes, Neuhaus's arguments in the IRD manifesto are remarkably similar to the themes articulated by evangelists like Francis Schaeffer and Jerry Falwell in that the greatest threats to American religion, and to Christianity in particular, were international communism, legalized abortion, and the misguided social witness of the political left.

The IRD manifesto reflected long-simmering tensions within mainline Protestant churches that were especially acute in American Methodism. For much of the twentieth century, Methodism had been at the center of the ecumenical Protestant establishment. While the Methodist Church would be overtaken by the Southern Baptist Convention in the 1960s as the largest Protestant church in the country, with over ten million members, Methodism was a denomination with a strong national membership base. Perhaps more than any other mainline denomination, Methodism played a leading role in the spread of the social gospel in twentieth-century American Protestantism. Its leaders crafted the first Protestant social creed, and Methodism had a preeminent role in the institutionalization of the social gospel in denominational and ecumenical bodies. Methodist leaders also were at the center of the civil rights movement and the anti–Vietnam War campaigns.

At the same time, Methodist churches had a long history of conservative resistance that dated from the founding of the Methodist Federation for Social Service in 1907. In 1967 influential conservatives in Methodism formed the Good News Movement, which emphasized biblical orthodoxy, stressing belief in the centrality of scripture, the substitutionary atonement, and the physical resurrection of Christ. The movement also castigated the social witness of Methodism, claiming that the church had moved away from a mandate to save souls as the primary means to engage in the reform of society. For many of the evangelicals in Good News, eradicating the influence of the social gospel was central to the organization's mission. For these leaders, the social gospel's emphasis on collective salvation obscured the importance of personal faith formation and of what these evangelicals saw as the timeless truths of scripture.

The Good News Movement, along with other Protestant evangelical groups that have enjoyed close affiliation with conservative lobby groups such as the Institute for Religion and Democracy, often resisted being identified with the doctrinal rigidity associated with early twentieth-century Protestant fundamentalism. Nevertheless, groups like Good News take a firm position that the basic teachings of Christianity are immutable. In the 1990s the Confessing Movement, an organization with ties to the Good News Movement, attacked liberals in the church for their theological relativism, and the sacrifice of United Methodism's "historic faith for political, therapeutic, sexual, or gender-based ideologies with religious veneers."[15]

The emphasis that Good News places on a return to scripture and church teaching was most publicly visible in late twentieth-century mainline Protestant debates over the inclusion of lesbian, gay, bisexual, and transgender persons. Until the 1970s, issues like abortion and LGBT rights were not major topics for discussion in mainline Protestant churches. It wasn't until 1972 that the United Methodist Church passed a resolution that declared homosexuality incompatible with Christian teaching. Over the course of the next two decades, United Methodist General Conferences endorsed stronger prohibitions against gay marriage as well as barring "self-avowed homosexuals" from being ordained.[16]

For many conservatives who resist ordaining gay and lesbian individuals, one persistent argument has been that any acceptance of homosexuality means embracing the predominant secular values of the world rather than what these leaders see as the timeless truths of Christianity. Like Francis Schaeffer in his critiques of "secular humanism," mainline Protestant evangelicals have argued that liberals who carry on the tradition of the social gospel are not only relativizing scripture in favor of social activism, but are being held captive by secular norms rather than gospel ones. "If you are being led by a spirit to do something that is contrary to the Word of God, you must test the spirit because it is clearly not the Spirit of God," one United Methodist evangelical asserted. While liberals elevate human knowledge over scripture, "we on the other hand believe that Jesus Christ is the same yesterday, today, and forever."[17]

The battle for LGBT rights in mainline denominations like the United Methodist Church underscored the deep religious divisions that exist in twenty-first-century American society. Religious conservatives who oppose LGBT rights tend to base their arguments on a traditional view of the family that emerges out of what they see as the timeless truth of the Bible. Liberals counter that the issue of LGBT inclusion is centered on a vision of God's inclusiveness, promoting the idea that God is actively engaged in driving out prejudice in the culture.

In their own way, each side of this social divide relies on different historical strands coming out of the social gospel legacy. For liberals, the central issues surrounding LGBT rights are inclusion, pluralism, and the comparisons between LGBT battles for justice and the civil rights movement.[18] Conservatives often see the issue as a conflict between a society governed by religious values and a secular society that excludes God. As these debates continue, however, a small but vocal group of evangelical Protestants, while embracing a more traditional theology, has channeled its understanding of that tradition in a politically progressive manner.

Evangelical Progressivism: A New Social Gospel?

While many evangelicals like Randall Terry and Ralph Reed identified Martin Luther King as a personal hero and a model of Christian faith and social action, there was little or no acknowledgment among these leaders of King's political radicalism, or the fact that his theology was heavily derived from the liberal Protestant legacy of the social gospel. In 2008 *Christianity Today*, a magazine with deep roots in the mid-twentieth-century legacy of American evangelicalism, contrasted the biblical Christianity of King to a dying brand of religious liberalism: "The belief that an 'experiential,' humanistic perspective on the Christian story is more accessible and appealing is proving not to be the case; several decades of this thin gruel have left us without any transcendent dimension to draw upon, either for social action or for individual regeneration."[19] This is a common perspective not only of religious conservatives, but also of proponents of what has been called "progressive evangelicalism."

This particular brand of evangelicalism helped to galvanize nineteenth-century movements for social change, such as abolitionism, and never fully disappeared from the American landscape. In the aftermath of the fundamentalist battles of the 1920s and 1930s, a group of evangelicals emerged who challenged what they saw as the social complacency of their tradition. In 1948 Carl Henry, a Baptist minister, published *The Uneasy Conscience of Fundamentalism*. Henry was clear that he was not interested in forging theological alliances with liberal modernists; however, he chastised many evangelicals for turning their backs on some of the major social issues of the time. "No evangelicalism which ignores the totality of man's condition dares respond in the name of Christianity," Henry asserted. "Though the modern crisis is not basically political, economic or social, fundamentally it is religious, yet evangelicalism must be armed to declare the implications of its proposed religious solution for the politico-economic and sociological context for modern life."[20]

Henry was part of a vanguard of religious leaders, including Billy Graham and Harold Ockenga, pastor of the historic Park Street Church in Boston, who became identified with the term "neo-evangelical." While these evangelicals often agreed on core doctrinal principles for defining their beliefs, they frequently embraced a more irenic view of other Christian communions, shunning the separatist fundamentalism associated with ministers such as Carl McIntire.[21] By the 1960s and 1970s, some of the leaders of the neo-evangelical movement moved in the direction of the Christian Right. However, in the 1960s, aspects of Henry's message were translated into more progressive models of social action by young evangelicals.

The modern tradition of progressive evangelicalism owes its inception to the social-political unrest in the late 1960s caused by the civil rights movement and the Vietnam War. Although members of this movement looked with pride to early nineteenth-century evangelical leadership in the abolitionist movement, the movement emerged as a reaction against most traditional evangelical complacency in the face of growing campaigns for social equality and antiwar activism. Drawn to the example of Martin Luther King, the primary spokespersons for this new movement, such as Ron Sider, Jim Wallis, John Howard Yoder, and Tony Campolo, threw their support behind the civil rights and antiwar movements, as well as backing political candidates who supported President Lyndon Johnson's "Great Society" social welfare programs designed to eliminate poverty in America. These activists were especially attracted to the progressive politics of political leaders like Senators Mark Hatfield and George McGovern, two politicians who embraced their evangelical backgrounds while pursuing a range of liberal political causes.

Many progressive evangelicals were drawn to George McGovern's 1972 presidential campaign. McGovern had impeccable credentials as an evangelical and a social gospel liberal. He was raised in a Wesleyan Methodist church, a mid-nineteenth-century evangelical denomination that had been formed prior to the Civil War as an antislavery church. McGovern had planned to enter the ministry, and for a time he attended Garrett Biblical Institute, where he heard sermons from the social gospel preacher Ernest Fremont Tittle, pastor of First Methodist Church in Evanston, Illinois. By the time of McGovern's presidential campaign, he was an active United Methodist layperson with a strong grounding in wider traditions of the Protestant social gospel and mid-twentieth-century Protestant ecumenical theology. In a 1972 essay written for a festschrift in honor of the Boston University School of Theology dean Walter G. Muelder, McGovern noted how the mainstream of the Judeo-Christian heritage, including the social gospel, had "been committed to aiding the dispossessed, striving for justice, and improving human conditions through political channels."[22] However, McGovern warned that while religion's role in the public square was important, he worried about religious zealotry that would create a self-righteousness that was resistant to political compromise: "The true believer is always a greater threat in politics than either the cynical realist or the naïve idealist."[23]

Support for McGovern in the 1972 presidential election among evangelical Protestants was small. However, it galvanized a faction of young evangelical leaders who saw in his candidacy the making of a wider movement of social engagement. A manifesto drafted by evangelical activists affirmed their support for McGovern, whose policies were seen as a greater reflection of God's will for humanity: "Social structures which favor the rich displease our God. Policies . . . which are designed to slow down or reverse racial progress grieve the One whose eternal Son became incarnate in the Middle East." While conceding that electing McGovern wouldn't usher in the kingdom of God, it "does offer the hope of taking some significant steps toward greater justice in national and international society."[24]

Despite McGovern's defeat, the cadre of evangelical activists that formed the group Evangelicals for McGovern expanded into a broader coalition to promote a progressive interpretation of religion and reform. In 1973 prominent evangelical activists led by Ron Sider formed Evangelicals for Social Action. Its principles, set forth in its founding document, "The Chicago Declaration," summarized many tenets of progressive evangelical social conscience, calling upon those in the movement to repent "of evangelical silence in the face of racism, materialism, militarism, sexism, and articulated the strongest statement to date from twentieth-century evangelicals in support of social justice."[25] In the final decades of the twentieth century, progressive evangelicals built alliances with many religious groups associated with mainline Protestantism and the religious left, especially surrounding issues of distributive economic justice, antiracism, and support of women's equality. However, they often parted company with liberals on one issue: abortion. Even as progressive evangelicals have endorsed a "pro-life" policy, the political suppositions surrounding their pro-life stance differ from those of conservatives. The historian Daniel K. Williams observes that these progressives differed from their conservative colleagues on how to frame the abortion issue. While conservatives took the strategy that the best way to change abortion policy was to vote for anti-abortion candidates and to overturn *Roe v. Wade*, progressive evangelicals advocated funding for social welfare programs to support pregnant women. Further, progressives had no interest in supporting "so-called prolife political candidates whose policies on nuclear arms buildup and other life issues [such as capital punishment] were diametrically opposed to their values."[26] Paradoxically, the progressive evangelical movement has often identified itself with "family values" issues favored by the religious right, such as its opposition to abortion and later in the twenty-first century on issues of marriage equality. Yet much of its social-economic advocacy has been reminiscent of the social gospel's historical advocacy for a redistribution of wealth, continuously emphasizing Jesus's preferential treatment of the poor.

The historian Brantley Gasaway has termed the progressive evangelical movement "politically homeless."[27] Although many of the movement's positions often paralleled the political positions taken by liberal Protestants, evangelicals like Sider and Wallis insisted that their social policies were determined by fidelity to scripture. Striking a public posture that echoed the rhetoric of the Christian Right, Ron Sider observed that "American public life needs to be shaped by biblical principles."[28] This stance has engendered criticism from secular (and some religious) reformers on the left who argue that progressive evangelicals, like their conservative counterparts, are infringing on the separation of church and state. However, in many ways progressive evangelicals manifest an earlier social gospel desire to create a form of "Christianized" society that, like Rauschenbusch's approach, embraces redistributive social-economic policies. The late twentieth-century tradition of progressive evangelicalism did not win the public prominence of conservative evangelical movements associated with the Christian Right. However, some of the movement's leaders, particularly Jim Wallis, have achieved a high degree of public visibility.

Like many progressive evangelicals coming out of the baby boom generation, Wallis was disillusioned by the cultural insulation that characterized the response of many evangelicals to the social issues of the 1960s. As a student at Michigan State University, Wallis had his first taste of activist politics through his involvement in the organization Students for a Democratic Society. In the aftermath of George McGovern's defeat in 1972, Wallis poured his efforts into journalism, becoming editor of *Sojourners* magazine, a publication that would ultimately become one of the most widely read publications of the Christian left. In the 1980s Wallis was at the center of a coalition of religious leaders who vigorously opposed the foreign policy initiatives of Ronald Reagan, helping to organize a wide range of public demonstrations against the escalation of nuclear weapons, including Reagan's Strategic Defense Initiative (popularly referred to as "Star Wars") in 1983.

Although Wallis was highly critical of religious conservatism, his work evinces certain historical characteristics of evangelical political activism, including many themes associated with social gospel leaders like Walter Rauschenbusch. In his 2005 book *God's Politics*, Wallis lamented the absence of religious voices in the public square of American politics. "Society and politics both shape and reflect our spiritual values, and these values are increasingly empty," he asserted. "How does a nation of endangered souls recover an authentic faith that is true to the gospel, the example of Jesus, the witness of the prophets, and the crushing needs of our times?"[29] While Wallis affirmed his belief in the separation of church and state, he believed that "spiritual values still undergird everything and are reflected in the society we live in, the social and political directions we choose, and the candidates we select."[30]

Although Wallis articulates a pluralistic view of religion's role in America, one that includes Christian and non-Christian voices, he embodies a long-standing tension in the history of American Protestantism. For Wallis, as for Walter Rauschenbusch, Francis Schaeffer, and Ralph Reed, religion's role was to shape the nation's political direction— even as these figures differed regarding the specific models of social reform that Christians should embrace. Yet, even as the use of the term "social gospel" might be anathema for some early twenty-first-century evangelicals like Rick Warren, we can see signs that Shailer Mathews's 1921 definition of the social gospel as "the application of the teaching of Jesus and the total message of the Christian salvation" has taken on varied meaning among a wide range of American evangelicals.

By the early twenty-first century, new currents of progressive evangelicalism were emerging in America. While sharing some affinities with progressive evangelicals like Jim Wallis, figures like Brian McLaren and Rob Bell were engaging models of belief and practice that often placed them at odds with others in the evangelical community. McLaren was one of the major voices behind the late twentieth-century "Emergent Church" movement. In the face of the perceived failures of modernity, evangelicals like McLaren called for a reconceptualization of Christianity that could reconcile disparate aspects of Christian tradition. Part of the appeal of McLaren to many "religious seekers" is that he embraces a wide range of theological beliefs and practices, including, to a degree, the political progressivism associated with the social gospel. McLaren's approach is also similar to that of many evangelicals who, like several earlier social gospel leaders, make commitment to specific doctrines secondary to a vibrant sense of religious experience.

Even more contentious than McLaren among many evangelicals has been Rob Bell. A graduate of Fuller Theological Seminary in California, Bell was the founding pastor of the Mars Hill Bible Church in Grandville, Michigan, which, like many nondenominational evangelical megachurches in the late twentieth century, rose from a handful of members to become one of the largest churches in America. By the early 2000s, however, Bell's evangelicalism increasingly embraced a more liberal theology. His 2007 best-selling book, *Love Wins*, stressed a vision of theological universalism, as well as a belief that Christian teaching had more to do with living holistic lives in the present than with getting into heaven.

As with many aspects of early twenty-first-century religion, it is hard to know whether the style of Christianity practiced by figures like Bell and McLaren is an anomaly or part of a wider shift in the American evangelical landscape. The sociologist James K. Wellman Jr. has noted that many leaders associated with emergent models of evangelicalism represented by McLaren and Bell defy easy theological categorization, in part because these leaders reject conventional labels like "liberal" and "conservative." At the same time, figures like Bell express a theological orientation that echoes themes from the earlier social gospel, using Christianity to support social engagement largely defined along the lines of liberal public policies. "Personal holiness is important," Bell asserted in a 2007 sermon, "but it makes some people miss the central things: justice, compassion, and mercy. . . . God isn't just interested in saving you, and God is not just interested in you and your purity. God wants to use us to do something about the greater suffering in the world."[31]

The late twentieth-century tradition of progressive evangelicalism reflects an effort to recover an antebellum Protestant tradition that combines conservative theologies with social radicalism. At the same time, many progressive evangelicals have been reluctant to identify with the tradition of the liberal social gospel and, like their politically conservative counterparts, have often caricatured the classic social gospel as a movement that failed to fully embrace the Bible.[32] Many progressive evangelical leaders continue to propagate earlier conservative and neo-orthodox stereotypes of the social gospel. In a hundredth-anniversary edition of Walter Rauschenbusch's 1907 book *Christianity and the Social Crisis*, the prominent evangelists Tony Campolo and Jim Wallis lauded Rauschenbusch's justice-oriented vision of Christianity. At the same time, their praise tends to reflect common caricatures of the social gospel employed by mid-twentieth-century theologians like Reinhold Niebuhr related to the social gospel's alleged overoptimistic assessment of human nature. "Walter Rauschenbusch's articulation of a Christian social ethic is an eloquent and necessary corrective to a privatized religion," Jim Wallis noted. "But his view of history sometimes misses the biblical reality of evil and the Christian notion of the kingdom of God that is both 'already' and 'not yet.'"[33] Tony Campolo added, "Rauschen-busch fails to grasp the radical sinfulness of the human race. . . . I wish Rauschenbusch had asserted the need for personal conversion in which an individual enters into a dialogical and transforming relationship with the living Christ."[34]

Rauschenbusch never discounted the reality of sin and evil. Accord-ing to social gospel idealists like Rauschenbusch, the attainment of a just society was a long-term proposition that required constant social engagement and struggle. He recognized that part of the systemic evil of modern capitalism was how it made good people become part of sys-temic networks of evil: "I say in all soberness that every rich man is the sad hero of a tragedy, and the more noble and wise and righteous he is by nature, the more tragic his fate."[35]

Some early twenty-first-century evangelicals have been more positive in their theological assessment of Rauschenbusch. "Walter Rauschen-busch gets the credit for shaking me out of my individualistic gospel coma," the evangelical pastor and author Tim Suttle noted in 2011. Rauschenbusch's "life and thought will offer those of us who are com-mitted to personal faith in Christ, as well as a gospel call to justice and mercy, an effective way to support all we are saying and doing theo-logically."[36] While a cross section of emerging evangelical leaders debate the merits of the classic social gospel movement associated with figures like Walter Rauschenbusch, the question of how the social gospel might develop in the twenty-first century, or even whether it is still viable, re-mains unclear.

Into the Twenty-First Century: The Social Gospel at the Crossroads

As we enter the twenty-first century, we can see how the social gospel has contributed to a broad legacy of American political liberalism through its championing of distributive economic justice, civil rights, antimilita-rism, and internationalism, rooted in a religious vision of nonviolence. However, the social gospel's sustainability for the future remains an open question. In 2015 the Pew Research Foundation released a report on the American religious landscape that updated an earlier 2007 study on religious participation rates in the United States. The study reveals significant declines in membership-participation for most religious groups in the country. Between 2007 and 2014, overall religious adherence dropped from 78.4 percent to 70.6 percent. This drop included a 3.1 percent membership decline in the Roman Catholic Church and a 3.4 percent decline in mainline Protestant denominations—the tradition that serves as the major historical caretaker for the legacy of the social gospel. Even evangelical churches, which grew steadily throughout the late twentieth century, showed signs of leveling off, dropping from a share of 26.3 percent in 2007 to 25.4 percent in 2014. Just as revealing, however, the survey notes that those who claim no religious affiliation, the so-called religious "nones," rose from 16.1 percent in 2007 to 22.8 percent in 2014.[37] These results raise a number of questions about how, and whether, the social gospel can be sustained as a vibrant tradition as the twenty-first century progresses.

Part of the challenge faced by contemporary religious leaders who hope for a renewal of the social gospel is a task that has plagued social gospelers since the era of John Ryan and Walter Rauschenbusch— namely, how to develop support on a grassroots level, particularly in American congregations. In 2004 the sociologist Mark Chaves summarized a point that many scholars have made for generations, that historically Americans have not primarily joined religious congregations for the purpose of becoming social-political activists. "The Social Gospel image of congregations deeply engaged in serving the needy of their communities has been for many a compelling normative vision for more than a century, but we should not let notions of what congregations *ought* to look like influence our assessment of what they do look like."[38] Chaves's assertion has been corroborated by numerous studies that have found that with the notable exception of many African American churches, Americans generally tend to disapprove of their congregations or denominations taking controversial stands on social-political questions.

The negative perception of religion's public role has been analyzed in the context of a widening division between secular and religious Americans. As part of an important study on American religious habits published in 2010, the economist Robert Putnam and the political scientist David Campbell observed the presence of a "God gap" in American politics, that is, "the tendency for highly religious Americans to favor the Republicans and for highly secular people to support the Democrats."[39] This God gap is evident in contemporary national debates on LGBT equality. Data suggest that proponents of LGBT rights tend to have little or no formal religious affiliation. Also, there is mounting evidence that the so-called millennial generation, Americans born roughly between 1982 and 2000, overwhelmingly support LGBT rights, including marriage equality, regardless of their religious affiliations. For much of the twentieth century, the social gospel movement advocated for an understanding of justice rooted in religious and cultural tolerance. However, the growing category of religious "nones" in the early twenty-first century raises questions about whether young Americans see religion, specifically religious institutions, as a benefit or a hindrance to building a pluralistic society. The sociologist Robert Wuthnow points out that the lack of civility surrounding issues such as abortion rights and marriage equality has alienated many millennials from religious institutions. "Religious leaders and policy makers need not abandon their principles to work for the common good, but working for the common good must be emphasized more forcefully if the culture wars are to be transcended."[40]

In the early twenty-first century many religious progressives have attempted to reclaim a prophetic voice to counter the visibility of the Christian Right. Several interfaith leaders have called on their constituents to address a wide range of political issues, including economic equality, racial justice, international peace, and LGBT rights. Indicative of this movement is the Network of Spiritual Progressives (NSP).

Principally founded by three religious activist and scholars, Michael Lerner (Jewish), Joan Chittister (Catholic), and Cornel West (Protestant), the NSP stresses the uniqueness of its religious and political vision. It contrasts itself with religious conservatives, who from the organization's perspective focus on power and domination, and liberals, who focus on the preservation of preexistent American institutions. At the same time, the NSP reform agenda largely embraces many predominant themes in the twentieth-century social gospel movement, especially linking capitalism to many of the political, economic, and spiritual problems of contemporary Americans. As the NSP statement of principles asserts, "We will rebuild our economy to provide economic security, fundamental equality, and meaningful work that contribute to some higher good beyond maximizing money or power."[41]

Organizations like the Network of Spiritual Progressives demonstrate that social gospel principles still retain their appeal, and that this historical movement still animates a wide range of liberal and radical religious leaders to pursue a social gospel–inspired vision of transforming American political institutions. However, the calls for radical social change that come from organizations like the NSP are being made at a time when the institutional base to act on these proposals is shrinking.

Although the classic social gospel did in one sense decline after World War I, due in part to the collapse of the Progressive Era coalition that helped bolster it, the movement continued to thrive among leaders in a range of religious and secular organizations that sustained its ideological worldview.[42] Throughout the history of the social gospel, we can see that its ideals inspired a number of institutions, including settlement houses in the urban North, "folk schools" in the rural South, and a range of religiously based organizations, such as the YMCA and YWCA, on university and college campuses across the country. These organizations provided critical contexts for leaders to meet, share ideas, and disseminate beliefs and strategies for action. We can also see how by the 1970s, many of these institutional networks were rapidly disappearing.

In 1972 *motive* magazine, long an iconic publication of religious radicalism in American Methodism, was shut down when the United Methodist Church ceased its funding. After its founding in the early 1940s, *motive* developed a strong reputation as a religious publication, and its cutting-edge style was widely acknowledged by the secular media. One person influenced by *motive* was Hillary Clinton, who received a subscription to the magazine from her youth pastor. By the time she graduated from Wellesley College in 1969, Clinton, who had supported Barry Goldwater in 1964, was firmly committed to a faith-based liberal politics that would characterize her subsequent political career.[43]

By the early 1970s, however, *motive*'s social radicalism, culminating with two issues in 1972 that focused on gay and lesbian rights, led the General Board of Higher Education of the United Methodist Church to cut the magazine's funding. The demise of *motive* magazine, a longtime symbol of youth-oriented, religiously motivated activism, signified a growing conservative reaction against the theological and political radicalism in mainline denominations. However, it also illustrates the decline of the organizational base that the social gospel had traditionally relied on to flourish as a movement. *motive*'s story reveals how a religious institution's desire to preserve a level of theological orthodoxy broke that denomination's connection to more radical voices outside the institutional church.

motive's demise is indicative of the decline of a wider historical base within American Protestantism that was devoted to nurturing and cultivating the social idealism of young people and that is critical for understanding the impact of the social gospel movement in America. By the end of the twentieth century, organizations like the World Student Christian Movement, the Student YMCA/YWCA, and a spate of denominationally funded campus ministries had either ceased to exist or were seriously truncated by dwindling financial resources. Robert Wuthnow notes that "traditionally, religion has been an important resource for networking, for maintaining intergenerational ties, and for transmitting values to adults as well as to children. It can continue to be in the future, but only if it faces the changes currently taking place among young adults."[44] However, many progressively aligned religious movements in the twenty-first century face the challenge of seeking to build this support in liberal religious institutions that face shrinking financial resources and that have become increasingly resistant to the left-liberal politics associated with the legacy of the social gospel.

Part of the social gospel's historical success was its ability to exist in the tension between religious institutions and more radical organizations. Many social gospel leaders and reformers, like Walter Rauschenbusch, spent their careers believing that they were part of a traditional Protestant culture that was at the center of the nation's social-political life. Yet their ideas were often disseminated by and influenced a range of more radical organizations and leaders found in a disparate range of bodies like the Federal Council of Churches, the YMCA, the Fellowship of Reconciliation, the Socialist Party, and a number of student organizations. While some of these organizations still exist, their connection to religious institutions has grown more tenuous. The Pew study on the current religious landscape draws attention not only to the dwindling membership in American religious bodies, but also to the decline in the institutional forces that had helped to shape the historical contours of the social gospel movement in America.

One indicator of the institutional decline of the social gospel is the fact that most people associated with "progressive" religious movements are in the academy or do their work outside religious institutions. Social gospel leaders of the late nineteenth and early twentieth centuries, such as Washington Gladden, Walter Rauschenbusch, and Stephen Wise, came out of pastoral contexts, in churches or synagogues. As the twentieth century progressed, most of the figures connected with the social gospel increasingly did their work in universities, colleges, and theological seminaries. The historian Eugene McCarraher reflects that by the end of the twentieth century, the Protestant and Catholic traditions that forged the social gospel movement in the twentieth century had become "therapeutic collages of belief and practice," and the movement's heirs exist "in genteel spiritual poverty."[45]

McCarraher's bleak assessment of the social gospel's future is borne out by many twenty-first-century secular activists who view religion, whether liberal or conservative, as the enemy of a progressive society. The grandson of Walter Rauschenbusch, the philosopher Richard Rorty, noted before his death in 2007 that while Rauschenbusch's social gospel presented a compelling reform vision, he viewed it as a last-gasp effort of Christianity to achieve relevancy in an increasingly secular world. "One hundred years ago, there was still a chance that the Christian churches would play a central role in the struggle for social justice—that Christian, rather than Marxist, ideas would inspire radical socio-political change." However, the reality of two world wars and the rise of communism epitomized the collapse of a world where religion could offer a political alternative to capitalism. "With a bit more luck, Rauschenbusch's dream could have come true"; however, "the likelihood that religion will play a significant role in the struggle for justice seems smaller now than at any time since *Christianity and the Social Crisis* was published." While conceding that religion still played a vital role in American society, Rorty lamented that this turn to religion was producing the kind of apocalyptic forms of individualist Christianity that Rauschenbusch fought against.[46]

Rorty's ambivalence toward the legacy of his grandfather's religious vision is shared by some high-profile figures of the political left who largely seem to support the notion of a "God gap" in America. In the

2016 presidential campaign, Vermont senator Bernie Sanders embraced many of the precepts of anticapitalism and support of democratic socialism that would have resonated with many social gospel leaders of an earlier era. However, the religious vision of Rauschenbusch's kingdom of God or Martin Luther King's "beloved community" is largely missing from Sanders's worldview.[47]

In sum, early twenty-first-century leaders who embrace labels such as "progressive Christian" or "religious progressive" face a difficult challenge not only in communicating their message but also in building broadly based social movements in the face of dwindling financial resources and cultural capital. Additionally, the growing association of religion (in particular, Protestant Christianity) with conservative policies that are connected with the anti-pluralist and conservative cultural stances of many evangelicals leaves many difficult questions facing those who yearn for a return to earlier visions of the social gospel.

Conclusion

In 2000 Richard Neuhaus issued a call for a redefinition of the historical concept of "Christian America." While conceding problems with the earlier application of this idea, Neuhaus still believed that America's unique religious heritage required that a person's faith be involved in the shaping of public discourse. Echoing Reinhold Niebuhr's stress on historical irony, Neuhaus conceded that "perennial attempts . . . to assert some grand national purpose within the world-historical scheme of things are usually Christian in inspiration but end by aspiring to take the place of Christianity." However, he argued that religion was necessary to cultivate a society of civility and shared values, noting that "any public philosophy that might be constructed, will not be democratically sustainable unless it engages in a fresh way the idea of Christian America."[48] Neuhaus's comments on the public role of religion highlight an important historical tension that both evangelicals and liberals repeatedly contest—namely, to what extent can and should religious beliefs define the nation's political agenda? Although the Christian Right made numerous gains in advocating for its public positions in the late twentieth century, heirs of the social gospel still remain visible in America, even if they face a precarious future.

In the early twenty-first century, signs of the long-standing social gospel emphasis on "social salvation" are still prominent. The election of Pope Francis I in 2013 spurred a renewed discussion in the United States on the role of religion in American politics. Francis appeals to many aspects of progressive Catholic social teachings—as well as the legacies of American reformers such as Dorothy Day and Martin Luther King—and his popularity suggests that the social gospel emphasis on reforming social structures continues to resonate in America.

At the same time, American religious decline, particularly among groups associated with the Protestant mainline, is part of a broader crisis faced by a wide range of religious institutions in the twenty-first century. The expansive range of institutional networks that helped to spawn and propagate many aspects of the social gospel have significantly declined, if not disappeared. For much of its history, the social gospel developed out of the creative, at times contentious, tension between liberal-progressive institutions and more radical social reform movements. In the early twenty-first century, mainline Protestant churches and their religious allies often claim the historical mantle of the classic social gospel. However, these institutions no longer enjoy the cultural capital or institutional networks to sustain and disseminate their visions.

Yet it is premature to say whether the social gospel, as a wider movement of religious idealism, will disappear. Historically, the movement showed an ability to evolve theologically, while grafting itself to a range of secular and religious institutions. This history reveals how the social gospel tradition has adapted itself to new social-historical contexts, even as it has stayed rooted in the idealism of its founding pioneers such as Washington Gladden, Reverdy Ransom, Walter Rauschenbusch, and John Ryan. Although what forms the social gospel may take in the future is an open-ended question, its history suggests that the tradition might very well adapt to the emerging realities of the twenty-first century, even as the institutional models that it used to thrive as a movement in the twentieth century have largely passed away.

Conclusion

The Social Gospel in American History

In June 2015 President Barack Obama delivered the eulogy for the Reverend Clementa Pinckney, pastor of the Emanuel African Methodist Episcopal Church in Charleston, South Carolina. The murder of Reverend Pinckney and eight of his parishioners by a white supremacist earlier that month had sparked fierce national debate about racism in America. While President Obama extensively discussed that broader history of racism in his eulogy, he also reflected on religion's role in combating it. As Obama observed, Pinckney's life bore witness to a vision of faith manifested not only in words, but in actions dedicated to changing society. Obama asserted "that to put our faith in action is about more than individual salvation, it's about collective salvation; that to feed the hungry and clothe the naked and house the homeless is not just a call for isolated charity but the imperative of a just society."[1]

Although Obama didn't use the term "social gospel" in his eulogy, the legacy of the social gospel is evident in the connection he drew between religion and the pursuit of systemic social change. Emerging out of a range of historical developments in the nineteenth century, the social gospel has played a major role in shaping the country's broader religious landscape and continues to animate discussions about religion's public role in the twenty-first century. As we saw in the introduction, our definition of the social gospel focuses on three broad themes. These themes were echoed in President Obama's Charleston eulogy.

The first theme—and in many ways the most important one in grounding this book—is that the social gospel represents a dynamic tradition of religious idealism. The social gospel movement went through extensive transitions as it developed in American history. However, one constant theme connects the beliefs of Washington Gladden in the late nineteenth century to those of Martin Luther King in the mid-twentieth century: the ideal of social salvation. That is, they all affirmed that prophetic forms of religion necessitated collective changes in the institutional makeup of society. Although Gladden's view of the kingdom of God differed from King's vision of the beloved community, each believed in a religiously based idealism that was rooted in the necessity of systemic social change. In different ways, they asserted that God, working through individuals, could root out injustice and create a nation that approximated the conditions of social equality.

In American Protestantism, this idealism has frequently opened proponents of the social gospel to accusations of being overly optimistic, if not naïve, about the possibilities of changing collective behavior. Also, the Protestant focus on Jesus as the supreme model to ground social reform is historically problematic for religious leaders coming out of Judaism and even Catholicism, a tradition that emphasizes the natural law teachings of the medieval era. However, there were important commonalities among, for example, John Ryan, Stephen Wise, Walter Rauschenbusch, and Martin Luther King: they all believed that religion was indispensable for developing a just society, that religious faith helped to shape social-ethical models designed, in a sense, to create the conditions of a "heaven on earth."

Although this objective sounds utopian, the figures who galvanized the social gospel movement never believed that the task would be easy, inevitable, or fully realized in any given historical context. Repeatedly, representatives of the social gospel balanced the themes of judgment and hope in their theologies. They preached, taught, and put into action a faith that God's judgment was upon the nation for sins such as poverty, militarism, and racism, while also lifting up visions of hope that the nation might be reformed. Rather than succumbing to pessimism, the social gospelers saw redemption through the ability to work in partnership with God for social justice. As William McGuire King observes, the social gospel conception of social salvation was fully realized when believers worked to change society, "when theological reflection became one with social action and with participation in the social struggles of humanity."[2] The social gospel, at its best, balanced a prophetic criticism of society's injustices with the hope that one day these injustices would be eliminated.

Throughout its history, the social gospel movement manifested an idealism that stressed the interconnection between one's religious tradition and the imperative to transform social-political structures. Rejecting literal interpretations of scripture and apocalyptic end time scenarios, social gospelers focused on using religion to address social problems and respond to injustices. While many social gospelers believed in the indispensable role of their religious institutions to create societal change, their idealism took root as a movement both within *and* outside these bodies.

The social gospel's idealism was found in both religious and secular institutions, which leads us to the second theme in this book—namely, that the social gospel contributed to broader social-political movements associated with the political left in American history. As noted in the introduction, Doug Rossinow's concept of an American "left-liberal" political tradition is critical to an understanding of the development of the social gospel movement. On one hand, the original period of the social gospel's ascendency in the late nineteenth century was characterized by a common faith, especially among Protestant social gospelers, that the spirit of Christianity could reform America along the lines of preexistent social institutions. However, in this same time period, the seeds of a more radical outlook were being sown by a range of social gospel leaders. The post–World War I social gospel engagement with issues such as racial justice and nonviolent direct action demonstrates how the core theological and political commitments of an earlier social gospel liberalism were being transformed by a wide range of groups and organizations, both within and outside mainline religious bodies.

What justifies referring to the social gospel as a long-standing movement in American religious history has as much to do with how it developed after 1920 as it does with its formative "classic" period in the late nineteenth and early twentieth centuries. While examining the contributions of church leaders like Harry Emerson Fosdick and Georgia Harkness is critical to understanding the evolution of the social gospel, the relationship of these leaders to organizations like the YMCA, the YWCA, the FOR, the Highlander Folk School, and the Socialist Party is also essential for an analysis of the diffusion of the social gospel across the broader fabric of American society. While Martin Luther King represents the culmination of the social gospel's influence in the twentieth century, his impact was magnified because his teachings were reinforced by groups like the YMCA and the FOR as well as a range of religiously based communities. Although this book has explored the social gospel's rise and decline in mainline religious institutions, it has also shown how the idealism of the original social gospel traveled a great distance from its point of origin in nineteenth-century American Protestantism—and in some fashion has survived the institutions that spawned its idealism.

An ongoing issue in interpreting the history of the social gospel is how to reconcile the movement's idealism, especially its faith in the social-ethical dimensions of Jesus's teachings, with specific models of political change. While the movement's leftist orientations often pushed it to embrace socialist models, many of its primary spokespersons, such as Rauschenbusch, frequently argued that God transcended any specific social political order. At the same time, Rauschenbusch was equally strident in his advocacy for a socialist political alternative to American capitalism. In the early twenty-first century, the democratic socialist ideals that galvanized many early twentieth-century social gospel leaders may seem remote to us, in an era where often the rhetoric of individual rights is seen as a central part of the American political canon. However, earlier social gospel leaders' vision of a cooperative society, based on the redistribution of economic power, continues to attract many followers, even as these ideas remain highly contentious in American public life.

Finally, exploring the historical arc of the social gospel allows us to see how the movement shifted its emphasis from an exclusive vision of America as a Protestant nation to one that affirmed the nation's pluralistic character. The one aspect of the social gospel movement that was most tied to late nineteenth-century Protestant hopes for "Christianizing" the nation was the ecumenical movement. Yet, as David Hollinger observes, it was largely through ecumenical bodies like the Federal Council and National Council of Churches that the social gospel contributed to "diminishing Anglo Protestant prejudice and embracing the varieties of humankind."[3] One of the most frequently leveled critiques against the social gospel was that it tended to view American culture in an uncritical fashion, making the movement susceptible to being co-opted by the social-political interests of the dominant culture.[4] To a degree, this reality came to pass in the mid-twentieth century, when many Protestant ecumenical leaders became enamored with their social status at the expense of being prophetic. It is perhaps ironic that the one Protestant leader who most epitomized this tension was Reinhold Niebuhr. Despite his persistent argument that liberal Protestants were naïve in their quest to create a society of perfect love, by the end of World War II Niebuhr had come to symbolize the ecumenical aspirations of mainline Protestantism to craft a global vision of American Protestant Christianity.

However, the cultural and political ambitions of leaders in the so-called Protestant establishment should not obscure the ways the social gospel signaled a growing embrace of religious and cultural pluralism. One of the paradoxes of the early social gospel was that it sought to reconcile its exclusive Protestant mission to Christianize America with its growing pluralistic tendencies. Despite their Protestant biases, leaders like Gladden and Rauschenbusch vehemently believed in the separation of church and state and strove, albeit not always successfully, to push beyond Protestant paternalism. Throughout the twentieth century, Protestant leaders in the social gospel tradition increasingly found themselves embracing different aspects of religious and cultural pluralism that moved far beyond the white Protestant world envisioned in the pages of Josiah Strong's *Our Country* in the 1880s. If one looks carefully at Martin Luther King's social thought, one sees how the theological personalism of Georgia Harkness, the natural law ethics of John Ryan, the historical "zeitgeist" of Walter Rauschenbusch, the tradition of the Hebrew prophets epitomized by Stephen Wise, the nonviolence of A. J. Muste, and the black church activism of Reverdy Ransom and Nannie Helen Burroughs came together in his life and the social movement that he led. King not only shows us how one person can change history, but reminds us how the voices of the past often carry far beyond their points of origin.

In the years since his martyrdom, many of Martin Luther King's heirs have struggled with how to link religion and politics in creative ways. The late twentieth-century efforts of many evangelicals to connect their religious beliefs to political engagement has caused a sort of backlash, whether from the left or the right, against religious groups that use their faith as the basis for political action. Demographic studies show not only a political divide between those who identify themselves as religious and those who do not, but also a growing wariness that equates religion with a lack of political tolerance.[5] Part of what Hollinger suggests about the broader history of liberal Protestantism is that those who came out of the liberal Protestant social gospel, in effect, worked themselves out of a job. One example can be seen in the historical development of one of the most important organizations in the dissemination of the social gospel in American history: the YMCA. The Y's decision in 2010 to drop the name "Christian" from its name demonstrates how the organization's mission has evolved beyond its evangelical Protestant roots. As the YMCA became more inclusive in its orientation, it found its historical sectarianism problematic and became, for all intents and purposes, a secular organization.[6]

Hollinger's interpretation of liberal Protestantism is borne out by the fact that many Americans who identify with the legacy of the social gospel today are largely comfortable with the growing religious and cultural pluralism of America. However, the history of the social gospel also reflects an ongoing desire to critique the culture that in many ways is still evident among those who carry on the mantle of this movement in the early twenty-first century. Whether those who pick up the mantle of the social gospel in the twenty-first century can re-create the prophetic visions that characterized the eras of Rauschenbusch, Fosdick, or King remains to be seen. However, many of the issues that the social gospel historically fought to uphold—a living wage for workers, a redistribution of economic wealth, racial justice, and a pluralistic society based on respecting religious and cultural differences—remain fiercely debated in the twenty-first century. The sociologist Steven Tipton notes that contemporary religious groups that want to advance a progressively based vision of justice that reclaims the legacy of the social gospel need to take on the role of "crucial questioners" of the dominant institutions in American life that are often committed to preserving class and economic privileges. These religious bodies "must tell the larger truth of human interdependence and shared responsibility" and "keep trying to live out this truth in exemplary ways that can reach into the fearful hearts of the righteous . . . and reach out beyond our economically segregated neighborhoods and national boundaries to embrace those who have so much less of everything except infinite value in the eyes of God."[7] In the context of political and economic polarization, renewed debates over racism, fears of terrorism, and Islamophobia, heirs of the social gospel might very well revive the spirit of many social gospel figures who saw religious tolerance as a core value.

The Social Gospel and Visions of Progress

The historian Christopher Lasch has noted that Americans "continue to believe in progress, in the face of massive evidence" that might have led them "to refute the idea of progress once and for all."[8] Lasch's comment is not far removed from the sentiment expressed by Reinhold Niebuhr, who, while critical of much of liberal theology, nevertheless maintained hope in the possibility that religion—specifically Christianity—would serve as a necessary resource capable of changing society. Despite Niebuhr's caricatures of liberal naïveté, the story of the social gospel presented in this book is a narrative of a dynamic and changing movement that, while embracing many different forms and ideas, remained rooted in core convictions. Proponents of the social gospel such as Walter Rauschenbusch, John Ryan, Stephen Wise, Georgia Harkness, Howard Thurman, and Martin Luther King were dreamers in that they believed in the possibility of a better world that emanated from their religious convictions. Yet their dreams of social change were connected to their faith that human efforts, in partnership with a loving God, would bring about justice, social equality, and a new reverence for the individual's role in society. Walter Rauschenbusch had reminded his readers that the social ideals of prophets may not be realized at a given historical moment; indeed, one of the social gospel's great successes was its ability to pass to successive generations a collective hope that permanent social change would one day occur. The history of the social gospel in American religion is a story of how this movement lived in the tension between the immediate need to act in the present and the desire to create long-term social change. It also demonstrates how a wide range of persons kept faith that social change would occur, even when they didn't necessarily see immediate results from their labors.

For some Americans living in the early twenty-first century, the term "social gospel" might be forever tied to a historical era that no longer exists in America. However, as long as the religious imperative to work for systemic social change persists in America, then the legacy of the social gospel will find ways to move into the future.

NOTES

INTRODUCTION

1 Martin Luther King, *Stride toward Freedom*, 91.

2 Reed, *Active Faith*, 67. See also Evans, *Histories of American Christianity*, 342–43.

3 Sources that provide interpretive definitions of the social gospel include Hopkins and White, *The Social Gospel*; Dorrien, *Soul in Society*; Ralph E. Luker, "Interpreting the Social Gospel: Reflections on Two Generations of Historiography," in Evans, *Perspectives on the Social Gospel*, 1–13; and Susan Hill Lindley, "Deciding Who Counts: Toward a Revised Definition of the Social Gospel," in Evans, *The Social Gospel Today*, 17–26.

4 Mathews's original use of this definition can be found in G. B. Smith, ed., *A Dictionary of Religion and Ethics* (New York: Macmillan, 1921), 416–17. An abridged version of this definition was also used in Charles Howard Hopkins's classic study of the social gospel in America, *The Rise of the Social Gospel in American Protestantism, 1865–1915*, 3. See also Wendy J. Deichmann Edwards and Carolyn De Swarte Gifford, "Introduction: Restoring Women and Reclaiming Gender in Social Gospel Studies," in Edwards and Gifford, *Gender and the Social Gospel*, 1–34.

5 The terms "progressive" and "progressivism" are subject to numerous definitions. Throughout most of this book, I use these terms to describe the theological and social-political liberalism that characterized much of the history of the social gospel movement, especially during the phase of the so-called classic social gospel of the late nineteenth and early twentieth centuries. I use "progressivism" to apply to a wide range of religious and secular movements that historically have emphasized the role of government in creating the conditions for social-economic equality (in other words, progressivism in my usage is roughly analogous to what would be referred to today as "liberalism"). This book often makes a distinction between the terms "radical" and "progressive," in that radicals sought political solutions that looked beyond preexisting social structures, historically characterized by a hostility toward capitalist-based economic solutions to the nation's social problems (often embracing models of political socialism). At the same time, many social gospelers—for example, Walter Rauschenbusch—often blended themes of political progressivism and radicalism in their social thought. Today the term "progressive" usually refers to persons who espouse more radical social-political solutions that call into question the viability of capitalist structures to achieve a just society. See Dorrien, *Economy, Difference, Empire*, 3–28.

6 My definition of the social gospel relies heavily on the work of Susan Hill Lindley, who identified the social gospel as a specific subcomponent in a wider movement of late nineteenth-century evangelical Protestant "social Christianity." See Lindley, "Deciding Who Counts."

7 Many scholars capitalize the term "Social Gospel" to refer to the movement's theological formation and institutional assimilation into American Protestantism that lasted from approximately 1880 until 1920. I prefer to use the lowercase term "social gospel" to indicate the movement's Protestant roots while also conveying that the tradition encompassed a wide range of religious and secular groups and social movements, culminating with the civil rights movement of the 1950s and 1960s.

8 This interpretive lens that sees the social gospel mostly as a response to the social-economic conditions of the late nineteenth century has influenced much of the historical writing on the social gospel. For an analysis on the historiography of the social gospel, see Luker, "Interpreting the Social Gospel."

9 The idea that the social gospel "died out" after World War I was widely espoused in American religious historiography for much of the twentieth century. See, for example, Ahlstrom, *A Religious History of the American People*.

10 The development of the social gospel after World War I tends to focus on the relationship between earlier models of social gospel liberalism and emerging currents of neo-orthodox (or crisis) theology associated in the 1930s with Reinhold Niebuhr. See Paul Carter, *The Decline and Revival of the Social Gospel*; Miller, *American Protestantism and Social Issues, 1919–1939*; and Donald B. Meyer, *The Protestant Search for Political Realism*. For an alternative interpretation of the social gospel after World War I, see William McGuire King, "The Emergence of Social Gospel Radicalism in American Methodism."

11 The relationship between the social gospel and Unitarianism was explored in Hopkins, *The Rise of the Social Gospel in American Protestantism*. See also Cauthen, *The Impact of American Religious Liberalism*; and Hutchison, *The Modernist Impulse in American Protestantism*.

12 See Timothy Smith, *Revivalism and Social Reform*; Dayton, *Discovering an Evangelical Heritage*; Luker, *The Social Gospel in Black and White*; and Gary Scott Smith, *The Search for Social Salvation*.

13 In many ways, the emergence of the social gospel in American Protestantism paralleled the rise of a popular form of premillennialism called dispensationalism. See Boyer, *When Time Shall Be No More*; and Sutton, *American Apocalypse*.

14 On this theme see, for example, Christopher H. Evans, "Walter Rauschenbusch and the Second Coming: The Social Gospel as Baptist History," in Harper, *Through a Glass Darkly*, 145–71.

15 Rauschenbusch, *Christianizing the Social Order*, 464.

16 On the broader development of theological liberalism in the late nineteenth century, see Hutchison, *The Modernist Impulse in American Protestantism*; on the rise of fundamentalism, see Marsden, *Fundamentalism and American Culture*.

17 Rauschenbusch, *Christianizing the Social Order*, 9.

18 Moore, *Religious Outsiders and the Making of Americans.*

19 See Duke, *In the Trenches with Jesus and Marx.*

20 See Hutchison, *The Modernist Impulse in American Protestantism*; Dorrien, *The Making of American Liberal Theology: Imagining Progressive Religion, 1805–1900*; and Evans, *Liberalism without Illusions.*

21 Gary Dorrien, "Social Salvation: The Social Gospel as Theology and Economics," in Evans, *The Social Gospel Today*, 101.

22 Quoted in Hudson, *Walter Rauschenbusch: Selected Writings*, 199.

23 See, for example, William McGuire King, "The Emergence of Social Gospel Radicalism: The Methodist Case."

24 For a summary of the relationship of the social gospel to modern biblical scholarship, see William McGuire King, "The Biblical Base of the Social Gospel."

25 See William McGuire King, "'History as Revelation' in the Theology of the Social Gospel"; and William McGuire King, "An Enthusiasm for Humanity."

26 As will be discussed in this book, the ethical passion of the social gospel movement was instrumental to the development in North America of what became known as "social ethics." See Dorrien, *Social Ethics in the Making.*

27 See Mead, *The Lively Experiment*, 177–83.

28 Dombrowski, *The Early Days of Christian Socialism in America.*

29 Rossinow, *Visions of Progress*, 4–5.

30 On the history of Catholic social teachings, see Abell, *American Catholicism and Social Action*; and Dolan, *The American Catholic Experience*. On American Judaism and the social gospel, see Michael A. Meyer, *Response to Modernity*; and Kleinberg, "Reform Judaism and the Jewish 'Social Gospel.'"

31 For a comparison of Rauschenbusch and Ryan, see Beckley, *Passion for Justice.*

32 Dorrien, *The New Abolition.*

33 One of the most important anthologies that helped reintroduce Walter Rauschenbusch to a new generation of Americans in the mid-twentieth century was edited by the president of Morehouse College, Atlanta, Benjamin Mays. See Mays, *A Gospel for the Social Awakening.*

34 This theme is explored in Hollinger, "After Cloven Tongues of Fire"; and *After Cloven Tongues of Fire*. See also Mislin, *Saving Faith.*

35 Finke and Stark, *The Churching of America, 1776–1990*, 271.

36 The question of the social gospel's relationship to a broader American consumer culture is examined by Curtis, *A Consuming Faith*. Although Curtis's analysis is helpful for an understanding of the cultural worldview of many early twentieth-century social gospel leaders, it doesn't take into account the ways that the theological commitments of the early social gospel movement evolved as the twentieth century progressed.

37 See, for example, Leigh Eric Schmidt, *Restless Souls: The Making of American Spirituality* (New York: Harper, 2002).

38 McKanan, *Prophetic Encounters.*

39 It is important to differentiate the African American freedom struggle of the nineteenth and twentieth centuries from the predominantly white social gospel of the Progressive Era. However, it is also vital for historians to examine the ways that various streams of these movements come together, especially in the life and thought of Martin Luther King Jr. See Luker, *The Social Gospel in Black and White*; White, *Liberty and Justice for All*; and Cook, "Martin Luther King, Jr. and the Long Social Gospel Movement."

40 See Tracy, *Direct Action*; and McKanan, *Prophetic Encounters*.

41 Part of Fosdick's contribution was that his books appealed to an emerging liberal religious culture in America during the 1920s and 1930s; see Hedstrom, *The Rise of Liberal Religion*.

42 See, for example, David P. King, "The West Looks East"; and Shaffer, "'A Missionary from the East to Western Pagans.'"

43 This downturn is underscored by the Pew Research Center in its report *America's Changing Religious Landscape*.

44 Ralph Luker traces the origins of the term "social gospel" to a reform-minded cleric, Harlan Paul Douglass, who used the term in relationship to racial reform efforts in the South. See Luker, *The Social Gospel in Black and White*, 1. The term was also used as the title of a periodical of a short-lived utopian community in Georgia that was established in the late nineteenth century. See Dombrowski, *The Early Days of Christian Socialism in America*, 132–70.

CHAPTER 1. "A PERFECT MAN IN A PERFECT SOCIETY"

1 Quoted in Handy, *The Social Gospel in America, 1870–1920*, 47.

2 See Heath W. Carter, *Union Made*, 48.

3 Handy, *The Social Gospel in America*, 38ff.

4 Quoted in Dorrien, "Social Salvation," 107.

5 See Handy, *A Christian America*.

6 See Timothy Smith, *Revivalism and Social Reform*; and Luker, *The Social Gospel in Black and White*.

7 On the development of American antebellum theology, see Noll, *America's God*; and Holifield, *Theology in America*.

8 See Hambrick-Stowe, *Charles G. Finney*.

9 Quoted in Gasaway, *Progressive Evangelicals and the Pursuit of Social Justice*, 5.

10 See Timothy Smith, *Revivalism and Social Reform*; and Dayton, *Discovering an Evangelical Heritage*.

11 See Cauthen, *The Impact of American Religious Liberalism*; and Dorrien, *The Making of American Liberal Theology: Imagining Progressive Religion*.

12 On Parker's impact on theological liberalism, see Dorrien, *The Making of American Liberal Theology: Imagining Progressive Religion*, 80–110; and Grodzins, *Radical Heretic*.

13 Theodore Parker, "The Transient and Permanent in Christianity," in Ahlstrom and Carey, *An American Reformation*, 140–41.

14   On Bushnell, see Mullin, *The Puritan as Yankee*.

15   See Noll, *The Old Religion in a New World*, 124; and Evans, *The Kingdom Is Always but Coming*, 51.

16   See Chicago, IL Population History, www.biggestuscities.com.

17   See Hofstadter, *Social Darwinism in American Thought*.

18   May, *Protestant Churches and Industrial America*, 51.

19   Quoted in ibid., 54.

20   Applegate, *The Most Famous Man in America*.

21   Quoted in May, *Protestant Churches and Industrial America*, 71.

22   See Wacker, "The Holy Spirit and the Spirit of the Age."

23   Dorchester, *Christianity in the United States*, 780. In his statistical tables for 1889, Dorchester pooled the major Protestant denominations together under the label "evangelical" and gave their total number as 45,063,627, compared to 7,855,294 Roman Catholics. See Dorchester, 784.

24   On the larger history of premillennialism in American history, see Boyer, *When Time Shall Be No More*; and Sutton, *American Apocalypse*.

25   See Evans, *Histories of American Christianity*, 202.

26   Walter Rauschenbusch traced his own social awakening to Strong's legacy. See Rauschenbusch, *Christianizing the Social Order*, 9.

27   See May, *Protestant Churches and Industrial America*, 116; and Hopkins and White, *The Social Gospel*, 56.

28   Wendy J. Deichmann Edwards, "Manifest Destiny, the Social Gospel and the Coming Kingdom: Josiah Strong's Program of Global Reform, 1885–1916," in Evans, *Perspectives on the Social Gospel*, 83.

29   Strong, *Our Country*, 53–54.

30   While Strong's work has received a measure of scholarly attention, a critical biography of his life has yet to be written. See Edwards, "Manifest Destiny, the Social Gospel and the Coming Kingdom," 81–116; and Edwards, "Women and Social Betterment in the Social Gospel Work of Josiah Strong," in Edwards and Gifford, *Gender and the Social Gospel*, 35–52.

31   Quoted in Hopkins and White, *The Social Gospel*, 59.

32   Rauschenbusch, *Christianizing the Social Order*, 394.

33   See C. George Fry, "The Social Gospel at the Crossroads of Middle America," in Evans, *Perspectives on the Social Gospel*, 67; and Dorrien, "Social Salvation," 108.

34   For an overview of the development of Gladden's theology, see Dorrien, *The Making of American Liberal Theology: Imagining Progressive Religion*, 304–18.

35   Quoted in Dorn, *Washington Gladden*, 59.

36   Washington Gladden, "The Church and the Kingdom," in Handy, *The Social Gospel in America*, 115–16.

37   Gladden, *The Christian Pastor and the Working Church*, 462.

38   See Fry, "The Social Gospel at the Crossroads of Middle America," 51–79. For a summary of Gladden's ministry in Ohio, see Boyer, "An Ohio Leader of the Social Gospel Movement."

39 Dorrien, "Social Salvation," 110.

40 Quoted in Gifford, *Writing Out My Heart*, 104.

41 Jean Miller Schmidt, "Reexamining the Public/Private Split: Reforming the Continent and Spreading Scriptural Holiness," in Richey, Rowe, and Schmidt, *Perspectives on American Methodism*, 235–38.

42 This process of institutionalization was especially evident in the nation's largest Protestant church in the late nineteenth century, the Methodist Episcopal Church. See William McGuire King, "Denominational Modernization and Religious Identity: The Case of the Methodist Episcopal Church," in Richey, Rowe, and Schmidt, *Perspectives on American Methodism*, 343–55.

43 On the impact of the American Missionary Association on the rise of the social gospel, see Luker, *Social Gospel in Black and White*, 9–29.

44 On the southern deaconess movement, see McDowell, *The Social Gospel in the South*.

45 Quoted in Rosemary Skinner Keller, "Women Creating Communities—and Community—in the Name of the Social Gospel," in Evans, *The Social Gospel Today*, 73.

46 Mathews, "The Development of Social Christianity in America," 379.

47 Handy, *The Social Gospel in America*, 192.

48 Du Bois, *The Souls of Black Folk*.

49 Quoted in White and Hopkins, *The Social Gospel*, 106–7.

50 See Higginbotham, *Righteous Discontent*.

51 Ibid., 221.

52 Quoted in Luker, *The Social Gospel in Black and White*, 184. A summary of Proctor's life can be found at the American National Biography Online, www.anb.org.

53 Luker, *The Social Gospel in Black and White*, 184.

54 Higginbotham, *Righteous Discontent*, 6.

55 See ibid.; and Richey, Rowe, and Schmidt, *The Methodist Experience in America*, 388ff.

56 Quoted in Luker, *The Social Gospel in Black and White*, 104. For a comprehensive discussion of Ida B. Wells's career, see Dorrien, *The New Abolition*, 85–123.

57 Quoted in Pinn, *Making the Gospel Plain*, 63.

58 Quoted in ibid., 67.

CHAPTER 2. INTERPRETING THE "GOLDEN RULE"

1 See Heath W. Carter, "Scab Ministers, Striking Saints"; and Heath W. Carter, *Union Made*.

2 Quoted in Norwood, *Sourcebook of American Methodism*, 491–92.

3 Stead, *If Christ Came to Chicago!*, 60.

4 Sheldon, *The Crucifixion of Philip Strong*, 208.

5 Ibid., 209.

6 On the role of the social gospel novel, see Susan Hill Lindley, "Gender and the Social Gospel Novel," in Edwards and Gifford, *Gender and the Social Gospel*, 185–201.

7 Dorn, "The Social Gospel and Socialism," 84.

8 Scudder, *On Journey*, 165.

9 Quoted in White and Hopkins, *The Social Gospel*, 168.

10 Quoted in ibid., 171.

11 See Pinn, *Making the Gospel Plain*, 18–19.

12 Ibid., xiv; and Dorrien, *Social Ethics in the Making*, 155. See also Bynum, "'An Equal Chance in the Race for Life.'"

13 Quoted in Pinn, *Making the Gospel Plain*, 189.

14 Quoted in ibid.

15 Quoted in ibid., 190.

16 Quoted in Dombrowski, *The Early Days of Christian Socialism in America*, 172.

17 Herron, *The Christian Society*, 137–38.

18 See Frederick, *Knights of the Golden Rule*.

19 Herron, *The Christian Society*, 137–38.

20 Studies of Harry Hopkins tend to gloss over his religious foundation; however, Grinnell clearly planted in him a spirit of religious idealism that carried into his later political work. On Hopkins, see Kurzman, *Harry Hopkins and the New Deal*; and Giffen and Hopkins, *Jewish First Wife, Divorced*. On the social gospel ethos at Grinnell College, see Bradley W. Bateman, "Born Again in 1904: John R. Commons and the Social Gospel," in Evans, *Perspectives on the Social Gospel*, 221–38.

21 Dorn, *Washington Gladden*, 199.

22 Peabody, *Jesus Christ and the Social Question*, 25–26; see also Dorn, "The Social Gospel and Socialism," 84–87.

23 Biographical details on Mathews from Dorrien, *Soul in Society*, 21–90; and Dorrien, *The Making of American Liberal Theology: Idealism, Realism, and Modernity, 1900–1950*, 181–215. See also Lindsey, *Shailer Mathews's Lives of Jesus*.

24 Mathews, *The Social Teaching of Jesus*, 54

25 Ibid., 181.

26 Ibid., 156.

27 Ibid., 157.

28 Mathews, "The Development of Social Christianity in America," 380.

29 Quoted in Dorn, "The Social Gospel and Socialism," 85–86.

30 Peabody, *Jesus Christ and the Social Question*, 90.

31 Quoted in Michael A. Meyer, *Response to Modernity*, 66.

32 For a comprehensive history of American Judaism, see Sarna, *American Judaism*.

33 See Michael A. Meyer, *Response to Modernity*, 82.

34 Ibid., 95–96.

35 Quoted in Kleinberg, "Reform Judaism and the Jewish 'Social Gospel,'" 129.

36 Quoted in ibid., 125.

37 See Gutstein, *A Priceless Heritage*; and Simonhoff, *Saga of American Jewry*.

38 Quoted in Feldman, "The Social Gospel and the Jews," 312. On the history of Temple Sinai, Chicago, see Brinkmann, *Sundays at Sinai*; and Olitzky, "Sundays at Chicago Sinai Congregation."

39 Quoted in Abell, *American Catholicism and Social Action*, 33.
40 Quoted in ibid., 56.
41 Quoted in Abell, *American Catholic Thought on Social Questions*, 208.
42 Ibid., 166–67.
43 *Rerum Novarum*.
44 *The United Methodist Hymnal* (Nashville: United Methodist Publishing House, 1989), 569.
45 See Boyer, *When Time Shall Be No More*; and Sutton, *American Apocalypse*.
46 Quoted in Hudson, *Walter Rauschenbusch: Selected Writings*, 94.
47 Quoted in ibid., 143–44.

CHAPTER 3. KINGDOM COMING

 1 Lyman, "Social Progress and Religious Faith," 148.
 2 Ibid., 156–57.
 3 Quoted in Evans, *The Kingdom Is Always but Coming*, 186.
 4 Quoted in Fosdick, *The Living of These Days*, 110.
 5 Rauschenbusch, *Christianizing the Social Order*, 121.
 6 Biographical studies on Rauschenbusch include Minus, *Walter Rauschenbusch*; and Evans, *The Kingdom Is Always but Coming*.
 7 Minus, *Walter Rauschenbusch*; and Evans, *The Kingdom Is Always but Coming*, 43.
 8 On the Brotherhood of the Kingdom, see Hopkins and White, *The Social Gospel in America*; and Hudson, *Walter Rauschenbusch: Selected Writings*.
 9 Quoted in Hudson, *Walter Rauschenbusch: Selected Writings*, 79.
10 Quoted in ibid., 98.
11 Rauschenbusch, *A Theology for the Social Gospel*, 157.
12 This original manuscript was ultimately published under the title *The Righteousness of the Kingdom*.
13 Ibid., 70.
14 Ibid., 71.
15 Rauschenbusch, *Christianity and the Social Crisis*, 90.
16 Ibid., 420.
17 Ibid., 372.
18 Ibid., 279.
19 Ibid., 421.
20 Mathews, "The Development of Social Christianity in America," 380.
21 Quoted in Hudson, *Walter Rauschenbusch: Selected Writings*, 210.
22 Rauschenbusch, *Christianizing the Social Order*, 125.
23 Ibid., 154.
24 Ahlstrom, *A Religious History of the American People*, vol. 2, 272.
25 See Oldstone-Moore, *Hugh Price Hughes*.
26 Barrett, *Work and Community in the Jungle*, 67.
27 Rossinow, "The Radicalization of the Social Gospel," 64.
28 Quoted in Duke, *In the Trenches with Jesus and Marx*, 64.

29 Eugene Link, *Labor-Religion Prophet*, 16–17.

30 Stanford, *Origin and History of the Federal Council of the Churches of Christ*, 397.

31 *United Methodist Hymnal*, 427.

32 See Richey, Rowe, and Schmidt, *The Methodist Experience in America*.

33 Quoted in Muelder, *Methodism and Society in the Twentieth Century*, 47.

34 Quoted in ibid., 48–49.

35 Welch, *As I Recall My Past Century*, 56.

36 Quoted in Voss, *Stephen S. Wise*, 35.

37 "Emil Gustav Hirsch," in *The Universal Jewish Encyclopedia*, vol. 5, 373–74.

38 Biographical notes on Wise are from Voss, *Stephen S. Wise*, xvii–xxi. See also Wise, *Challenging Years*.

39 Quoted in Urofsky, *A Voice That Spoke for Justice*, 62.

40 Wise, *Challenging Years*, 96.

41 Quoted in Urofsky, *A Voice That Spoke for Justice*, 96.

42 Wise, *Challenging Years*, 118.

43 See Luker, *The Social Gospel in Black and White*, 24–29; and Dorrien, *The New Abolition*, 65–66.

44 Voss, *Stephen S. Wise*, 42.

45 On the history of Ford Hall, see Meyers, *Democracy in the Making*. A complete list of Ford Hall speakers can be found at www.fordhallforum.org.

46 Quoted in Evans, *The Kingdom Is Always but Coming*, 155.

47 On Ryan's life, see Beckley, *Passion for Justice*, 110–87; and Dorrien, *Social Ethics in the Making*, 185–215.

48 Ryan, *A Living Wage*, 3.

49 Ibid., 8.

50 Quoted in Abell, *American Catholic Thought on Social Questions*, 240.

51 Ryan, *A Living Wage*, 24.

52 Quoted in Abell, *American Catholic Thought on Social Questions*, 241.

53 Ryan, *Distributive Justice*, 432–33.

54 Dolan, *The American Catholic Experience*, 343–44.

55 Scudder, *On Journey*, 180.

56 Ibid., 84.

57 Corcoran, *Vida Dutton Scudder*, 23.

58 Scudder, *On Journey*, 81.

59 Hinson-Hasty, *Beyond the Social Maze*.

60 While scholars have debated the relationship between Jane Addams and the social gospel, a significant scholarly corpus details how Addams's life and thought relate to the social gospel. See Stebner, *The Women of Hull House*; Schultz, "Jane Addams, Apotheosis of Social Christianity"; and Kittelstrom, *The Religion of Democracy*, 309–49.

61 See Hinson-Hasty, *Beyond the Social Maze*, 5.

62 Scudder, *On Journey*, 136.

63 Ibid., 384.

64 Quoted in Corcoran, *Vida Dutton Scudder*, 55.
65 Quoted in Dorn, "The Social Gospel and Socialism," 99.
66 See Fishburn, *The Fatherhood of God and the Victorian Family*.
67 On the Men and Religion Forward movement, see Putney, *Muscular Christianity*, 137–43.
68 Rauschenbusch, *Christianizing the Social Order*, 20.
69 Scudder, *On Journey*, 388.
70 Ibid., 390.
71 McCarraher, *Christian Critics*, 12.
72 Hirsch, "Religious Education and Moral Efficiency," 133.
73 Lyman, "Social Progress and Religious Faith," 164–65.
74 Rauschenbusch, *Christianizing the Social Order*, 29.
75 Ibid., 7.
76 Ibid., 42.
77 Ibid., 55.
78 McConnell, "The Causes of Pre-Millenarianism," 181.

CHAPTER 4. "THE CHURCH STANDS FOR . . ."

1 See Ahlstrom, *A Religious History of the American People*, vol. 2, 271; and Handy, *A Christian America*.
2 Quoted in Stanford, *Origin and History of the Federal Council of Churches of Christ*, 271.
3 For an overview of the relationship between the social gospel and the rise of the American Protestant ecumenical movement, see Gorrell, *The Age of Responsibility*.
4 Macfarland, "The Progress of Federation among the Churches," 392.
5 Quoted in Hopkins and White, *The Social Gospel*, 206.
6 Robert A. Schneider, "Voices of Many Waters: Church Federation in the Twentieth Century," in Hutchison, *Between the Times*, 102.
7 Macfarland, "The Progress of Federation among the Churches," 400.
8 Quoted in Stanford, *Origin and History of the Federal Council of Churches of Christ*, 500.
9 William R. Hutchison, "Protestantism as Establishment," in Hutchison, *Between the Times*, 3–20.
10 Macfarland, "The Progress of Federation among the Churches," 406.
11 William McGuire King, "The Emergence of Social Gospel Radicalism: The Methodist Case," 441.
12 Ward, *The Social Creed of the Churches*, 191.
13 Quoted in Voss, *Stephen S. Wise*, 74–75.
14 Quoted in ibid., 49.
15 Burnidge, "The Business of Church and State."
16 Quoted in Arthur S. Link, *The Papers of Woodrow Wilson*, vol. 35, 330. See also Burnidge, "The Business of Church and State," 661; and Gorrell, *The Age of Responsibility*.

17 Arthur S. Link, *The Papers of Woodrow Wilson*, 335.

18 Quoted in Putney, *Muscular Christianity*, 172.

19 Abbott, *The Twentieth Century Crusade*, 64.

20 Ibid., 87.

21 Quoted in Voss, *Stephen S. Wise: Servant of the People*, 74.

22 Quoted in Dorn, *Washington Gladden*, 431.

23 Quoted in Miller, *Harry Emerson Fosdick*, 77–78.

24 See Hopkins, *John R. Mott*.

25 Hopkins, *History of the Y.M.C.A. in North America*, 629.

26 Wilson, *Fifty Years of Association Work among Young Women*, quoted in introduction.

27 Rice, *A History of the World's Young Women's Christian Association*, 126.

28 Eddy, *Eighty Adventurous Years*, 113.

29 Ibid., 118–19.

30 For perspectives on the broader ramifications of the twentieth-century Protestant student movement domestically and internationally, see Robert, "The First Globalization"; and Rossinow, "'The Break-Through to New Life.'"

31 Quoted in Evans, *The Kingdom Is Always but Coming*, 288.

32 Quoted in Hudson, *Walter Rauschenbusch: Selected Writings*, 198–99.

33 Rauschenbusch, *A Theology for the Social Gospel*, 158.

34 Ibid., 128–29.

35 Quoted in Evans, *The Kingdom Is Always but Coming*, 316.

36 Quoted in Duke, *In the Trenches with Jesus and Marx*, 97.

37 Quoted in David Nelson Duke, "Harry F. Ward, Social Gospel Warrior in the Trenches," in Evans, *Perspectives on the Social Gospel*, 205; and Duke, *In the Trenches with Jesus and Marx*, 104.

38 On the history of Union Theological Seminary, New York, see Coffin, *A Half Century of Union Theological Seminary*.

39 Ward, "The Present Task of Christian Ethics," 21.

40 Ibid., 26.

41 McConnell, *By the Way*, 213.

42 See Fox, *Reinhold Niebuhr*.

43 William McGuire King, "The Emergence of Social Gospel Radicalism," 445.

44 McConnell, *Democratic Christianity*, 55.

45 Quoted in Abell, *American Catholicism and Social Action*, 202–3.

46 Ward and Edwards, *Christianizing Community Life*, 158.

47 Ibid., 144.

48 See Handy, *A Christian America*; and Ernst, *Moment of Truth for Protestant America*.

49 Quoted in Handy, *A Christian America*, 164.

50 On the history of the Interchurch World Movement, see Ernst, *Moment of Truth for Protestant America*.

51 Quoted in Ensley, "The Interchurch World Movement and the Steel Strike of 1919," 217.

52 Interchurch World Movement, *Report on the Steel Strike*, 3–4.

53 Ibid., 81.

54 Ibid., 20–33.

55 Muelder, *Methodism and Society*; Ensley, "The Interchurch World Movement and the Steel Strike of 1919."

56 Wise, *Challenging Years*, 73.

57 Quoted in Voss, *Stephen S. Wise*, 153.

58 Ward, "Twenty Years of the Social Creed," 502.

59 See Rossinow, "The Radicalization of the Social Gospel."

60 Quoted in Duke, *In the Trenches with Jesus and Marx*, 102.

61 *Christian Century*, "Since Rauschenbusch—What?," 887.

62 Ibid.

63 Ibid., 888.

64 Visser't Hooft, *The Background of the Social Gospel in America*, 186.

CHAPTER 5. "SINCE RAUSCHENBUSCH—WHAT?"

1 McConnell, "What Shall the Churches Do with the Young Radicals?," 406.

2 See Paul Carter, *The Decline and Revival of the Social Gospel*; Miller, *American Protestantism and Social Issues*; and Donald B. Meyer, *The Protestant Search for Political Realism*.

3 See William McGuire King, "The Emergence of Social Gospel Radicalism in American Methodism"; and William McGuire King, "The Emergence of Social Gospel Radicalism: The Methodist Case."

4 William McGuire King, "The Emergence of Social Gospel Radicalism: The Methodist Case," 447–48.

5 Quoted in Evans, *Social Gospel Liberalism and the Ministry of Ernest Fremont Tittle*, 125.

6 Quoted in Sayre, "The Story of the Fellowship of Reconciliation."

7 Danielson, *American Gandhi*, 54.

8 Thomas wrote that "in so far as any one man or any one book, or series of books, made me a Socialist, it was probably Walter Rauschenbusch and his writings." Quoted in Sharpe, *Walter Rauschenbusch*, 415.

9 Quoted in Seidler, *Norman Thomas, Respectable Rebel*, 72.

10 McKanan, "The Implicit Religion of Radicalism."

11 See Donald B. Meyer, *The Protestant Search for Political Realism*, 49–53.

12 See William McGuire King, "The Emergence of Social Gospel Radicalism in American Methodism"; and William McGuire King, "The Emergence of Social Gospel Radicalism: The Methodist Case."

13 Eddy, *Eighty Adventurous Years*, 120.

14 See Appelbaum, *Kingdom to Commune*.

15 Page, *Dollars and World Peace*, 204.

16 Page, *Jesus or Christianity*, 230–31.

17 Ibid., 248.

18 Fosdick, *The Living of These Days*, 293.

19 Ibid., 110.

20 Dorrien, *The Making of American Liberal Theology: Idealism, Realism, and Modernity*, chap. 6.

21 Jones, *Social Law in the Spiritual World*, 218.

22 For a discussion of Fosdick's role in the fundamentalist-modernist controversy, see Fosdick, *The Living of These Days*; and Miller, *Harry Emerson Fosdick*.

23 See Hedstrom, *The Rise of Liberal Religion*.

24 See Coffman, *The Christian Century and the Rise of the Protestant Mainline*, 12–32, 222.

25 On Niebuhr's early career, see Fox, *Reinhold Niebuhr*.

26 Reinhold Niebuhr, "Christianity and Contemporary Politics," 498.

27 Ibid., 501.

28 Reinhold Niebuhr, "What the War Did to My Mind," 1161, 1163.

29 McKanan, "The Implicit Religion of Radicalism," 752.

30 Chappell, "Training Women," 509.

31 Miriam J. Crist, "Winifred L. Chappell," in Thomas and Keller, *Women in New Worlds*, 362.

32 Quoted in Crist, "Winifred L. Chappell," 369.

33 Gellman and Roll, *The Gospel of the Working Class*, 116.

34 See Eugene Link, *Labor-Religion Prophet*; and Duke, *In the Trenches with Jesus and Marx*.

35 Ward, "Religion Confronts a New World," 147.

36 For an analysis of Ward's evolving views of the Soviet Union, see Rossinow, "The Radicalization of the Social Gospel"; and Rossinow, "'The Model of a Model Fellow Traveler.'"

37 Ward, *In Place of Profit*, 16–17.

38 Ibid., 107.

39 Smith, *Moscow over Methodism?*, 7.

40 Hopkins, *History of the Y.M.C.A. in North America*, 524.

41 See Keller, *Georgia Harkness*.

42 See ibid.; and Dorrien, *The Making of American Liberal Theology: Idealism, Realism, and Modernity*, 390–414.

43 Reinhold Niebuhr, *An Interpretation of Christian Ethics*, 160–61.

44 As many scholars have observed, Niebuhr's critique of liberalism tended to avoid sustained engagement with more rigorous proponents of liberalism such as Walter Rauschenbusch. Christopher Lasch accurately notes that Rauschenbusch's mature theology anticipated many of the predominant themes in Niebuhr's thought: "Rauschenbusch not only denied the efficacy of political strategies based solely on moral suasion; he tried to revive elements of theological orthodoxy that liberals, he thought, had prematurely surrendered." See Lasch, *The True and Only Heaven*, 380.

45 For example, see Miles, *Georgia Harkness*, 165–69.

46 Quoted in Keller, *Georgia Harkness*, 183–84.

47 Quoted in Miles, *Georgia Harkness*, 154.

48 Quoted in ibid., 156.

49 Quoted in Hollinger, "After Cloven Tongues of Fire," 40. The entire catalog of *motive* is available online through the Boston University Center for Global Christianity, housed at Boston University School of Theology, http://sth-archon.bu.edu.

50 Eddy, *Eighty Adventurous Years*, 209.

51 Quoted in Shaffer, "'A Missionary from the East to Western Pagans,'" 590.

52 Quoted in ibid., 592.

53 Rembert Gilman Smith, *Moscow over Methodism?*, 52–53.

54 See Shaffer, "'A Missionary from the East to Western Pagans'"; and David P. King, "The West Looks East."

55 Danielson, "'In My Extremity I Turned to Gandhi,'" 383. See also Danielson, *American Gandhi*.

56 Ernest Fremont Tittle, "Can Democracy Be Made to Work?" *motive*, February 1941, 9.

57 Hinson-Hasty, "The Future of the Social Gospel," 61. Although scholars have noted the connection between the social gospel and New Deal reform, historians tend to gloss over the religious influences on the key New Deal architects. In addition to Harry Hopkins, Roosevelt's secretary of the agriculture and later vice president, Henry A. Wallace, reflected strong affinity with the social gospel. For a broader overview, see Kleinman, *A World of Hope, a World of Fear*.

58 On Rustin, see Levine, *Bayard Rustin and the Civil Rights Movement*; and D'Emilio, *Lost Prophet*.

59 Gerlach and Hine, *People, Power, and Change*.

CHAPTER 6. ACHIEVING THE "BELOVED COMMUNITY"

1 Thurman, *Jesus and the Disinherited*, 35.

2 Vincent Harding, foreword to *Jesus and the Disinherited*.

3 Pinn, *Making the Gospel Plain*, 165.

4 Thurman, *With Head and Heart*, 10.

5 For biographical details on Thurman's early life, see Fluker, *The Papers of Howard Washington Thurman*, vol. 1, xxxi–lxxxvi.

6 Thurman, *With Head and Heart*, 54.

7 Ibid., 51.

8 Jelks, *Benjamin Elijah Mays*, 44–45.

9 See Mays, *A Gospel for the Social Awakening*; and Luker, *The Social Gospel in Black and White*, 321–22.

10 For a summary of Mays's career, see Dorrien, *The Making of American Liberal Theology: Idealism, Realism, and Modernity*, 415–30.

11 See Jelks, *Benjamin Elijah Mays*.

12 Quoted in Bergler, "Youth, Christianity, and the Crisis of Civilization," 279.

13 Mays, *Born to Rebel*, 241–42.

14 In many ways, the efforts of religiously based socialists in the 1920s and 1930s to create a democratic socialist political alternative went further in Canada than in the United States. In the late 1930s, a Canadian social gospel minister, J. S. Woodsworth, founded the Cooperative Commonwealth Party (later renamed the New Democratic Party). In the mid-twentieth century, the New Democratic Party, associated with the leadership of two former ministers strongly influenced by the social gospel, Tommy Douglas and Stanley Knowles, championed a range of public welfare initiatives, including national health insurance legislation. See Phillips, *A Kingdom on Earth*; and Van Die, *Religion and Public Life in Canada*.

15 See Bell, *The Stockholm Conference*.

16 On the broader history of the Federal and National Council of Churches, see Findlay, *Church People in the Struggle*; and Gill, *Embattled Ecumenism*.

17 Gill, *Embattled Ecumenism*, 33; and Schneider, "Voice of Many Waters," 110.

18 See William McGuire King, "The Reform Establishment and the Ambiguities of Influence," in Hutchison, *Between the Times*, 122–40.

19 Quoted in Edwards, "'God's Totalitarianism,'" 297.

20 See Oxnam, *I Protest*.

21 Quoted in Miller, *Bishop G. Bromley Oxnam*, 284.

22 Quoted in ibid., 283–84.

23 Dulles, "Six Pillars of Peace."

24 See Will, *A Will for Peace*, 79–88.

25 Hoopes, "God and John Foster Dulles," 160.

26 Day has been the subject of numerous critical studies. For an overview of her life and thought, see Dorrien, *Social Ethics in the Making*, 361–77.

27 McCarraher, *Christian Critics*, 51–52. See also Edwards, "'God's Totalitarianism.'"

28 Mays, *Born to Rebel*, 354.

29 Martin Luther King, *Stride toward Freedom*, 100. For overviews of King's thought, see Ansbro, *Martin Luther King*; Burrow, *Personalism*; and Smith and Zepp, *Search for the Beloved Community*.

30 Martin Luther King, *Strength to Love*, 70.

31 Ibid., 74–75.

32 Mays, *Born to Rebel*, 265–66.

33 On Johns, see Branch, *Parting the Waters*, 1–26.

34 See Kaplan, *Spiritual Radical*.

35 Quoted in ibid., 225.

36 For an example of James Cone's critique of white social gospel leaders, see *The Cross and the Lynching Tree*.

37 Martin Luther King, "Letter from Birmingham Jail," in Washington, *Testament of Hope*, 292.

38 William McGuire King, "An Enthusiasm for Humanity," 68.

39 Martin Luther King, "Letter from Birmingham Jail," 297.

40 Ibid., 293.

41 Martin Luther King, "I Have a Dream," in Washington, *Testament of Hope*, 19.

312313

42 Martin Luther King, "Letter from Birmingham Jail," 300.

43 Washington, *Testament of Hope*, xxi.

44 Martin Luther King, *Strength to Love*, 51.

45 Quoted in Hoopes, "God and John Foster Dulles," 159.

46 See David W. Wills, "An Enduring Distance: Black Americans and the Establishment," in Hutchison, *Between the Times*, 168–92.

47 Gill, *Embattled Ecumenism*, 139.

48 See Ramsey, *Who Speaks for the Church?*; and Evans, *Liberalism without Illusions*, 96.

49 Gill, *Embattled Ecumenism*, 257–78; for a discussion of the impact of the 1960s on youth participation in religious bodies, see Putnam and Campbell, *American Grace*.

50 While many scholars have observed a heightened radicalism in Martin Luther King's later years, other scholars have noted that King's radicalism emerged out of his long-standing theological idealism, rooted in the personalist theology of the social gospel. See Cook, "Martin Luther King, Jr. and the Long Social Gospel Movement."

51 Martin Luther King, "A Time to Break Silence," in Washington, *Testament of Hope*, 234.

52 Ibid., 243.

53 Martin Luther King, "Remaining Awake through a Great Revolution," in Washington, *Testament of Hope*, 274.

54 Martin Luther King, "Our God Is Marching On!," in Washington, *Testament of Hope*, 230.

55 Mays, *Born to Rebel*, 359.

56 Ibid., 360.

57 Cone, *A Black Theology of Liberation*, 39.

58 Ibid., 41.

59 McCarraher, *Christian Critics*, 171–72.

60 Howard Thurman, "Religion in a Time of Crisis," quoted in Fluker, *The Papers of Howard Washington Thurman*, vol. 2, 348.

61 Findlay, *Church People in the Struggle*, 224.

62 See, for example, Finke and Stark, *The Churching of America*.

CHAPTER 7. AN EVANGELICAL SOCIAL GOSPEL?

1 Quoted in Raushenbush, "Rick Warren and the Social Gospel," Beliefnet, n.d., www.beliefnet.com. See also Suttle, *An Evangelical Social Gospel?*, 74.

2 Hollinger, "After Cloven Tongues of Fire," 21.

3 On Schaeffer, see Hankins, *Francis Schaeffer and the Shaping of Evangelical America*; and Williams, *God's Own Party*, 136–43.

4 Quoted in Williams, *God's Own Party*, 140.

5 See Balmer, *The Making of Evangelicalism*; Williams, *God's Own Party*; and Balmer, *Redeemer: The Biography of Jimmy Carter*.

6 Quoted in Williams, *God's Own Party*, 156.
7 Hankins, *Francis Schaeffer and the Shaping of Evangelical America*, 197.
8 See Jewett, *Mission and Menace*.
9 Reed, *Active Faith*, 10. For a fuller description of the rise of the Christian Right, see Williams, *God's Own Party*.
10 Reed, *Active Faith*, 42.
11 See Evans, *Histories of American Christianity*, 339–46.
12 For an overview of the neoconservative political phenomenon, see Dorrien, *Economy, Difference, Empire*, 187–213.
13 Quoted in Tipton, *Public Pulpits*, 161.
14 Quoted in ibid.
15 Quoted in Case, *Evangelical and Methodist*, 259.
16 See Janet Forsythe Fishburn, "The Social Gospel, Gender, and Homosexuality: Then and Now," in Evans, *The Social Gospel Today*, 126–45.
17 Quoted in Tipton, *Public Pulpits*, 124.
18 See Wellman, *Evangelical vs. Liberal*.
19 Quoted in Evans, *Liberalism without Illusions*, 127.
20 Quoted in Timothy Tseng and Janet Furness, "The Reawakening of the Evangelical Social Consciousness," in Evans, *The Social Gospel Today*, 116.
21 Assessments of Billy Graham's historical legacy vary tremendously. For a comprehensive review of Graham's life and legacy, see Wacker, *America's Pastor*. For a less favorable assessment of Graham's legacy, see Gary Dorrien, "Ironic Complexity: Reinhold Niebuhr, Billy Graham, Modernity, and Racial Justice," in *Economy, Difference, Empire*, 66–84.
22 George McGovern, "Political Participation—a Christian View," in Deats, *Toward a Discipline of Social Ethics*, 228.
23 Ibid., 230.
24 Quoted in Tseng and Furness, "The Reawakening of the Evangelical Social Consciousness," 123.
25 Ibid.
26 Daniel K. Williams, "Progressive Evangelicals' Campaign against Abortion," in Steensland and Goff, *The New Evangelical Social Engagement*, 211–12.
27 Gasaway, *Progressive Evangelicals and the Pursuit of Social Justice*, 155.
28 Quoted in ibid., 56.
29 Wallis, *God's Politics*, 36.
30 Ibid., 36–37.
31 Quoted in Wellman, *Rob Bell and a New American Christianity*, 102–3.
32 See, for example, Tseng and Furness, "The Reawakening of the Evangelical Social Consciousness," 124–25.
33 Jim Wallis, "What to Do," in Raushenbush, *Christianity and the Social Crisis in the 21st Century*, 345.
34 Tony Campolo, "A Response from an Evangelical," in Raushenbush, *Christianity and the Social Crisis in the 21st Century*, 77–78.

35 Rauschenbusch, *Christianizing the Social Order*, 309.
36 Suttle, *An Evangelical Social Gospel?*, 18–19.
37 Pew Research Center, *America's Changing Religious Landscape*.
38 Chaves, *Congregations in America*, 93. See also Evans, *Liberalism without Illusions*, 146.
39 Putnam and Campbell, *American Grace*, 576.
40 Wuthnow, *After the Baby Boomers*, 232.
41 See Network of Spiritual Progressives, http://spiritualprogressives.org.
42 Chaves, *Congregations in America*; Putnam and Campbell, *American Grace*.
43 See Elizabeth Dias, "Hillary Clinton: Anchored by Faith," *Time*, March 23, 2016, http://time.com; and "The Faith of Hillary Clinton," Calvin College, March 23, 2016, www.calvin.edu.
44 Wuthnow, *After the Baby Boomers*, 232.
45 McCarraher, *Christian Critics*, 189.
46 Richard Rorty, "Buds That Never Opened," in Raushenbush, *Christianity and the Social Crisis in the 21ˢᵗ Century*, 349; see also Evans, *Liberalism without Illusions*, 29.
47 On Sanders's secularism, see Lauren Markoe and Cathy Lynn Grossman, "Five Faith Facts about Bernie Sanders: Unabashedly Irreligious," Religion News Service, January 31, 2016, www.religionnews.com.
48 Quoted in Gaustad and Noll, *A Documentary History of Religion*, 685.

CONCLUSION
1 "Remarks by the President in Eulogy for the Honorable Reverend Clementa Pinckney," June 26, 2015, www.whitehouse.gov.
2 William McGuire King, "'History as Revelation' in the Theology of the Social Gospel," 129.
3 Hollinger, "After Cloven Tongues of Fire," 21.
4 See, for example, H. Richard Niebuhr, "The Social Gospel and the Mind of Jesus."
5 Putnam and Campbell, *American Grace*.
6 Hollinger, "After Cloven Tongues of Fire," 48.
7 Tipton, *Public Pulpits*, 411–12.
8 See Lasch, *The True and Only Heaven*, 13.

BIBLIOGRAPHY

PRIMARY SOURCES

Abbott, Lyman. *The Twentieth Century Crusade*. New York: Macmillan, 1918.

Abell, Aaron I., ed. *American Catholic Thought on Social Questions*. Indianapolis: Bobbs-Merrill, 1968.

Ahlstrom, Sydney, and Jonathan Carey, eds. *An American Reformation: A Documentary History of Unitarian Christianity*. Middleton, CT: Wesleyan University Press, 1985.

Bell, George K., ed. *The Stockholm Conference 1925: The Official Report of the Universal Christian Conference on Life and Work Held in Stockholm, 19–30 August, 1925*. London: Humphrey Milford, 1926.

Chappell, Winifred. "Training Women for City, Home and Foreign Missionary Service." *Religious Education* 11 (February 1916): 508–11.

Christian Century. "Since Rauschenbusch—What?" 43 (July 15, 1926): 886–88.

Coffin, Henry Sloane. *A Half Century of Union Theological Seminary, 1896–1945*. New York: Scribner's, 1954.

Dorchester, Daniel. *Christianity in the United States from the First Settlement Down to the Present Day*. New York: Hunt and Eaton, 1890.

Du Bois, W. E. B. *The Souls of Black Folk*. 1903. Online access at www.bartleby.com

Dulles, John Foster. "Six Pillars of Peace: Cement Unity Now with Organized World Collaboration." Presentation, New York, March 18, 1943. Available at www.ibiblio.org.

Eddy, Sherwood. *Eighty Adventurous Years: An Autobiography*. New York: Harper and Brothers, 1955.

Fluker, Walter E., ed. *The Papers of Howard Washington Thurman*. Vol. 1. Columbia: University of South Carolina Press, 2009.

———. *The Papers of Howard Washington Thurman*. Vol. 2. Columbia: University of South Carolina Press, 2012.

Fosdick, Harry Emerson. *The Living of These Days*. New York: Harper and Brothers, 1956.

Gaustad, Edwin S., and Mark A. Noll, eds. *A Documentary History of Religion in America since 1877*. Grand Rapids: Eerdmans, 2003.

Gifford, Carolyn De Swarte, ed. *Writing Out My Heart: Selections from the Journal of Frances Willard*. Urbana: University of Illinois Press, 1995.

Gladden, Washington. *The Christian Pastor and the Working Church*. New York: Scribner's, 1898.

Handy, Robert T., ed. *The Social Gospel in America, 1870–1920*. New York: Oxford University Press, 1966.

Herron, George David. *The Christian Society.* Reprint, New York: Johnson Reprint Corporation, 1969.

Hirsch, Emil G. "Religious Education and Moral Efficiency." *Religious Education* 4 (June 1909): 129–38.

Hopkins, Charles Howard. *History of the Y.M.C.A. in North America.* New York: Association Press, 1951.

Hopkins, Charles Howard, and Ronald White, eds. *The Social Gospel: Religion and Reform in Changing America.* Philadelphia: Temple University Press, 1976.

Hudson, Winthrop, ed. *Walter Rauschenbusch: Selected Writings.* New York: Paulist, 1984.

Interchurch World Movement. *Report on the Steel Strike of 1919.* New York: Harcourt, Brace and Howe, 1920.

Jones, Rufus M. *Social Law in the Spiritual World.* Philadelphia: Winston, 1904.

King, Martin Luther, Jr. *Strength to Love.* Philadelphia: Fortress, 1963.

———. *Stride toward Freedom.* New York: Harper and Row, 1958.

Link, Arthur S., ed. *The Papers of Woodrow Wilson.* Vol. 35. Princeton: Princeton University Press, 1980.

Lyman, Eugene. "Social Progress and Religious Faith." *Harvard Theological Review* 7 (April 1914): 139–65.

Macfarland, Charles S. "The Progress of Federation among the Churches." *American Journal of Theology* 21 (July 1917): 392–410.

Mathews, Shailer. "The Development of Social Christianity in America during the Past Twenty-Five Years." *Journal of Religion* 7 (July 1927): 376–86.

———. *The Social Teaching of Jesus: An Essay in Christian Sociology.* London: Macmillan, 1897.

Mays, Benjamin E. *Born to Rebel.* New York: Scribner's, 1971.

———, ed. *A Gospel for the Social Awakening: Selections from the Writings of Walter Rauschenbusch.* New York: Association Press, 1950.

McConnell, Francis J. *By the Way: An Autobiography.* New York: Abingdon-Cokesbury, 1952.

———. "The Causes of Pre-Millenarianism." *Harvard Theological Review* 12 (April 1919): 179–92.

———. *Democratic Christianity: Social Problems of the Church in the Days Just Ahead.* New York: Macmillan, 1919.

———. "What Shall the Churches Do with the Young Radicals?" *Journal of Religion* 4 (July 1923): 398–412.

Miles, Rebekah, ed. *Georgia Harkness: The Remaking of a Liberal Theologian; Collected Essays from 1929–1942.* Louisville: Westminster John Knox, 2010.

motive Magazine. Online archive, Boston University Center for Global Christianity. http://sth-archon.bu.edu.

Niebuhr, H. Richard. "The Social Gospel and the Mind of Jesus." *Journal of Religious Ethics* 16 (Spring 1988): 115–27.

Niebuhr, Reinhold. "Christianity and Contemporary Politics." *Christian Century* 41 (April 14, 1924): 498–501.

————. *An Interpretation of Christian Ethics*. New York: Meridian, 1956.

————. "What the War Did to My Mind." *Christian Century* 45 (September 27, 1928): 1161–63.

Norwood, Frederick A., ed. *Sourcebook of American Methodism*. Nashville: Abingdon, 1982.

Oxnam, G. Bromley. *I Protest: My Experience with the House Committee on Un-American Activities*. New York: Harper, 1954.

Page, Kirby. *Dollars and World Peace*. New York: Doran, 1927.

————. *Jesus or Christianity: A Study in Contrasts*. Garden City, NY: Doubleday, Doran, 1929.

Peabody, Francis Greenwood. *Jesus Christ and the Social Question*. New York: Macmillan, 1900.

Pinn, Anthony B., ed. *Making the Gospel Plain: The Writings of Bishop Reverdy C. Ransom*. Harrisburg, PA: Trinity Press International, 1999.

Rauschenbusch, Walter. *Christianity and the Social Crisis*. New York: Macmillan, 1907.

————. *Christianizing the Social Order*. Waco: Baylor University Press, 2010.

————. *The Righteousness of the Kingdom*. Nashville: Abingdon, 1968.

————. *A Theology for the Social Gospel*. New York: Macmillan, 1917.

Raushenbush, Paul, ed. *Christianity and the Social Crisis in the 21ˢᵗ Century*. New York: HarperOne, 2008.

Reed, Ralph. *Active Faith: How Christians Are Changing the Soul of American Politics*. New York: Free Press, 1996.

Rerum Novarum: Encyclical of Pope Leo XIII on Capital and Labor. May 15, 1891. Available at Vatican website, http://w2.vatican.va.

Rice, Anna V. *A History of the World's Young Women's Christian Association*. New York: Woman's Press, 1947.

Ryan, John A. *Distributive Justice: The Right and Wrong of Our Present Distribution of Wealth*. New York: Macmillan, 1916.

————. *A Living Wage*. Rev. ed. 1906; New York: Macmillan, 1920.

Sayre, John Nevin. "The Story of the Fellowship of Reconciliation: 1915–1935." Pamphlet. Boston University School of Theology Library. 1935.

Scudder, Vida Dutton. *On Journey*. New York: Dutton, 1937.

Sharpe, Dores Robinson. *Walter Rauschenbusch*. New York: Macmillan, 1942.

Sheldon, Charles. *The Crucifixion of Philip Strong*. Toronto: Poole Publishing, n.d. Available at Internet Archive, https://archive.org.

Smith, Rembert Gilman. *Moscow over Methodism?* Houston: University Press, 1950.

Stanford, Elias B. *Origin and History of the Federal Council of Churches of Christ in America*. Hartford, CT: Scranton, 1916.

Stead, William. *If Christ Came to Chicago!* Chicago: Laird and Lee, 1894.

Strong, Josiah. *Our Country: Its Possible Future and Its Present Crisis*. New York: Baker and Taylor, 1885.

Thurman, Howard. *Jesus and the Disinherited*. Rev. ed. Boston: Beacon, 1996.

————. *With Head and Heart: The Autobiography of Howard Thurman*. San Diego: Harcourt Brace Jovanovich, 1979.

The Universal Jewish Encyclopedia: An Authoritative and Popular Presentation of Jews.
Vol. 5. New York: Universal Jewish Encyclopedia, 1941.

Visser't Hooft, Willem. *The Background of the Social Gospel in America.* Reprint, St.
Louis: Bethany, 1963.

Voss, Carl Hermann, ed. *Stephen S. Wise: Servant of the People; Selected Letters.* Philadelphia: Jewish Publication Society of America, 1969.

Ward, Harry F. *In Place of Profit: Social Incentives in the Soviet Union.* New York: Scribner's, 1933.

———. "The Present Task of Christian Ethics." *Union Theological Seminary Bulletin* 2
(November 1918): 21–29.

———. "Religion Confronts a New World." *Christian Century* 49 (February 3,
1932):146–48.

———. *The Social Creed of the Churches.* New York: Abingdon, 1914.

———. "Twenty Years of the Social Creed." *Christian Century* 45 (April 19, 1928): 502–4.

Ward, Harry F., and Richard Henry Edwards. *Christianizing Community Life.* New
York: Abingdon, 1917.

Washington, James, ed. *Testament of Hope: The Essential Writings of Martin Luther
King, Jr.* San Francisco: Harper and Row, 1985.

Welch, Herbert. *As I Recall My Past Century.* New York: Abingdon, 1962.

Wilson, Elizabeth. *Fifty Years of Association Work among Young Women.* Reprint,
Farmingdale, NY: Dabor Social Science Publications, 1978.

Wise, Stephen. *Challenging Years: The Autobiography of Stephen Wise.* New York:
Putnam's, 1949.

SECONDARY SOURCES

Abell, Aaron I. *American Catholicism and Social Action: A Search for Social Justice,
1865–1950.* Garden City: Hanover House, 1960.

Ahlstrom, Sydney. *A Religious History of the American People.* 2 vols. Garden City, NY:
Image Books, 1975.

Ansbro, John J. *Martin Luther King, Jr.: The Making of a Mind.* Maryknoll: Orbis, 1984.

Appelbaum, Patricia Faith. *Kingdom to Commune: Protestant Pacifist Culture between
World War I and the Vietnam Era.* Chapel Hill: University of North Carolina
Press, 2009.

Applegate, Debby. *The Most Famous Man in America: The Biography of Henry Ward
Beecher.* New York: Three Leaves, 2006.

Balmer, Randall. *The Making of Evangelicalism: From Revivalism to Politics and Beyond.*
Waco: Baylor University Press, 2010.

———. *Redeemer: The Biography of Jimmy Carter.* New York: Basic Books, 2014.

Barrett, James R. *Work and Community in the Jungle: Chicago's Packinghouse Workers,
1894–1922.* Urbana: University of Illinois Press, 1987.

Beckley, Harlan. *Passion for Justice: Retrieving the Legacies of Walter Rauschenbusch,
John A. Ryan, and Reinhold Niebuhr.* Louisville: Westminster John Knox, 1992.

Bergler, Thomas E. "Youth, Christianity, and the Crisis of Civilization, 1930–1945." *Religion and American Culture* 24 (Summer 2014): 259–96.

Boyer, Paul. "An Ohio Leader of the Social Gospel Movement: Reassessing Washington Gladden." *Ohio History* 116 (2009): 88–100.

———. *When Time Shall Be No More: Prophecy Belief in Modern American Culture.* Cambridge, MA: Belknap, 1992.

Branch, Taylor. *Parting the Waters: America in the King Years, 1954–63.* New York: Simon and Schuster, 1988.

Brinkmann, Tobias. *Sundays at Sinai: A Jewish Congregation in Chicago.* Chicago: University of Chicago Press, 2012.

Burnidge, Cara L. "The Business of Church and State: Social Christianity in Woodrow Wilson's White House." *Church History* 82 (September 2013): 659–66.

Burrow, Rufus, Jr. *Personalism: A Critical Introduction.* St. Louis: Chalice Press, 1999.

Bynum, Cornelius L. "'An Equal Chance in the Race for Life': Reverdy C. Ransom, Socialism, and the Social Gospel Movement, 1890–1920." *Journal of African American History* 93 (Winter 2008): 1–20.

Carter, Heath W. "Scab Ministers, Striking Saints: Christianity and the Class Conflict in 1894 Chicago." *American Nineteenth Century History* 11 (September 2010): 321–49.

———. *Union Made: Working People and the Rise of Social Christianity in Chicago.* New York: Oxford University Press, 2015.

Carter, Paul. *The Decline and Revival of the Social Gospel.* Ithaca: Cornell University Press, 1954.

Case, Riley B. *Evangelical and Methodist: A Popular History.* Nashville: Abingdon, 2004.

Cauthen, Kenneth. *The Impact of American Religious Liberalism.* New York: Harper and Row, 1962.

Chaves, Mark. *Congregations in America.* Cambridge: Harvard University Press, 2004.

Coffman, Elesha J. *The Christian Century and the Rise of the Protestant Mainline.* New York: Oxford University Press, 2013.

Cone, James. *A Black Theology of Liberation.* Philadelphia: Lippincott, 1970.

———. *The Cross and the Lynching Tree.* Maryknoll, NY: Orbis, 2011.

Cook, Vaneesa. "Martin Luther King, Jr. and the Long Social Gospel Movement." *Religion and American Culture* 26 (Winter 2016): 74–100.

Corcoran, Theresa. *Vida Dutton Scudder.* Boston: Twayne, 1982.

Curtis, Susan. *A Consuming Faith: The Social Gospel and Modern American Culture.* Baltimore: Johns Hopkins University Press, 1991.

Danielson, Leilah C. *American Gandhi: A. J. Muste and the History of Radicalism in the 20th Century.* Philadelphia: University of Pennsylvania Press, 2015.

———. "'In My Extremity I Turned to Gandhi': American Pacifists, Christianity, and Gandhian Nonviolence, 1915–1941." *Church History* 72 (June 2003): 361–88.

Dayton, Donald. *Discovering an Evangelical Heritage.* New York: Harper and Row, 1976.

Deats, Paul, ed. *Toward a Discipline of Social Ethics: Essays in Honor of Walter George Muelder.* Boston: Boston University Press, 1972.

D'Emilio, John. *Lost Prophet: The Life and Times of Bayard Rustin.* New York: Free Press, 2000.

Dolan, Jay P. *The American Catholic Experience.* Garden City, NY: Doubleday, 1985.

Dombrowski, James. *The Early Days of Christian Socialism in America.* New York: Columbia University Press, 1936.

Dorn, Jacob H. "The Social Gospel and Socialism: A Comparison of the Thought of Francis Greenwood Peabody, Washington Gladden, and Walter Rauschenbusch." *Church History* 62 (March 1993): 82–100.

———. *Washington Gladden.* Columbus: Ohio State University Press, 1966.

Dorrien, Gary. *Economy, Difference, Empire: Social Ethics for Social Justice.* New York: Columbia University Press, 2010.

———. *The Making of American Liberal Theology: Idealism, Realism, and Modernity, 1900–1950.* Louisville: Westminster John Knox, 2003.

———. *The Making of American Liberal Theology: Imagining Progressive Religion, 1805–1900.* Louisville: Westminster John Knox, 2001.

———. *The New Abolition: W. E. B. Du Bois and the Black Social Gospel.* New Haven: Yale University Press, 2015.

———. *Social Ethics in the Making: Interpreting an American Tradition.* Malden: Wiley-Blackwell, 2011.

———. *Soul in Society: The Making and Renewal of Social Christianity.* Minneapolis: Fortress, 1995.

Duke, David Nelson. *In the Trenches with Jesus and Marx: Harry F. Ward and the Struggle for Social Justice.* Tuscaloosa: University of Alabama Press, 2003.

Edwards, Mark Thomas. "'God's Totalitarianism': Ecumenical Protestant Discourse during the Good War, 1941–1945." *Totalitarian Movements and Political Religions* 10 (September–December 2009): 285–302.

Edwards, Wendy J. Deichmann, and Carolyn De Swarte Gifford, eds. *Gender and the Social Gospel.* Urbana: University of Illinois Press, 2003.

Ensley, Philip C. "The Interchurch World Movement and the Steel Strike of 1919." *Labor History* 13, no. 2 (1972): 217–30.

Ernst, Eldon G. *Moment of Truth for Protestant America: Interchurch Campaigns following World War I.* Missoula, MO: Scholars Press, 1972.

Evans, Christopher H. *Histories of American Christianity: An Introduction.* Waco: Baylor University Press, 2013.

———. *The Kingdom Is Always but Coming: A Life of Walter Rauschenbusch.* Grand Rapids: Eerdmans, 2004.

———. *Liberalism without Illusions: Renewing an American Christian Tradition.* Waco: Baylor University Press, 2010.

———, ed. *Perspectives on the Social Gospel: Papers from the Inaugural Social Gospel Conference at Colgate Rochester Divinity School.* Lewiston: Edwin Mellen, 1999.

———. *Social Gospel Liberalism and the Ministry of Ernest Fremont Tittle: A Theology for the Middle Class*. Lewiston: Edwin Mellen, 1996.

———, ed. *The Social Gospel Today*. Louisville: Westminster John Knox, 2001.

Feldman, Egal. "The Social Gospel and the Jews." *American Jewish Historical Quarterly* 58, no. 3 (1969): 308–29.

Findlay, James F., Jr. *Church People in the Struggle: The National Council of Churches and the Black Freedom Movement, 1950–1970*. New York: Oxford University Press, 1993.

Finke, Roger, and Rodney Stark. *The Churching of America, 1776–1990: Winners and Losers in Our Religious Economy*. New Brunswick: Rutgers University Press, 1992.

Fishburn, Janet Forsythe. *The Fatherhood of God and the Victorian Family: The Social Gospel in America*. Philadelphia: Fortress, 1981.

Fox, Richard. *Reinhold Niebuhr: A Biography*. San Francisco: Harper, 1985.

Frederick, Peter J. *Knights of the Golden Rule: The Intellectual as Christian Social Reformer in the 1890s*. Lexington: University of Kentucky Press, 1976.

Gasaway, Brantley W. *Progressive Evangelicals and the Pursuit of Social Justice*. Chapel Hill: University of North Carolina Press, 2014.

Gellman, Erik S., and Jarod Roll. *The Gospel of the Working Class: Labor's Southern Prophets in New Deal America*. Urbana: University of Illinois Press, 2011.

Gerlach, Luther, and Virginia Hine. *People, Power, and Change: Movements of Social Transformation*. Indianapolis: Bobbs-Merrill, 1970.

Giffen, Allison, and June Hopkins, eds. *Jewish First Wife, Divorced: The Correspondence of Ethel Gross and Harry Hopkins*. Lanham, MD: Lexington, 2003.

Gill, Jill K. *Embattled Ecumenism: The National Council of Churches, the Vietnam War, and the Trials of the Protestant Left*. DeKalb: Northern Illinois University Press, 2011.

Gorrell, Donald K. *The Age of Responsibility: The Social Gospel in the Progressive Era, 1900–1920*. Macon: Mercer University Press, 1988.

Grodzins, Dean. *Radical Heretic: Theodore Parker and the Rise of Transcendentalism*. Chapel Hill: University of North Carolina Press, 2003.

Gutstein, Morris A. *A Priceless Heritage: The Epic Growth of Nineteenth Century Jewry*. New York: Block, 1953.

Hambrick-Stowe, Charles. *Charles G. Finney and the Spirit of American Evangelicalism*. Grand Rapids: Eerdmans, 1996.

Handy, Robert. *A Christian America: Protestant Hopes and Historical Realities*. New York: Oxford University Press, 1984.

Hankins, Barry. *Francis Schaeffer and the Shaping of Evangelical America*. Grand Rapids: Eerdmans, 2008.

Harper, Keith, ed. *Through a Glass Darkly: Contested Notions of Baptist Identity*. Tuscaloosa: University of Alabama Press, 2012.

Hedstrom, Matthew S. *The Rise of Liberal Religion: Book Culture and American Spirituality in the Twentieth Century*. New York: Oxford University Press, 2013.

Higginbotham, Evelyn Brooks. *Righteous Discontent: The Women's Movement in the Black Baptist Churches*. Cambridge: Harvard University Press, 1993.

Hinson-Hasty, Elizabeth L. *Beyond the Social Maze: Exploring Vida Dutton Scudder's Theological Ethics*. New York: Clark, 2006.

———. "The Future of the Social Gospel." *Theology Today* 66 (June 2009): 60–73.

Hofstadter, Richard. *Social Darwinism in American Thought*. Boston: Beacon, 1992.

Holifield, E. Brooks. *Theology in America: Christian Thought from the Age of the Puritans to the Civil War*. New Haven: Yale University Press, 2003.

Hollinger, David A. *After Cloven Tongues of Fire*. Princeton: Princeton University Press, 2013.

———. "After Cloven Tongues of Fire: Ecumenical Protestantism and the Modern American Encounter with Diversity." *Journal of American History* 98 (June 2011): 21–48.

Hoopes, Townsend. "God and John Foster Dulles." *Foreign Policy* 13 (Winter 1973–1974): 154–77.

Hopkins, Charles Howard. *John R. Mott: A Biography*. Grand Rapids: Eerdmans, 1979.

———. *The Rise of the Social Gospel in American Protestantism, 1865–1915*. New Haven: Yale University Press, 1940.

Hutchison, William R., ed. *Between the Times: The Travail of the Protestant Establishment, 1900–1960*. Cambridge: Cambridge University Press, 1989.

———. *The Modernist Impulse in American Protestantism*. Cambridge: Harvard University Press, 1976.

Jelks, Randal Maurice. *Benjamin Elijah Mays, Schoolmaster of the Movement: A Biography*. Chapel Hill: University of North Carolina Press, 2012.

Jewett, Robert. *Mission and Menace: Four Centuries of American Religious Zeal*. Minneapolis: Fortress, 2008.

"The Jewish Training School of Chicago." Unpublished essay. Department of History, University of Illinois at Chicago, n.d. www.uic.edu.

Kaplan, Edward K. *Spiritual Radical: Abraham Joshua Heschel in America, 1940–1972*. New Haven: Yale University Press, 2007.

Keller, Rosemary Skinner. *Georgia Harkness: For Such a Time as This*. Nashville: Abingdon, 1992.

King, David P. "The West Looks East: The Influence of Toyohiko Kagawa on American Mainline Protestantism." *Church History* 80 (June 2011): 302–20.

King, William McGuire. "The Biblical Base of the Social Gospel." In *The Bible and Social Reform*, edited by Ernest R. Sandeen. Philadelphia: Fortress, 1982.

———. "The Emergence of Social Gospel Radicalism in American Methodism." Ph.D. dissertation, Harvard University, 1977.

———. "The Emergence of Social Gospel Radicalism: The Methodist Case." *Church History* 50 (December 1981): 436–49.

———. "An Enthusiasm for Humanity: The Social Emphasis in Religion and Its Accommodation in Protestant Theology." In *Religion and Twentieth-Century American Intellectual Life*, edited by Michael J. Lacey. Cambridge: Cambridge University Press, 1989.

———. "'History as Revelation' in the Theology of the Social Gospel." *Harvard Theological Review* 76, no. 1 (1983): 109–29.

Kittelstrom, Amy. *The Religion of Democracy: Seven Liberals and the American Moral Tradition.* New York: Penguin, 2015.

Kleinberg, Darren. "Reform Judaism and the Jewish 'Social Gospel.'" *Reform Jewish Quarterly* 56 (Fall 2009): 119–34.

Kleinman, Mark L. *A World of Hope, a World of Fear: Henry A. Wallace, Reinhold Niebuhr, and American Liberalism.* Columbus: Ohio State University Press, 2000.

Kurzman, Paul A. *Harry Hopkins and the New Deal.* Fairlawn, NJ: Burdick, 1974.

Lasch, Christopher. *The True and Only Heaven: Progress and Its Critics.* New York: Norton, 1991.

Levine, Daniel. *Bayard Rustin and the Civil Rights Movement.* New Brunswick: Rutgers University Press, 2000.

Lindsey, William D. *Shailer Mathews's Lives of Jesus: The Search for a Theological Foundation for the Social Gospel.* Albany: State University of New York Press, 1997.

Link, Eugene. *Labor-Religion Prophet: The Times and Life of Harry F. Ward.* Boulder: Westview, 1984.

Luker, Ralph E. *The Social Gospel in Black and White: American Racial Reform, 1885–1912.* Chapel Hill: University of North Carolina Press, 1991.

Marsden, George. *Fundamentalism and American Culture.* Rev. ed. New York: Oxford University Press, 2005.

May, Henry F. *Protestant Churches and Industrial America.* New York: Harper and Row, 1949.

McCarraher, Eugene. *Christian Critics: Religion and the Impasse in Modern American Social Thought.* Ithaca: Cornell University Press, 2000.

McDowell, John Patrick. *The Social Gospel in the South: The Woman's Home Mission Movement in the Methodist Episcopal Church, South.* Baton Rouge: Louisiana State University Press, 1982.

McKanan, Dan. "The Implicit Religion of Radicalism: Socialist Party Theology, 1900–1934." *Journal of the American Academy of Religion* 78 (September 2010): 750–89.

———. *Prophetic Encounters: Religion and the American Radical Tradition.* Boston: Beacon, 2012.

Mead, Sidney. *The Lively Experiment: The Shaping of Christianity in America.* New York: Harper and Row, 1963.

Meyer, Donald B. *The Protestant Search for Political Realism, 1919–1941.* Berkeley: University of California Press, 1960.

Meyer, Michael A. *Response to Modernity: A History of the Reform Movement in Judaism.* New York: Oxford University Press, 1988.

Meyers, Arthur S. *Democracy in the Making: The Open Forum Lecture Movement.* Lanham, MD: University Press of America, 2012.

Miller, Robert Moats. *American Protestantism and Social Issues, 1919–1958.* Chapel Hill: University of North Carolina Press, 1958.

———. *Bishop G. Bromley Oxnam: Paladin of Liberal Protestantism.* Nashville: Abingdon, 1990.

———. *Harry Emerson Fosdick: Pastor, Preacher, Prophet.* New York: Oxford University Press, 1985.

Minus, Paul. *Walter Rauschenbusch: American Reformer.* New York: Macmillan, 1988.

Mislin, David. *Saving Faith: Making Religious Pluralism an American Value at the Dawn of the Secular Age.* Ithaca: Cornell University Press, 2015.

Moore, R. Laurence. *Religious Outsiders and the Making of Americans.* New York: Oxford University Press, 1985.

Muelder, Walter G. *Methodism and Society in the Twentieth Century.* Nashville: Abingdon, 1961.

Mullin, Robert Bruce. *The Puritan as Yankee: A Life of Horace Bushnell.* Grand Rapids: Eerdmans, 2002.

Noll, Mark. *America's God: From Jonathan Edwards to Abraham Lincoln.* New York: Oxford University Press, 2002.

———. *The Old Religion in a New World: The History of North American Christianity.* Grand Rapids: Eerdmans, 2002.

Oldstone-Moore, Christopher. *Hugh Price Hughes: Founder of a New Methodism, Conscience of a New Nonconformity.* Cardiff: University of Wales Press, 1999.

Olitzky, Kerry M. "Sundays at Chicago Sinai Congregation: Paradigm for a Movement." *American Jewish History* 74 (June 1985): 356–68.

Pew Research Center. *America's Changing Religious Landscape.* May 12, 2015. www.pewforum.org.

Phillips, Paul T. *A Kingdom on Earth: Anglo-American Social Christianity.* University Park: Pennsylvania State University Press, 1995.

Putnam, Robert D., and David E. Campbell. *American Grace: How Religion Unites and Divides Us.* New York: Simon and Schuster, 2010.

Putney, Clifford. *Muscular Christianity: Manhood and Sports in Protestant America, 1880–1920.* Cambridge: Harvard University Press, 2001.

Ramsey, Paul. *Who Speaks for the Church?* Nashville: Abingdon, 1967.

Richey, Russell E., Kenneth E. Rowe, and Jean Miller Schmidt, eds. *The Methodist Experience in America: A History.* Nashville: Abingdon, 2010.

———. *Perspectives on American Methodism: Interpretive Essays.* Nashville: Kingswood, 1993.

Robert, Dana L. "The First Globalization: The Internationalization of the Protestant Missionary Movement between the World Wars." *International Bulletin of Missionary Research* 26 (April 2002): 50–66.

Rossinow, Doug. "'The Break-Through to New Life': Christianity and the Emergence of the New Left in Austin, Texas, 1956–1964." *American Quarterly* 46 (September 1994): 309–340.

———. "'The Model of a Model Fellow Traveler': Harry F. Ward, the American League for Peace and Democracy, and the 'Russian Question' in American Politics, 1933–1956." *Peace and Change* 29 (April 2004): 177–20.

———. "The Radicalization of the Social Gospel: Harry F. Ward and the Search for a New Social Order, 1898–1936." *Religion and American Culture* 15 (Winter 2005): 63–106.

———. *Visions of Progress: The Left-Liberal Tradition in America.* Philadelphia: University of Pennsylvania Press, 2008.

Sarna, Jonathan. *American Judaism: A History.* New Haven: Yale University Press, 2004.

Schmidt, Leigh Eric. *Restless Souls: The Making of American Spirituality.* New York: Harper, 2002.

Schultz, Rima Lunin. "Jane Addams, Apotheosis of Social Christianity." *Church History* 84 (March 2015): 207–19.

Seidler, Murray B. *Norman Thomas, Respectable Rebel.* Syracuse: Syracuse University Press, 1967.

Shaffer, Robert. "'A Missionary from the East to Western Pagans': Kagawa Toyohiko's 1936 U.S. Tour." *Journal of World History* 24 (September 2013): 577–621.

Simonhoff, Harry. *Saga of American Jewry, 1865–1914.* New York: Arco, 1959.

Smith, Gary Scott. *The Search for Social Salvation.* Lanham, MD: Lexington, 2000.

Smith, Kenneth L., and Ira G. Zepp. *Search for the Beloved Community: The Thinking of Martin Luther King, Jr.* Valley Forge: Judson, 1971.

Smith, Timothy. *Revivalism and Social Reform.* New York: Abingdon, 1957.

Stebner, Eleanor J. *The Women of Hull House: A Study of Vocation and Friendship.* Albany: State University of New York Press, 1997.

Steensland, Brian, and Philip Goff, eds. *The New Evangelical Social Engagement.* New York: Oxford University Press, 2013.

Suttle, Tim. *An Evangelical Social Gospel? Finding God's Story in the Midst of Extremes.* Eugene, OR: Cascade, 2011.

Sutton, Matthew Avery. *American Apocalypse: A History of Modern Evangelicalism.* Cambridge: Belknap, 2014.

Thomas, Hilah F., and Rosemary Skinner Keller, eds. *Women in New Worlds: Historical Perspectives on the Wesleyan Tradition.* Nashville: Abingdon, 1981.

Tipton, Steven M. *Public Pulpits: Methodists and Mainline Churches in the Moral Argument of Public Life.* Chicago: University of Chicago Press, 2008.

Tracy, James. *Direct Action: Radical Pacifism from the Union Eight to the Chicago Seven.* Chicago: University of Chicago Press, 1996.

Urofsky, Melvin I. *A Voice That Spoke for Justice: The Life and Times of Stephen S. Wise.* Albany: State University of New York Press, 1982.

Van Die, Marguerite, ed. *Religion and Public Life in Canada: Comparative and Historical Perspectives.* Toronto: University of Toronto Press, 2001.

Voss, Carl Hermann. *Rabbi and Minister: The Friendship of Stephen S. Wise and John Haynes Holmes.* Cleveland: World, 1964.

Wacker, Grant. *America's Pastor: Billy Graham and the Shaping of a Nation.* Cambridge: Harvard University Press, 2014.

———. "The Holy Spirit and the Spirit of the Age in American Protestantism, 1880–1910." *Journal of American History* 72 (June 1985): 45–62.

Wallis, Jim. *God's Politics: Why the Right Gets It Wrong and the Left Doesn't Get It*. San Francisco: HarperSanFrancisco, 2005.

Wellman, James K. *Evangelical vs. Liberal: The Clash of Christian Cultures in the Pacific Northwest*. New York: Oxford University Press, 2008.

———. *Rob Bell and a New American Christianity*. Nashville: Abingdon, 2012.

White, Ronald C. *Liberty and Justice for All: Racial Reform and the Social Gospel*. San Francisco: Harper and Row, 1990.

Will, Herman. *A Will for Peace: Peace Action in the United Methodist Church*. Washington, D.C.: General Board of Church and Society, 1984.

Williams, Daniel K. *God's Own Party: The Making of the Christian Right*. New York: Oxford University Press, 2010.

Wuthnow, Robert. *After the Baby Boomers*. Princeton: Princeton University Press, 2007.

INDEX

Ockenga, Harold, 206
Open and Industrial Church League, 88
The Outlook (magazine), 114
Oxford University, 91, 99
Oxnam, G. Bromley, 111, 173–74

pacifism, 146, 154, 158–59, 161, 176; development after World War I, 136–37, 139, 141, 145; influence upon the FOR, 137–38; relationship to nonviolent direct action tactics, 159–60, 162
Packingtown (Chicago), 87
Page, Kirby, 139–41
Pallen, Condé, 70
Palmer, Phoebe, 23
Parker, Theodore, 24–25, 34
Payne, Daniel, 53–54
Peabody, Francis Greenwood, 57–58, 63–64
pentecostalism, 75
People's Institute of Applied Religion (PIAR), 149
perfectionism, 23, 54
Perkins, Frances, 147
Perry, Rick, 201
personalism, 61, 153, 177–78
Pew Research Foundation (Religious Landscape Survey), 212–13, 216–17
Phillips, John, 84
Pinckney, Clementa, 221
Pittsburgh Platform (1885), 67, 92
The Plot Against Christianity (Dilling), 151
pluralism, 194–95, 205; legacy of social gospel, 11, 18, 225–26
Plymouth Congregational Church (Brooklyn), 27, 73, 114
political left, 2, 4; relationship to the social gospel, 9, 136, 149, 153, 217
Poor People's Campaign (1968), 187
postmillennialism, 4–5, 23, 28, 114; connection to the social gospel, 5, 25, 34, 49
Presbyterian churches, 22, 74, 109, 122–23, 191

premillennialism, 5, 28–29, 73, 110; response of social gospelers to, 50, 63, 74, 81, 105, 201
Proctor, Henry Hugh, 43
Progress and Poverty (George), 31
Progressive Era, 2, 3, 7, 31, 33, 108, 215
progressive evangelicalism, 205–6, 211; comparisons to the Christian Right, 208–9; and George McGovern campaign, 207–8; relationship to the classic social gospel, 209, 211
Prohibition, 128–29
Protestant establishment, 108, 174, 183–84, 203, 225
Protestantism, 2, 3, 7,12, 222; Christian Right, 201–3, declining influence of, 217–18; and Federal Council of Churches, 110–11; origins of the social gospel, 22, 25, 32, 37–38, 41, 46. *See also* Christian America; "Christianizing"; ecumenical movement; evangelicalism; liberal Protestantism; National Council of Churches
Pullman strike (1894), 47–48
Putnam, Robert, 213

Quakers, 142, 162

racism, 136, 140, 143; confronted by Benjamin Mays and Howard Thurman, 165–170. *See also* Black Social Gospel; social gospel
Ransom, Reverdy, 53; Christian socialism of, 54–55; later career of, 166–67; views on racism in America, 45–46
the Rapture, 28, 110
Rauschenbusch, August, 79
Rauschenbusch, Walter, 74–75, 79–85, 105, 119–120; emerging radicalism, 75, 79; influence on Martin Luther King, Jr., 181, 191; New York City ministry of, 74, 90; theological beliefs and, 78–79, 81, 83

Reagan, Ronald, 197, 199, 209
Reed, Ralph, 1, 199–201
The Red Network (Dilling), 151
Reform Judaism, 65–68; anti-Zionism
    and, 92; commitment to social reform,
    68; development in the nineteenth
    century, 65–66; relationship to Prot-
    estant reformers, 68; uses of the Bible,
    68, 90
religious left, 4, 18, 122, 194, 208
religious "nones," 213–14
religious outsiders, 7
religious right. *See* Christian Right
Report of the Steel Strike, 129. *See also*
    Interchurch World Movement
Republican Party, 138, 144, 199
Rerum Novarum, 71–73, 95
Rethinking Mission (Hocking), 156
Riis, Jacob, 49
Ritschl, Albrecht, 60–61
Riverside Church (New York City),
    143, 186. *See also* Fosdick, Harry
    Emerson
Robertson, Frederick, 52
Robins, Henry Burke, 168
Rochester Theological Seminary, 78, 80,
    168
Rockefeller, John D., 80, 84
Rockefeller, John D., Jr., 128, 143
Roe v. Wade (1973), 196–97, 208
Roman Catholicism, 29, 30, 64, 144, 213,
    219; comparisons to Protestant reform
    efforts, 69, 72–73, 96, 98; views toward
    social reform, 69–70, 71–72, 78, 95,
    125, 176
Roosevelt, Franklin D., 146–47, 171
Roosevelt, Theodore, 89
Rorty, Richard, 217
Rossinow, Doug, 10
Royce, Josiah, 121
Ruskin, John, 99
Russian Revolution, 127
Rustin, Bayard, 161–62

Ryan, John, 95–97; Bishop's Program
    Report, 125; and the New Deal, 147, 161;
    views toward democratic socialism, 98

Salvation Army, 5, 99
Sanders, Bernie, 218
Sankey, Ira, 81
Schaeffer, Francis, 195–98
Schaff, Philip, 60
Schleiermacher, Friedrich, 58–59, 60, 64
Schumann, Samuel, 94
Scudder, Vida Dutton, 52, 98–103; affinity
    with John Ruskin, 99; embrace of
    Anglo-Catholicism, 99; political so-
    cialism and, 101; relationship to Walter
    Rauschenbusch, 100; settlement house
    movement, 100"
secular humanism, 196, 198, 204
settlement house movement, 38, 46, 52,
    54, 62, 85–86, 88, 100, 106, 147
"seven sister" churches, 109
Seymour, William, 75
Sheldon, Charles, 48–51. See also *In His
    Steps*; "What Would Jesus Do?"
Sider, Ron, 206, 208–9
Sinclair, Upton, 87
"single-tax," 31, 53, 71, 80, 97
Sisters of St. Joseph, 69
Small, Albion, 61–62
Smith, Alfred E., 144
Smith, Kenneth "Snuffy," 178
The Social Aspects of Christianity (Ely), 39
social creed, 89–90, 108–10
social gospel, 1–2, 221; and anti-
    Catholicism, 15, 68; and anti-Semitism,
    84; as applied Christianity/religion,
    2, 47–48, 52, 56, 88, 149; in Canada,
    243n14; and Christian democracy,
    154; "Christianizing" America, 22, and
    Christian Right, 193, 198, 200–201; 73,
    84, 107, 162; defined, 2–3; eight-hour
    workday and, 53, 161; foreign missions,
    118, 156; immigration and, 29–30, 38,

World War I, 8, 97, 104, 108, 113, 118, 119,
122, 127, 135, 136
World War II, 9, 143, 160, 161, 171, 172, 174
Wuthnow, Robert, 214, 216

Yoder, John Howard, 206
Young Men's Christian Association
(YMCA), 116–17, 118–19, 152, 226;
interwar conferences, 141; social

gospel leanings of, 117, 118, 141; views
toward race/racism, 170; World War I
chaplains, 119, 136
Young Women's Christian Association
(YWCA), 116–19, 136, 139, 141, 152,
216

Zionism, 92
Zinn, Howard, 155

ABOUT THE AUTHOR

Christopher H. Evans is Professor of the History of Christianity at Boston University. He is the author of several books, including *Histories of American Christianity: An Introduction*; *Liberalism without Illusions: Renewing an American Christian Tradition*; and *The Kingdom Is Always but Coming: A Life of Walter Rauschenbusch*.

Made in the USA
Coppell, TX
09 November 2020

41033097R00163